MICHAEL BEROLZHEIMER

1866–1942   HIS LIFE AND LEGACY

EDITED AND PUBLISHED BY
MICHAEL G. BEROLZHEIMER

WITH CONTRIBUTIONS BY

ANDREA BAMBI,
DIETLIND BRATENGEYER,
SVEN BRUNTJEN,
REBECCA FRIEDMAN,
JOSEPH GOLDYNE,
UWE HARTMANN,
ANDREAS HEUSLER,
HORST KESSLER,
BERNHARD PURIN,
PETER SCHWARZ,
VANESSA-MARIA VOIGT,
PETRA WINTER,
AND GARY A. ZIMMERMAN

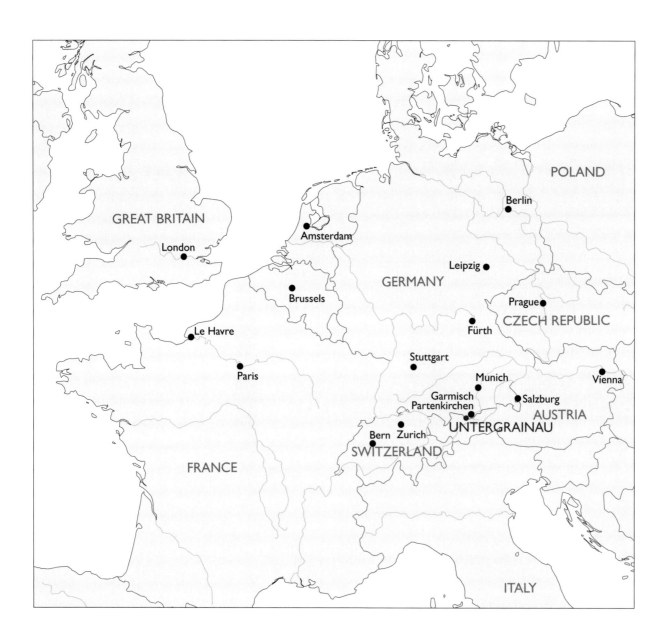

GREAT BRITAIN

London

POLAND

Berlin

Amsterdam

GERMANY

Leipzig

Brussels

Prague

CZECH REPUBLIC

Le Havre

Fürth

Stuttgart

Paris

Munich

Vienna

Garmisch
Partenkirchen

Salzburg

AUSTRIA

UNTERGRAINAU

Bern Zurich

SWITZERLAND

FRANCE

ITALY

CONTENTS

MUNICH, UNTERGRAINAU, NEW YORK

JUDAISM AND GENEALOGY

THE BEROLZHEIMER COLLECTION

APPENDICES

Michael Bersolzheimer

PREFACE

There were many cross-currents of events which led to this book about my great-uncle and namesake, Dr. Michael Berolzheimer. Without the knowledge, research, and dedication of the distinguished authors who have molded a story out of fragments of history, this book could not have been written. I owe them an immeasurable debt of gratitude.

Dr. Michael's art collection and genealogical writings represent the core of these fragments. Art collectors maintain meticulous records to prove the provenance of each piece. Family members preserve important papers which sooner or later attract someone's interest. Municipal and state archives house the clues which lead to important discoveries. Museums nurture people who pursue the process of discovery. And today, we benefit from access to countless records on the Internet.

My great-uncle Michael's story is of interest not only to his family. This publication also represents a way to better understand the era in which he lived; especially the contrast between Michael's idyllic life in Untergrainau and the devastating consequences of the Nazi era. Through Michael's story we rediscover the events of his times, leading to a different perspective of our own lives. We also discover the intellectual, studious, detailed, and romantic character of a remarkable man.

Shortly after my birth, Michael sent my parents a beautiful, long letter about the history of the name Michael. At the age of twelve, I was given Michael's desk, part of the furniture my father had purchased from his estate. At the age of sixty-five, and still knowing very little about him, I inherited many of Michael's etchings. Three years later a stranger asked for the addresses of Michael's heirs by e-mail. Suddenly I had to face many questions: Who was this person after whom I was named? How might I honor his memory? How should I honor my own German heritage?

In the last years of her life, my wife, Yoshiko (1945–2012), encouraged me to complete this personal journey. It is to her I dedicate this book.

Michael G. Berolzheimer
Saitama, Japan / September 2014

FOREWORD

This book is more than a biography. To capture a life between the covers of a book, to relate a personal history with all its unpredictable turns of events and ultimately logical development is an ambitious task. It would appear arrogant to dare the seemingly impossible, to narrate how an individual's personality and character develops, changes, and matures: how the "human" in a person gains in intensity, how emotions—hopes, fears, longings, passions, and many other emotive states—become intermingled with talents and skills, experience and chance, shaping an individual's mindset, honing special characteristics, and finally defining a person's unique qualities.

A publication such as this is primarily an experiment. An experiment to draw nearer to a person who lives on solely in scant written recollections, in a few archival fragments, and a number of rediscovered photos, and who—for quite some time—has not held a prominent place in the memories of his successors. The generation of "contemporary witnesses" mostly passed on long ago. Only very few are left who are still able to tell of Dr. Michael Berolzheimer (*fig. 1*) from their own personal encounters, from their own experiences, and from the times they lived through together. This book is accordingly an attempt to reconstruct events. And since the term "reconstruction" is inherently a creative undertaking, it should be conceded that writing a biography frequently touches on the speculative. How something was, how events unfolded and the course they followed cannot always be proven beyond doubt. Stories can be deduced, explained, and implied. But they cannot be substantiated. History, on the other hand, is scholarship which records and explains past events. And the same is true for the genre "biography." Nonetheless, the experiment to record the story of Michael Berolzheimer's life has been tackled. This publication tells the story of a man whose life links two centuries which could not be more different.

Michael Berolzheimer was born and grew up in the supposedly "good old days." However, the glorified idyll of the Prince Regent period in Bavaria was ultimately forced to confront the tensions and challenges of a crisis-ridden modern era. During Berolzheimer's lifetime the implacable clash between tradition and progress took its course; he witnessed the destructive confrontation between the complacency of the bourgeoisie and the avant-garde spirit of optimism.

fig. 1 Michael Berolzheimer outside the front door at Hügel am Weg

Berolzheimer's life was also marked by the major, devastating catastrophes of the times. He experienced the horrors of World War I, which was to be such a definitive turning point, and in a much greater, more profound and tragic form, the crime to humanity perpetrated by the Nazis—the genocide of the Jews. The complexity and tragedy of these decades, which irrevocably changed and distorted the plans of whole generations and nations, are reflected in the protagonist's life. Berolzheimer attempted to elude the aggressive abuse and violent interventions over the course of time through his own particular form of inner emigration. His wealth enabled him to withdraw into his private sphere and to live out the ambitions of a critically wise member of the educated class, brought up honoring the traditional, classical values of his family and society. As an independent scholar and art collector Berolzheimer could afford intellectual introspection and withdrew—at least for some of the time—from the profane world with its loud, dazzling, and in many cases morbid and violent afflictions. In contrast to Munich as the regional capital and royal seat, the country oasis of Untergrainau in the heart of the Bavarian mountains was not only an ideal hideaway for intellectual escapism but also a shelter for a gentle, sensitive character. His marriage to Melitta Schweisheimer in his late thirties, after a long wait, was the ultimate fulfillment of a happiness that was to remain untroubled until 1933. With Hitler's rise to power, life became more and more difficult for the Berolzheimers. Being of Jewish extraction, Michael was to experience exclusion and the deprivation of his rights—a process which encroached step by step and gradually came to a head. The highly respected local resident, a doctor of jurisprudence and well regarded art expert was made into a publically stigmatized social outcast through the racial fanaticism of the Nazis. In summer 1938, he saw himself forced to leave his homeland. The emigrant—in reality a displaced person—was more than seventy years old at this time. He died on June 5, 1942, in New York.

The initial idea and starting point for this book evolved around the question of the fate of those works in Dr. Michael Berolzheimer's important art collection which he did not manage to take with him to the United States. The question was posed by his great-nephew and namesake, Michael G. Berolzheimer, who—as custodian to a certain extent of Berolzheimer's legacy—wanted to know more about the injustice that befell his ancestor "Uncle Michael" after 1933. The scope of the project developed and expanded from the initial research work to clarify questions of art provenance. Apart from Berolzheimer as a collector, the person himself increasingly became the focus of this undertaking. And with good reason. Can a collection possibly be regarded as an abstract assortment of objects without taking the personality of the collector into consideration?

In the case of this unusual project, the generally dialog-free search for traces of a collector or art dealer, being the fundamental focus of provenance research, turned into a discussion spanning continents and generations. The idea for this book started in 2009 with an e-mail enquiring about Dr. Michael and a question about Anselm Feuerbach's *Woman with a Fan*. What followed were trial forays into museum archives, which brought the first traces of Berolzheimer to light in the circle of the great art historian and museum director Hugo von Tschudi. Although the Pinakothek Museums in Munich had not profitted at the time from the confiscation of his art collection, they had equally done nothing to protect him. What is an institution's duty in the face of its own history, when seventy-

five years later it is confronted with the extreme injustice that befell one of its
important former associates? Michael Berolzheimer, advisor to the Pinakothek
Museums and contemporary of Hugo von Tschudi, was robbed of his exceptional
art collection and there is nothing today to remind us of him in the city or region
in which he chose to live.

It was therefore fortunate that the idea for a book project could be treated
with the same level of awareness by representatives of the Bayerische Staatsgemäldesammlungen (Bavarian State Picture Collections), the Münchner Stadtarchiv
(Munich City Archives), and the Jewish Museum Munich. Through this attempt
to render visible what had once been lost once, these institutions have been
able to contribute to enhancing the collective memory and illuminating and
reconstructing a forgotten chapter in Munich's municipal and museum history.
Discussions with Michael G. Berolzheimer in the Stadtarchiv, as well as the
meeting in Untergrainau in "Uncle Michael's" villa, served to launch this project,
a project which from the very outset was met with great enthusiasm by all
participants. The institutions connected with this undertaking (the Bavarian State
Picture Collections, the Munich City Archives, and the Jewish Museum Munich)

consider this project unique and are grateful for having been given such an opportunity.

The remaining section of Michael Berolzheimer's art collection was dispersed among public and private collections in Germany and Austria after 1938 without its provenance being considered relevant or subject to research. This can, on the one hand, be attributed to the mood of the post-war period, when memories of art ownership had been lost or were simply ignored during the huge rebuilding effort. Decades of major exhibition cycles followed, which degraded the compilation of oeuvre catalogs to the not-so-popular field of specialist research, and placed the subject of provenance right at the bottom of the list. However, as a result of the Washington Conference on Holocaust-Era Assets, held in 1998 and attended by delegates from forty-four countries, the issue of the restitution of assets confiscated in 1933–45 was addressed. Based on the recommendations made, museums and other public institutions began to examine their holdings and check the provenance of their art works.

For prints and other works on paper, however, provenance research is extremely complex and seldom without its problems. Public collections, whose holdings of prints can easily run into six to seven digits, rarely had complete catalogs of works, nor was it usual for private collectors to mark their prints with their own collector stamps. If these metadata do not exist, how is Berolzheimer's collection to be traced? In our case, to aggravate this situation, "Uncle Michael's" collection was not in the public eye. The time it finally did attract attention, however, is linked to the darkest and most dramatic episode in the collector's biography, namely the brief period leading up to and immediately following Berolzheimer's emigration.

The part of Berolzheimer's collection left behind in Untergrainau was auctioned at Weinmüller's in Munich on November 30, 1938, and on March 9 and 10, 1939, in the owner's absence. By chance, auction catalogs found while pursuing post-war restitution claims, with Berolzheimer given as the provenance, included hand-written notes with the names and details of several successful bidders. These included the Kupferstichkabinett of the Staatliche Museen Preußischer Kulturbesitz (Museum of Prints and Drawings in Berlin), the Albertina in Vienna, the Kunsthalle Bremen, the Staatliche Graphische Sammlung München, the Städtische Galerie im Lenbachhaus in Munich, and the Städel in Frankfurt, to mention just a few institutions. Apart from the enormity of the injustice of these illegal confiscations, it is the acquisition of confiscated works by museums in particular, made in such a matter-of-fact and seemingly legal manner, which—in retrospect—still seems shocking to this day. Several works owned by Michael Berolzheimer have been restituted in the past (*figs 2, 3*). However, many claims are outstanding and are still being pursued by his heirs at the time of publishing.

During our first meeting with the publisher, the interest of all participants was awakened. We have been able to provide the background history of Munich and Bavaria as well as its art scene, and we gratefully acknowledge the considerable support of an extensive network of experts in various fields who have contributed to providing a broader view of Dr. Michael Berolzheimer's life. We are all equally grateful to Michael G. Berolzheimer for allowing us to accompany him on his quest to find out more about his ancestor "Uncle Michael."

fig. 3   Flemish, 17th century. *View of a Dutch Village*,
pen in brown ink, restituted by the Albertina, Vienna

Fürth i. B. Berolzheimerianum

donated to the town of Fürth
by Heinrich Berolzheimer
1836 - 1906
built in 1911, destroyed in 1945
rebuilt in 1956
by the city of Nürnberg

a statue in a niche, covered by the ivy, is of Prince
Regent Luitpold of Bavaria (1821 - 1912)
married 1844 Princesse Augusta of Austria (1825 - 1864)

See letter 19 March 1931

INTRODUCTION

Michael Berolzheimer was born on February 22, 1866, in the city of Fürth, not far from Nuremberg in Northern Bavaria, Germany, the third son of Heinrich Berolzheimer and his wife, Lina. Heinrich was descended from a long line of established and distinguished Franconian Jews, and at a young age had inherited a fifty-percent share in a pencil factory which had been founded in Fürth by his father, Daniel, and his business partner, Leopold Illfelder. Over the years, Heinrich had built the company up to global importance. He established offices in London and New York, and finally built a pencil factory in the United States which thrived on the vast resources of the North American continent and world-wide demand. Unwittingly, he also split the family by taking two of his sons, Emil and Philip, to the USA at the end of the nineteenth century, where they established roots and became the American branches of his family.

Heinrich traveled back and forth between the continents, learning about the advantages of a good public education system in America. He became a benefactor in his native town, funding the "Berolzheimerianum" (*fig. 1*), a spectacular edifice for a public education organization, including a public library. He died shortly before its grand opening in 1906.

During his lifetime, Heinrich was awarded the St. Michael's Cross for his philanthropy by Prince Luitpold of Bavaria. The honorary citizenship of Fürth was also bestowed on him as well as that of Nuremberg, his place of retirement. Together with his sons, he had provided funding for the building of the Luitpold Haus—a public education facility which is now the city library—as well as the Künstlerhaus, an art gallery.

Michael Berolzheimer's upbringing was based on German history and culture, and marked by his Jewish heritage. His frequent trips around Europe exposed him early on to foreign cultures, unfamiliar places, new ideas, and different ways of life.

Berolzheimer served for a brief period as a young man in the Fürth regiment of the Bavarian army, but was soon discharged for health reasons. A lingering heart ailment affected him all his life, as did bad hearing. Nevertheless, he had a sharp, logical mind and went on to study law at the universities of Würzburg, Munich, and Leipzig. He established a law practice, but his interests were drawn to the thriving art community in Munich and to genealogy. Fine arts and cultural

fig. 1   The "Berolzheimerianum" in Fürth

art objects became a passion of his. He started collecting graphic works, traveled to France and Italy for art's sake, and commissioned a ceiling painting by a Munich artist for his newly built country house in Untergrainau.

Berolzheimer was a patient man. He had to wait until he was thirty-seven years old to marry the woman he loved, Melitta Dispeker, who divorced her first husband, Eugen Schweisheimer, to be with Berolzheimer. Michael and Melitta had no children together, but Berolzheimer cared deeply for Melitta's three children from her first marriage, Waldemar, Nelly, and Robert, and later for their children too.

For nearly twenty years the house "Hügel am Weg" in Untergrainau in the mountains south of Munich, became the center of their happy family life (*fig. 2*). Every year for over a decade they moved seasonally from Munich to the Bavarian

fig. 2   Hügel am Weg

alpine hamlet, until—in 1919—they finally decided to give up polluted city life and settle permanently in the fresh mountain air of Untergrainau.

Melitta was a loving, socially polished, and outgoing woman who provided the counterpoint to Berolzheimer's quiet, studious, concentrated life. She was a gracious hostess to frequent visitors, and with local domestic help ran her household with a kind but firm hand. The garden surrounding the large property was everybody's favorite place, and there was never a shortage of flowers in the rooms of the well-appointed house.

Berolzheimer himself became engrossed in the detailed research of his family. Old gravestones in Jewish cemeteries were crumbling and Hebrew documents stored in the synagogues were becoming unreadable to the younger "worldly" generations. When Theodor Harburger was charged with the documentation of Jewish graves and artifacts in Bavaria, Berolzheimer found a great source of information for his research. Even more important was his friendship with the rabbi, Dr. Max Freudenthal, another genealogist. The extensive correspondence Berolzheimer enjoyed with Harburger, Freudenthal, and other interested genealogists, as well as his contributions to related publications, kept him at his desk for hours on end, frequently on his own and deep in thought, as he concentrated on making copious notes which were later used in his writings.

Berolzheimer was not only tracing his own family's history, but also researching that of many interrelated Jewish families in the Franconia region in the process. His detailed findings and comments have thankfully survived and are accessible today on-line through the Leo Baeck Institute in New York. As a result of Jewish persecution during the Nazi era and the destruction brought about by World War II, few authentic Jewish genealogical sources have survived intact. Berolzheimer's genealogical work has since become one of the primary sources for Franconian Jewish family research.

Living in a relatively remote corner of the countryside, Michael and Melitta were largely sheltered from the political upheaval in Munich and the rest of the country for quite some time, although they were fully aware of developments. Ultimately the anti-Semitic decrees introduced by Hitler affected their lives as well. In 1936, Melitta's oldest son, Waldemar, emigrated with his family to America after being prohibited from practicing as a doctor. The four children of Melitta's daughter, Nelly, were sent to boarding school in Italy that same year, because they were refused public schooling in Germany. By 1938, Nelly and her husband, Leopold Friedberg, sought permission to emigrate, as did Melitta's son, Robert, and his wife, Lilly.

Berolzheimer and Melitta had visited Michael's brother, Philip, in America, in winter 1933, when Hitler's power was already starting to grow ominously. They traveled to New York once again in 1937 to visit Waldemar and most probably to organize their own emigration. The annexation of Austria in March 1938, the decree for the meticulous recording of Jews' assets in April 1938, and the desecration of the Munich Synagogue (*see p. 37*) abruptly ordered by Hitler in June 1938 were like final warning bells.

The Berolzheimers packed their belongings and left Germany on July 26, 1938, just two days before an order was issued to confiscate their passports. They first went to Zurich, Switzerland, for a few weeks until they managed to secure passage aboard the SS Washington (*fig. 3*), which departed Le Havre, France, to New York on September 8, 1938. One condition for being granted an

fig. 3　SS Washington, colored postcard, c. 1938

emigration permit was for the Berolzheimers to leave part of their art collection behind. This was later sent to auction (*see p. 149 ff.*). All proceeds of the auctioned items were confiscated by the government and never reached Berolzheimer.

In spite of their worries about family members and friends left behind among the political turmoil in Europe, Michael and Melitta spent their remaining years in America relatively happily. They both died in summer 1942; Michael on June 5, Melitta following him just fifteen days later on June 20. They were buried side by side in the Beth-El Cemetery in Queens, New York, next to Michael's brother, Philip, who had died just two weeks earlier on May 22.

In December 1938, nine months before the outbreak of World War II, both Michael and Melitta signed rather complicated wills with a view to the prevailing situation. With Melitta's son, Waldemar, appointed executor by default for both testaments, they had planned an orderly transfer of their possessions. They could not foresee the drastic consequences of Hitler losing the war, the Allied Forces occupying Germany, the Americans taking over the administration in Bavaria, and the eventual legislation to restitute property taken unlawfully.

Berolzheimer's art collection and his properties left behind in Germany became part of an extended restitution effort by his executor. Locating his artworks—auctioned under duress and bought by various institutions and private individuals without the proceeds ever reaching the owner—is still an ongoing project, aided by the New York Holocaust Claims Centre. Berolzheimer's ownership of his much-loved villa, Hügel am Weg, and land in Untergrainau, was easier to prove; the house was restituted and parcels of real estate eventually sold.

The financial aspect surrounding Michael Berolzheimer's art collection drove a wedge between the Schweisheimer heirs. Contact among the Berolzheimer descendents was cut, and family knowledge of Berolzheimer's life and legacy disappeared with the death of his nephew, Charles.

Charles Berolzheimer was a favorite nephew of Michael's and shared many of his traits. Very well educated and widely traveled, both for pleasure and business reasons, Charles visited his uncle several times in Germany. He felt a great affection and loyalty towards his German uncle, naming his second son, Michael, after him. With the outbreak of World War II, Charles volunteered for the army. He was deployed in the European war theater and witnessed first hand the horrors of war. Like so many others, he closed his mind to these memories and refused to pass on any information which had to do with Germany to his sons—including information about his uncle.

Restitution inquiries instigated by the Graphics Art Collection at the Albertina in Vienna, Austria, which had bought several drawings and works on paper owned by Michael Berolzheimer at an auction in 1939, ultimately led to more questions being asked. Since that time it has been a lengthy and fascinating process spanning more than fifteen years to find the answers.

This book traces the rediscovery of a remarkable life.

Map of Bavaria, Germany, showing places and regions
mentioned in the book, with the names of other
German states and neighboring countries

MUNICH   UNTERGRAINAU   NEW YORK

MICHAEL BEROLZHEIMER IN MUNICH

Places and their residents always form a symbiotic entity. A city without citizens is unthinkable. Topographical features are only turned into familiar places through those who live there. And people, biographies, and fates are always influenced by the places to which they are linked. The question therefore begs to be asked—what was Munich like when Michael Berolzheimer first arrived in the city as a young man in 1885, a city which would be his home for the next thirty or so years? What did the Jewish student from Franconia, a region in what was then the Kingdom of Bavaria, who went on to become an attorney and counselor at the royal court, feel about the forward-looking provincial capital in southern Germany? To gain a better perspective, things need to be placed in a wider context.

Munich around 1850: This was a period that marked the city's transition from an unremarkable provincial capital to a German metropolis of universal appeal. Urban development had been given a lasting impulse by visionary projects initiated by Ludwig I—that philhellenist and admirer of architecture—who ascended the throne in 1825 (*fig. 2*). The king declared city planning to be a political undertaking. Although his expansion plans and construction projects turned Munich into a massive building site for decades, his frequently quoted desire "to turn Munich into a city that will bring such honor to Germany, that nobody can claim to know Germany without having seen Munich,"[1] served as a catalyst for further developments in the regional capital. In the years that followed, striking architectural gems were built, which no metropolis of rank could consider being without.

It was Ludwig's creative drive, his persistence, and his power of persuasion, which soon led to Bavaria's capital being able to secure a place of honor alongside other traditional centers of culture in Europe.[2] Munich's transition into the proud cultural and administrative center of southern Germany took place on several levels, and influenced various spheres and sections of the city's local community with differing intensity. The architectural achievements and innovative urban planning under Ludwig I were just one side of the coin. Other major factors, which also had a decisive impact on the developing self-confidence of the ambitious "Athens on the Isar" (*fig. 1*), included the reorganization of state administrative bodies by the reformist Maximilian von Montgelas into a modern

fig. 1   Aerial view of Königsplatz, with
the cathedral church in the background, c. 1916

fig. 2   Ludwig I, c. 1860

33

and effective centralized entity and the introduction of new local by-laws (1817/18), the formation of the archbishopric of Munich and Freising, including the suffragan dioceses of Augsburg, Passau, and Regensburg (1821), and moving the university from Landshut to Munich (1826). Finally, the link to the railroad network (1839) created new possibilities for economic expansion (*figs 3, 4*). It took these changes to turn the new Munich into a "mix of Old Munich and an 'Athens on the Isar,' an artists' metropolis, which helped promote tourism, a mixture of easy-going provincialism, and cosmopolitan worldliness."[3]

At the beginning of the nineteenth century, Munich had a population of about 60,000, and there was no sign of its steady growth slowing down. By the middle of the century that number had risen to more than 121,000. It was no longer the Bavarian nobility seeking the proximity of the Wittelsbach court which influenced the social configuration of the city, but the ambitious quest for representation by the well-to-do, upper middle classes. The Industrial Revolution had also had an impact on the city. Within a few decades, Munich had become the most important industrial center in Bavaria. As a result of this dynamic urban development the Bavarian capital and seat of the royal family was extremely attractive to people from Upper Bavaria, Swabia, and Franconia, especially in the second half of the nineteenth century. Munich's development into a regional capital, not just in name but as the actual center of the Kingdom of Bavaria, resulted in a steady increase in the number of new residents from surrounding areas, who saw promising opportunities in Munich and hoped for economic growth and career opportunities.

Munich's shift from a small, introspective city and seat of the Prince-Elector, to a metropolis of the arts, culture, and commerce of international standing, brought with it significant social changes (*fig. 5*). In addition to the rather reserved, independent-minded characters of Old Munich—whose unique mixture

fig. 3   View of Munich station, c. 1925

fig. 4   Square in front of Munich station, c. 1900, hand-colored postcard

fig. 5 View of the Palace of Justice, Karlsplatz, Munich, c. 1900, hand-colored postcard

of charm and grumpiness embodied the values typically found among craftspeople and farmers—an academic, intellectual, and particularly artistic elite emerged, attracted by the development boom and seemingly never-ending state contracts. In the middle of the century, a Swedish visitor to Munich commented with candid admiration: "Munich has such an immeasurable richness of artists at the moment, which is no surprise if one knows they are pouring in from all parts of Germany to study and achieve a high level of perfection. What Rome still is to all artists in the world, Munich is to Germany."[4] A wealthy and educated middle class was emerging in Munich, superseding the aristocracy and adopting the leading role the latter had played until then. Executive civil servants, high-ranking military officers, academics, entrepreneurs, bankers, doctors, attorneys, and wealthy men of independent means lived side by side with locally respected figures—the craftspeople, innkeepers, house owners, and farmers of Old Munich—to create a new urban society. Perfectly in keeping with the spirit of the times and influenced by the Enlightenment, political liberalism, and republican ideals, the bourgeoisie assertively claimed its share in social and political decision-making processes. The principle of local self-government was reinforced, and the desire of its citizens for a political say in their own affairs assumed a new dimension.

There were certainly several understandable motifs and good reasons which prompted Michael Berolzheimer to move to Munich at the end of October 1885,

immediately after being dismissed from compulsory military service due to heart
trouble. It was here, at the renowned Ludwig-Maximilians-Universität (*fig. 6*),
that he wanted to study law. It was here that a sound foundation for his future
life was to be laid. For a young man born into a highly-regarded family with its
roots in Franconia, keen to learn and interested in history and culture, Munich
would doubtlessly have been the logical place to study, as he had relatives in
Munich and other family members had also studied law there. A comparable
combination of such a high standard of living and first-class academic and
cultural opportunities was otherwise only to be found in Berlin or Vienna—with
the disadvantage of living a considerable distance from home. That the Bavarian
royal city already had a sizable Jewish community at the end of the nineteenth
century and a correspondingly developed ritual and cultural infrastructure, also
spoke in Munich's favor.

   After lengthy negotiations and tedious discussions, the building of a representative main synagogue had been started in 1884. Located not far from the
cathedral, the Frauenkirche, the synagogue was unequaled, not just in southern
Germany but far beyond its borders too. The design chosen was by the Munich
architect Albert Schmidt, who with his Neo-Romanesque, single-aisled building,
proposed an impressive and distinct urban landmark in the heart of the city.

fig. 6   The main university buildings, where two of
Munich's major boulevards, Ludwigstrasse and Leopold-
strasse meet just to the north of the city center, c. 1905

After a construction period of almost three years, the synagogue was completed in summer 1887 (*fig. 7*). With 1,000 prayer chairs for men and 800 for women, it was, in its day, the third-largest Jewish house of worship in the German Empire after the synagogues in Berlin and Breslau. Critics called the new building "an utterly unique work of pronounced individuality, a memorial not just to the master who designed it, but to the times in which it was built."[5]

The building of the new synagogue was a remarkable testimony to the social confidence of the Jewish community in Munich at the end of the nineteenth century. Situated on a prominent site and visible to everybody from afar, the synagogue marked an unmistakable change in the relationship between its builders and the non-Jewish world. The imposing structure was a proud demonstration of how the Jewish congregation had now become part of Munich society. The banishing of the synagogue in the past to the fringes of the predominantly Catholic city had now given way to this bold, public sign of recognition. Or to phrase it differently, not only did the middle classes prosper towards the close of the nineteenth century, but a diverse and prosperous Jewish society was also developing at the same time. It is not without reason that the last decade of the nineteenth and the first of the twentieth century are described as "the golden age of Jewish life in Munich."[6]

fig. 7 The main synagogue on Herzog-Max-Strasse, 1889

For devout Jews contemplating a move to Munich, it was certainly significiant that Jewish life had now become an integral part of the city's social fabric. This was probably also true for Michael's parents, Heinrich and Karoline (Lina) Berolzheimer, who had a decisive influence on their son's future plans. There was a strong sense of Jewish identity and religious zeal in the family, and indeed, until his move temporarily to New York in 1886, Heinrich Berolzheimer remained a board member of the Israelite Congregation in Fürth and a highly respected member of the Jewish community.[7]

In fall 1885, Michael Berolzheimer moved to Munich after two semesters in Würzburg. Although he officially still held residence status in Fürth, and later on in Nuremberg, the next few years were marked by frequent moves. On October 30, the nineteen-year-old matriculated at the university. At first he lodged on the second floor of a handsome building from the *Gründerzeit* period, at Herzogspitalstrasse 12 (*fig. 8*), in the heart of city.[8] His landlord was Thomas Siegl, a middle-ranking civil servant working as chief conductor, who sought to better his meager income by taking in student lodgers.[9] Just six months later, Berolzheimer moved round the corner to Sonnenstrasse 27. And as of April 1887, we find him not far from the university to the northwest of the city centre, at Gabelsbergerstrasse 5/I, where he took lodgings at the master tailor Mathias Rösch's.[10]

fig. 8 Herzogspitalstrasse 12, Berolzheimer's first lodgings in Munich, c. 1910

fig. 9 Burgstrasse 6, c. 1920

In those days, a certain mobility with a frequent change of address was nothing unusual—especially among students—as with "just a little baggage" it was easy to move from one place to the next, pushing one's belongings in a hand-cart. The man living in furnished rooms, an unmarried tenant with a suitcase but without any relatives or other dependents, was typical of the times.

The young Michael Berolzheimer also lived at several other addresses scattered around the inner city during his time in Munich. In April 1891, he was registered as living at Burgstrasse 6 (fig. 9), just a few yards from the central square, Marienplatz, where Berolzheimer lodged on the third floor for nearly two years. This time his landlord was the fuel merchant Johann Baptist Bauer.[11] It was also in 1891 that Berolzheimer successfully sat the *Staatsexamen*, the state law exam.[12] From the end of March 1893, we find him at Jägerstrasse 3b, renting a room on the fourth floor from Babette Hölzl, a court counselor's widow.[13]

By the age of twenty-six, Berolzheimer had gained a doctorate in law and decided to become an attorney. According to an entry in the listing of attorneys in the city, he opened his first law office at Dienerstrasse 7/III on August 28, 1892;[14] in 1894, he moved into more representative premises at Neuhauser Strasse 33/I (figs 10, 11). Fittingly, there was a tavern on the ground floor of the property by the name of "Zum Gefängnis" (Jail Inn), which conjures up many an allusion. On both occasions he shared the office with the politically-active, fellow attorney Dr. Benedikt Bernheim (1862–1924), whose wife Rosa Oettinger was related to Berolzheimer through their common great-great-grandfather, Hirsch Berolzheimer.[15] Only much later did Dr. Michael Berolzheimer rent an office for his legal practice on his own—at Neuhauser Strasse 7/II, as of July 31, 1917.[16]

During the second half of the 1890s and in the early 1900s, Berolzheimer went to Nuremberg on several occasions and for different lengths of time, to stay with his parents, who had moved there from Fürth in August 1889.[17] His brothers would come from America at this time, sometimes accompanied by their families, and Berolzheimer enjoyed lengthy summer vacations with his family. His mother, however, was most probably ailing at that time, and died in 1901. His father died five years later after a long illness.

Berolzheimer returned to Munich at the end of September 1898, and moved into an apartment at Ainmillerstrasse 9/I in the Schwabing neighborhood (fig. 12). Even though Berolzheimer frequently traveled in subsequent years, the attorney's life remained centered on Munich, where his future wife Melitta Schweisheimer was living with her husband and their three children (see p. 50).

Berolzheimer applied for citizenship and residence rights in the Bavarian capital and seat of the royal court in summer 1903. This was generally a privilege only bestowed with extreme caution and after detailed checks by the local authorities, and only given to applicants with sufficient funds and an excellent reputation. Applicants were charged a fee of 150 Marks, which would have amounted to a small fortune in those days.[18]

For Berolzheimer, neither the fee nor character references were a problem. The city gladly granted him citizenship without the usually thorough investigations. However, he was not able personally to pick up the official citizenship and residency certificate made out in October 1903, as he was away on a lengthy trip abroad. A note from his housekeeper, Maria Braun, written on the receipt slip, states quite clearly: "Herr Dr. Berolzheimer is abroad in Rome. May possibly stay a year." A little later, Berolzheimer contacted the city magistrate's office.

Written on headed writing paper from the Hotel de la Paix & Helvetia in Rome, where he was staying, he asked "with the greatest respect" if it were possible "to postpone the matter until March 1, 1904, bearing in mind that I will most likely be absent from Munich during the winter months."[19] This request was granted without any difficulty, and the official presentation of citizenship and residence rights in Munich was made in March 1904.[20]

Much speaks for the assumption that this trip to Rome in October 1903 was in fact the honeymoon of a newly married couple—Berolzheimer having married Melitta Schweisheimer, née Dispeker, in London on September 26, 1903. It is likely that the couple had actually known each other at least since the mid 1890s, but Melitta was married at that time to Eugen Schweisheimer, a banker from Munich. That marriage produced two sons and one daughter.

Despite her love for Berolzheimer, Melitta was not ready to apply for divorce out of consideration for her young children. It was not until 1903, after an eight-year-long trial of patience, that she was granted a divorce and Michael and Melitta were able to marry. The journey to Italy may therefore have been the result of a longstanding yearning for privacy and intimacy.

After their return in 1904, Berolzheimer rented an apartment for himself and his wife on the fourth floor at Franz-Joseph-Strasse 21, in the immediate neighborhood of where he had previously lived. One of the other tenants in the house was the renowned neurologist Leonhard Seif (1866–1949), one of the psychoanalytical dissidents around Carl Gustav Jung and Alfred Adler. The composer and pianist Bernhard Stavenhagen (1862–1914), a gifted musician and student of Liszt, also lived in the same house. He was director of the University of Music and Performing Arts Munich, and was highly regarded internationally.

Michael and Melitta Berolzheimer therefore found themselves in a well connected, socio-cultural environment at the beginning of the twentieth century. The couple, both now in their forties, would have been considered part of Munich's upper middle class society. But Michael and Melitta had nothing in common with the fleeting members of the local establishment, who had gained status and wealth as part of the urbanization process. Nor did they imitate court rituals by wallowing in their own importance or—to ensure that they did not slip into oblivion whatever happened—by maintaining an eternal presence in appropriate social circles, in *salons*, and at *soirées*. In the relevant chronicles and journals of the day, there is no mention of the Berolzheimers. And a search for the name Berolzheimer in local daily papers—the most important medium for news at the time, which reported in detail virtually every aspect of city life—is also in vain. Berolzheimer was not a person in the public eye in spite of his social status and his profession as an attorney. It may even be assumed that he consciously avoided publicity and the inquisitive gaze of the public. In the few photographs which exist, he appears as a serious looking, focussed, and composed man, emerging as a reserved and quiet intellectual only at second glance. He was a person who kept his distance, who was no friend of the camera—the prying eye of the photographer. Instead, a friend of the arts and sciences can be seen, a well educated, clear-sighted researcher with a sense of perseverance. In short, an analytical mind interested in widening his knowledge; someone who is dedicated to the appreciation and collection of art for its own sake, not because the social reward of having a collection built around a work's importance and quality leads to a better reputation and greater prestige, but rather because of a private

fig. 10 Excerpt from the Munich address register, 1904

fig. *11* Neuhauser Strasse 33, 1910

inclination and personal passion. Or in the words of his great-nephew and namesake, Michael G. Berolzheimer: "… a man of vast knowledge and deep intellect, but also of great sensitivity, commitment, and compassion."[21]

There is much to support this unpretentious image of a modest and financially independent Berolzheimer and his insatiable appetite for knowledge. There is not just his genuine love of nature and the Bavarian mountains, which had nothing to do with any false romanticism or folkloric notions. His lengthy trips abroad, often lasting several months, to England, France, and Italy, for example, prevented an all too close, too restricting dependence on the social circles of Munich, since belonging to any particular social group required continuous presence. That was something the Berolzheimers neither wanted nor were able to do. In addition, Berolzheimer developed an interest in a socially rather isolating discipline—genealogy. This time-consuming and frequently expensive passion is a science behind closed doors, which in spite of considerable expenditure produces little return at times—a field for meticulous and persevering researchers, not for presumptuous, academic show-offs.

Nevertheless, Berolzheimer always kept a close eye on the events of the day and commented on them perceptively. The few letters preserved in the family archives reveal a clear-sighted analyst, who understood how to interpret the developments and confusion of the period. In 1924, he painted a vivid picture of the situation in Germany and Munich to his twenty-two-year-old nephew, Charles, who lived in New York. Even at this early date, Berolzheimer sketched a sobering image of Germany's future prospects: "It is just as dangerous on a political level. On the left, the Bolshevik flood is rising, which will show at the next election to the Reichstag in a most distinct and disastrous way, and on the right, the reactionary, anti-Semitic, anti-Catholic, nationalistic wave is rising higher and higher. As you know, the court case against Hitler, General Ludendorff, and others is presently being held in Munich, which gives an idea of the dangerous situations that are constantly threatening Germany. And this process of decay in Germany will naturally spread to all of Europe, and has in fact already started."[22] The short, emphatic, and prophetic letter ends with a quotation from Horace's *Letters*: "Quidquid delirant reges, plectuntur Achivi" (Whatever folly the rulers embark upon, it is the ordinary people who bear the consequences).

In 1919, Melitta and Michael Berolzheimer moved permanently from Munich to Untergrainau— a small village close to Garmisch-Partenkirchen at the foot of the Bavarian Alps—having decided to settle in "Hügel am Weg". Over the years, their summer house had become a much cherished and indispensable focal point in their lives.

fig. 12 A view of Ainmillerstrasse in Schwabing, later a center of bohemian life and the haunt of German Expressionist artists, c. 1905

1   Hans-Rüdiger Schwab (ed.), *München. Dichter sehen eine Stadt,* Stuttgart 1990, p. 58.

2   Richard Bauer, "Stadt und Stadtverfassung im Umbruch" in: Hans-Rüdiger Schwab (ed.), *Geschichte der Stadt München,* Munich 1992, p. 273.

3   Ralf Zerback, "Unter der Kuratel des Staates" in: ibid., p. 288.

4   Hans-Joachim Kissling, "Ein zeitgenössischer schwedischer Bericht über die Entstehung des ludwigischen Münchens: T.G.Rudbeck's *Det Nya München"* in: *Zeitschrift für Bayerische Landesgeschichte* 43 (1980), p. 644 f.

5   Leo Baerwald, Ludwig Feuchtwanger (eds), *Festgabe. 50 Jahre Hauptsynagoge München, 1887–1937,* Munich 1937, p. 75.

6   Elisabeth Angermair, "Eine selbstbewusste Minderheit (1892–1918)" in: Richard Bauer, Michael Brenner (eds), *Jüdisches München. Vom Mittelalter bis zur Gegenwart,* Munich 2006, p. 110.

7   Michael Berolzheimer, *Geschichte der Familie Berolzheimer* (handwritten manuscript), Berolzheimer Family Archives, Stockton, USA.

8   All addresses have been taken from: Stadtarchiv München PMB B 223.
    From 1885–1904 Michael Berolzheimer was registered as living at the following addresses in Munich (and Starnberg, a short distance to the southwest of Munich in 1898).
    October 30, 1885   Herzogspitalstrasse 12/I (left), c/o Siegl
    May 3, 1886   Sonnenstrasse 27I, c/o Kleckamm
    April 26, 1887   Gabelsbergerstrasse 5/I, c/o Rösch
    April 21, 1891   Burgstrasse 6/III (left), c/o Bauer
    March 31, 1893   Jägerstrasse 3b/II, c/o Hölzl
    July 1, 1898   Maximilianstrasse 68 (Starnberg)
    September 28, 1898   Ainmillerstrasse 9/I c/o Frank
    October 10, 1904   Franz-Joseph-Strasse 21/III

9   Munich address register, 1886.

10 Munich address register, 1887.

11 Munich address register, 1892.

12 Stadtarchiv München RAK 2278.

13 Munich address register, 1893.

14 Bayerisches Hauptstaatsarchiv München, Justice Dept. 20380.

15 Munich address registers, 1893, 1895.

16 Stadtarchiv München PMB B 223.

17 Entry in Fürth registry dated 09/18/1903, Stadtarchiv München EBA 1903/424.

18 As a form of orientation and for an approximation of the value in US dollars today, see Appendix.

19 Letter of 10/30/1903 from Dr. Michael Berolzheimer to the city magistrate in Munich, Stadtarchiv München EBA 1903/424.

20 Note on official registration form of 04/12/1904, Stadtarchiv München PMB B223.

21 Michael G. Berolzheimer, "Overview of Dr. Michael Berolzheimers's Life (1866–1942)," unpublished manuscript, 2011.

22 Letter of 03/17/1924, Berolzheimer Family Archives, Stockton, Box 35, Folder 23.

"We feel very comfortable here …"

MELITTA AND MICHAEL BEROLZHEIMER: THIRTY YEARS IN UNTERGRAINAU

"We have become very used to living in the country, do not yearn for city life, and enjoy being in our little house every day. The vegetables are growing splendidly, and in the fall we want to extend the vegetable garden and build a greenhouse, where we can store the plants in the winter. We always have lots of visitors; yesterday for instance we hosted a cozy evening party with sixteen people. When fall arrives with its fog and short days, only then do we think of returning to the city …."

Melitta Berolzheimer (1867–1942) wrote this letter on August 3, 1908, in Untergrainau to her brother-in-law, Philip, and his wife, Clara, in the USA. Her husband, Michael (1866–1942), added:

"We feel very comfortable here, the air is wonderful, the countryside beautiful, and our little house most pleasant …."[1]

In 1908, Melitta and Michael Berolzheimer spent their first summer in the house in Untergrainau which had been completed earlier that year. Its location alone made them feel happy. The new house was just over half a mile from the village, on a small hillock, with an unrestricted view of the Wetterstein and Germany's highest mountain, the Zugspitze, further to the west. The hillock lies between Untergrainau station and a lake, the Eibsee, and appropriately, gave the new home its name "Hügel am Weg" — "the hill on the path" (*fig. 1*).

UNTERGRAINAU IN THE SHADOW OF THE ZUGSPITZE

What did Untergrainau look like in those days? The parish lies on the banks of the River Loisach, some sixty-two miles south of Munich in a region known as Werdenfelser Land. The village itself is 2450 feet above sea level and was amalgamated with the district of Garmisch in 1908, which was later expanded to form the administrative area of Garmisch-Partenkirchen. The parish covers a total area of just over six square miles. The only neighboring village is Obergrainau,

fig. 1 "Hügel am Weg," Untergrainau, the Berolzheimers' country home, c. 1910

with a population in 1910 of 402. The parish of Obergrainau borders the smaller village of Untergrainau to the west, south, and east. To the north, the boundary of Untergrainau is defined by the Loisach.[2]

And what sort of governance structure did an Upper Bavarian village have? The village had a mayor, a village priest, and a teacher. When the Berolzheimers moved to Untergrainau, the mayor was Mathias Bader, who held this office from 1907 through 1919. He carried out his official duties at that time from the front parlor of his own home. His brother, Johann Bader (*fig. 2*), had become mayor of Obergrainau one year earlier and remained in office until removed by the Nazis in 1939. Other mayors of Untergrainau during the time the Berolzheimers lived there were Josef Kraus (1919–25) and Anton Bader (1925–37).[3]

In 1908, the Catholic priest of Grainau—as the combined villages are known—was Prebendary Ludwig Lanzl, who held this position from 1901–11. He lived in the rectory, then called the "Benefiziatenhaus," on Kirchbichl in Obergrainau next to the church and cemetery.[4] Some time later, Michael Berolzheimer worked with one of Lanzl's successors, Prebendary Karl Herdegen, to ensure that a memorial to those who fell in World War I was built in Grainau.

The old schoolhouse is also on Kirchbichl. The building in its present form was built in 1912. The school director at this time was the local priest who taught alongside another teacher. It was not until the new school was built that teaching duties were separated from the Catholic benefice.[5]

Around 1810, Untergrainau was purely a farming community (*figs 3, 4*) with some twenty-two properties and a population of 113.[6] A hundred years later, the parish of Untergrainau—as the Berolzheimers would have known it— had fifty-two properties with a total population of 250. The growth of the village is shown in Table 1.[7]

Relatively speaking, there was what could almost be called a "building boom" in Grainau from 1895 onward, reflected in the number of building appli-

fig. 2 Local council members, c. 1930, with the mayor from 1906–1933, Johann Bader, on the right

cations submitted from both villages to the regional council office in Garmisch. While there had barely been more than three applications a year before, this number "swelled" from 1896 and in subsequent years to between ten and twenty.[8] Two developments contributed to this. From around 1880, the market towns of Garmisch and Partenkirchen were keen to promote the summer tourist trade. The Kainzenbad, a natural swimming and recreational area near Partenkirchen, which still exists to this day, drew many visitors. In 1883, the twin-towns attracted a total of 3,724 guests.[9] After the Murnau-to-Partenkirchen stretch of the railroad was completed in 1889, that number shot up, with 16,116 staying in Garmisch and 18,228 in Partenkirchen.[10] The wave of tourists also reached as far as Grainau. In summer 1910, Obergrainau recorded 1,675 guests staying a total of 7,534 nights.[11] Grainau experienced its first tourist boom in 1913, one year after the cross-border Ausserfern railway line was opened between Garmisch and Tyrol in Austria, as this meant that both villages, which each had its own station, could be reached directly by train.

	Residents	Properties	Of which villas and larger houses
1895	177	39	–
1910	250	65	11
1925	397	100	26
1937	700	140	–

Table 1: Number of residents and properties in Untergrainau

fig. 3   Cows being herded to their pastures, Untergrainau, c. 1930

Both villages were however still heavily dependent on agriculture. An animal census in 1910 shows that there were 361 head of cattle, 170 sheep, and 50 pigs in Obergrainau, and 194 cattle, 96 sheep, 18 pigs, and 3 goats in Untergrainau.[12]

Another development can also be seen in Table 2. The foothills of the Alps and its valleys were not only "discovered" by tourists, but by well situated, upper middle class families from the cities as well, who could afford a second home here. Country houses and villas were generally built on especially attractive sites in this scenic area. Spending the summer months in one's own four walls was very much *en vogue*. This had already started in the 1850s on Lake Starnberg to the southwest of Munich, reaching Garmisch and Partenkirchen in the 1870s, and Untergrainau later. By 1910, eleven villas had been built in Untergrainau, including that of the Berolzheimers. But what brought Michael Berolzheimer to Untergrainau in the first place?

	Untergrainau	Obergrainau	Grainau (combined)
1910	–	1675	–
1913	1007	7277	8284
1922	1806	6152	7958
1934	3977	7885	11,862
1938	–	–	23,523

Table 2: Development in the number of visitors to Grainau between 1910 and 1938[13]

PROFESSIONAL CAREER

Well read, educated, and meticulous—and a romantic; according to family members these were Berolzheimer's outstanding traits.[14]

Michael (*fig. 5*) was born on February 22, 1866, in Fürth in northern Bavaria and grew up with his three siblings, Emil (1862–1922), Philip (1867–1942), and Frida (1870–1942) in a cosmopolitan, Jewish, upper middle class family. His father, Heinrich Berolzheimer (1836–1906) was a successful entrepreneur and partner of a Fürth pencil manufacturing business. In 1868, Heinrich founded a branch office in America. In 1883 and 1885, his two sons, Emil and Philip, moved to the USA. Heinrich returned to Germany in 1889 as a wealthy man and settled in Nuremberg. He was made an honorary citizen of Fürth in 1904 and of Nuremberg in 1905 in recognition of his generous endowments—the "Berolzheimerianum," a public education facility in Fürth, and the "Luitpoldhaus," a natural science museum in Nuremberg.[15]

Michael Berolzheimer graduated from Nuremberg high school in August 1884 and enrolled at the Julius-Maximilians-Universität in Würzburg for the winter and summer semesters 1884/85. He was called up for military training in 1885 in Würzburg, but was declared unfit for service because of heart problems.[16] From October 1885 through October 1886 he studied law at the University of Munich, changed to Leipzig University for the winter semester, and returned to

fig. 4　Oxen and cart below a wayside cross on Loisachstrasse, c. 1930

fig. 5   Dr. Michael Berolzheimer in Hügel am Weg,
c. 1930

Munich in summer 1887. He completed his final two semesters in Würzburg.
Berolzheimer passed his first theoretical exam in August 1888, his second practical
exam in June 1892, and was officially admitted as attorney at the Royal Regional
Court of Appeal in Munich on August 28, 1892.[17]

Between 1894 and 1914, his name appeared in the annual "Hof und
Staatshandbuch" (court and state index) for the Kingdom of Bavaria as a court-
accredited attorney at law.[18] As a man of independent means, Berolzheimer's
financial situation allowed him to focus on his own interests, especially art and
genealogical research. From his father he had inherited part of his wealth, and
also received dividends from the Eagle Pencil Company in New York. His wife,
Melitta, had financial means of her own.[19]

It would seem that Berolzheimer's work as an attorney was more a sideline.
Back in 1913, Prince Ludwig—later King Ludwig III of Bavaria—had bestowed

the honorary title "Hofrat" (court counselor) on the attorney Michael Berolz-heimer, who used it proudly from that date onward (*fig. 6*). In 1915, he had his name taken off the list of practicing attorneys as he was planning to move from Munich to Untergrainau for good. However, due to the lack of legal representatives during World War I, he made his services available again and was reinstated as attorney on May 12, 1917. In 1919, he switched to the district court of Garmisch, but in 1922 finally dispensed with the title "Justizrat" (counselor of justice), as this would have required greater presence at court as an attorney. On reaching the age of sixty-five in 1931, he retired officially. Until his retirement, he had assisted many local people from Grainau in legal matters, mostly without charging them.[20]

FAMILY LIFE

Melitta Schweisheimer (née Dispeker) and Michael Berolzheimer are said to have met for the first time in London in 1894. Melitta was married to the Munich banker Eugen Schweisheimer and had three children, Waldemar "Waldi" (1889–1986), Nelly (later Friedberg; 1891–1971) and Robert (1894–1963). It must have been love at first sight since Melitta promised to marry Michael as soon as her youngest son, Robert, was five years old. However, Michael became very ill around 1900, possibly from a heart condition, and the promise was not fulfilled until a few years later. Melitta and Eugen were divorced on May 29, 1903. Michael and Melitta married four months later on September 26, 1903, in London. At first they continued to live in Munich. The three children lived with their father, but visited "Mama and Uncle Michael" often and for lengthy periods.[21]

BUILDING HÜGEL AM WEG

Michael Berolzheimer had been fascinated by the mountains since he was young. In 1884, after leaving school when he was eighteen, he undertook a study trip on foot and by train across the Alps to Italy.[22]

After their wedding, Melitta and Michael Berolzheimer visited Untergrainau for the first time together in 1905.[23] Both must have decided on the spot to make the small village their future home. Berolzheimer acquired just under 3¾ acres of land on the local road from Garmisch to Eibsee, and barely a year after their visit he submitted plans for a country house called "Hügel am Weg" to the local authorities in Untergrainau on June 15, 1906. The property comprised three parcels of land (cadastral plots 729, 732, 734), which previously belonged to three different local families.

The plan submitted by the architectural practice Herms and Mattar of Munich was for a rendered brick house with decorative woodwork, typical of farmhouses in the region. For the roof cladding, beaver-tail tiles with rounded bottom edges were foreseen rather than than the customary wooden shingles. The planning engineer from the district office in Garmisch, Carl Schweyer,

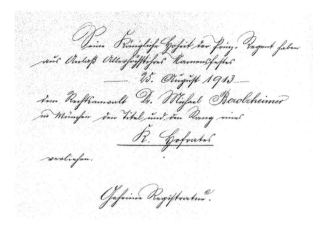

fig. 6 Berolzheimer was granted the honorary title "Hofrat" (Court Counselor) on August 25, 1913

fig. 7 A second plan for Hügel am Weg was submitted in 1907; here: the ground floor

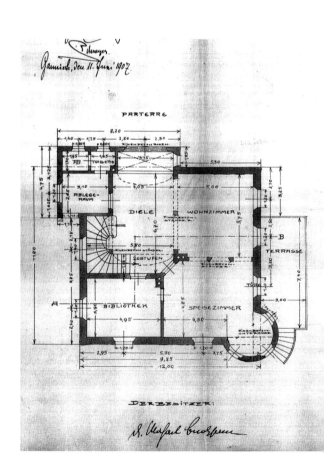

Bau- resp. Abbruchs-Beginn-Anzeige.

however, insisted on numerous changes being made to the general design. In particular, he did not give permission for an unusually flat pitch of the roof to be used with the tiles wanted. In addition, Berolzheimer had to give up a strip of his property for the planned widening of the district road.

Excavation work by the Munich construction company J. Kalb & Co. started on November 5, 1906 (*fig. 8*).[24] On March 21, 1907, Berolzheimer submitted a revised plan (*fig. 7*), which fulfilled all official requirements,[25] and approval was given by Untergrainau council on June 19, 1907, for the new country residence to be connected to the local water supply.[26]

The appearance of the house had by now been changed considerably. It had turned into a typical "Werdenfelser Haus," in the local venacular—a style of building in Upper Bavaria found from around 1900 through 1930, frequently referred to as "countrified Jugendstil".[27] A similar "Werdenfelser Haus" was also built in the hamlet of Hammersbach in the parish of Obergrainau in 1909—the Hotel Madl. While a bay window is all that can be seen of the old building today, the appearance of Michael and Melitta's Hügel am Weg has remained virtually unchanged. Looking at it from the south, the building seems quite small as the lower floor is not visible. Its true size only really becomes evident from the north.

The layout inside has remained unchanged as well. On the lower floor, the *souterrain*, are the kitchen, pantries, and staff accommodation. On the ground floor, with the front door on the south façade, are the reception rooms. The large entrance hall, the living room with Delft wall tiles and ceiling paintings, the study with its Swiss pine panelling (*fig. 9*), and the original wooden panelling in the dining room with its bay window, are all still intact. The bedrooms and guest rooms, including two large bathrooms each with bath tubs, are on the first upper floor and under the roof. All rooms of the main floor upstairs have access to a balcony that runs around the house.

fig. 8 Document confirming the start of building work on Hügel am Weg, dated November 5, 1906

fig. 9 The study with Swiss pine panelling photographed in 2011

After a construction period of just a little more than a year, the mayor of Unter-grainau, Mathias Bader, informed the district office on November 23, 1907, that Dr. Michael Berolzheimer's country house had now been completed. Hügel am Weg was given the official house number: 47⅙.[28]

THE DELFT ROOM

Among the Berolzheimer's friends was the painter Paul Roloff (1877–1951), who lived with his family in a studio apartment on Adalbertstrasse in the Schwabing district of Munich. In 1907/1908 he prepared sketches of paintings for the wooden ceiling in the living room in Untergrainau (*fig. 10*). The six oil ceiling paintings (*fig. 11*) depict the "Expulsion from Paradise" and still survive to this day. The first scene shows Eve in a hilly landscape with native deciduous trees offering the apple rather hesitatingly to Adam. The two figures are separated by a spring scene with crocuses, gentians, and a cone-laden fir tree in the middle. The second scene depicts the couple, having been expelled from Paradise, and the Archangel Michael, separated by a fall landscape with an apple tree bearing ripe fruit in a meadow with autumn crocuses. The snake with a bizarre head winds itself around the trunk of the tree. All these paintings are noteworthy from an art historical point of view, since they are among Roloff's most expressive paintings in which biblical themes and nudes are combined.[29]

The ceiling paintings contrast with the hand painted, blue Delft tiles[30] from the eighteenth and nineteenth centuries, depicting biblical motifs, which cover three of the walls (*figs 12, 13*).[31] Built-in, glass-fronted display cabinets and cupboards fill the fourth wall. The original furnishings with the tiles, the *Kachel-ofen*—a traditional ceramic stove—and the clock have survived unaltered.

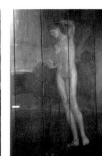

PROPERTY

Between 1910 and 1914, Berolzheimer acquired additional land in Untergrainau:

- Around 1910, the "Krackermoos Meadow" of just under 4 acres (cadastral plot no. 744), and the adjacent 1¼-acre "Braendl" field (no. 745½); now divided into some 17 plots and built on.

- A ¼-acre meadow in "Untergrainauer Feld" with a path to the district road (no. 741½); now owned by the village of Grainau.

- The "Krepbach Meadows" with a wood (nos. 305, 307(?)/307), amounting to approx. 17⅓ acres, which were bought from public ownership after the bed of the Krepbach stream was realigned in the 1920s; now owned by the village of Grainau.

- The "Entgelt-Eggart" of just under 1½ acres, which runs along the Krepbach stream (no. 731); now owned by the village of Grainau.

- The "Hassaraut," beyond the parish boundary in the Loisach valley (cadastral plot nos. 1023,1023/4), extending to just under 7 acres; still in private ownership.[32]

Berolzheimer bought the parcel of land, the "Hassaraut," before 1914, and as with his other property, permitted the previous owner to farm it as before.[33] The "Entgelt-Eggart" and the "Hassaraut" later played an important role when the family emigrated.

fig. 12 Detail of the Delft Room in 2011

fig. 13 Detail of the Delft Room in 2011

GUESTS AND NEIGHBORS

Until 1919, the Berolzheimers continued to spend the winters in Munich, but in the summer Hügel am Weg became the center of family life, where they liked to host their distinguished guests who included musicians, painters, artists, writers, and theologians. In the letter cited at the beginning of this essay, Melitta mentions a "cozy evening party with sixteen people," which she had enjoyed the day before. Guests had included the rabbi Dr. Max Freudenthal (1868–1937), with whom Michael had extensive correspondence, and the well-known art historian Theodor Harburger (1887–1949), who enthused about the beautiful house in Untergrainau.[34]

The guestbook from 1904 to 1908 still exists (*see pp. 88–93*), and is a reminder of the many guests who enjoyed the Berolzheimers' generous hospitality in both Untergrainau and Munich. Among them was Michael's father, Heinrich, in 1905, his brother Philip from the USA, the Munich architect Gerhard Herms, who designed Hügel am Weg, and Arthur Hirth, the son of the well-known Munich publisher Georg Hirth.[35] The Hirths were the next-door neighbors to the east, about 200 yards away, and were good friends of the Berolzheimer family. Their house is also still standing today (*fig. 14*).

BEROLZHEIMER AND HIS LOVE OF ART

With the move to his new house, Berolzheimer began to collect prints, essentially historical and modern graphic works and etchings. In the following thirty years, an extensive art collection evolved which was housed in the villa in Untergrainau. The collecting activity reached its peak in the 1920s.[36]

In early summer 1912, the Berolzheimers went to France and visited Auguste Rodin (1840–1917) in his studio at the Villa des Brillants in Meudon near Paris. Berolzheimer bought two figures cast in bronze from the famous sculptor, who had gained international acclaim for his modern sculptural works and statues. One was the larger-than-life sized statue *Saint Jean-Baptiste*, showing St. John the Baptist—a lean yet muscular, striding figure.[37] The statue was a cast of one of the greatest works by the artist and was placed in the garden of Hügel am Weg in such a perfect spot that Rodin thanked Berolzheimer personally on July 7, 1912, for the beautiful site he had found for it (*fig. 16*).[38]

The second Rodin bronze, *L'homme au nez cassé* (The Man with the Broken Nose, *fig. 15*) stood on Berolzheimer's desk. Only a few casts were made of this bust of 1864 with its striking head. Berolzheimer was presumably very fond of the two sculptures as he took both of them with him to the USA. *Saint Jean-Baptiste* was later sold in 1945,[39] and *L'homme au nez cassé* in 2010 (*see p. 174*).

Two stone sculptures were also among Berolzheimer's favorites. One is the bust, the "Marble Sophocles," showing the well-sculpted head of a bearded Greek man. It was originally in Munich before being taken to Untergrainau, where it was placed on another desk in the so-called "Stone Room" under the roof. The second sculpture was the "Stone Magdalena," a bust which found a place in the entrance hall in Untergrainau. Both were also taken to the USA and remained in the possession of the family.[40]

fig. 14 Haus Hirth, the neighboring house to the east of Hügel am Weg, c. 1910

fig. 15 Auguste Rodin, *L'homme au nez cassé*

fig. 16 The larger-than-life bronze statue by Auguste Rodin (1840–1917) of *Saint Jean-Baptiste* preaching, in the garden at Hügel am Weg, c. 1912

Berolzheimer did not just keep his eyes open for works to add to his own art collection. When he lived in Munich, he was a voluntary expert for the Acquisitions Committee at the Alte Pinakothek art museum and worked freelance for the Graphische Sammlung München—the Prints Collection. He was also a member of the Deutsche Orient-Gesellschaft (German Oriental Society). He was especially fascinated by the history of the Hittites, whose traces were first found in 1905. Many well-known Munich figures were members of the society, including Crown Prince Rupprecht of Bavaria, whom Michael knew personally and held in high esteem.[41] It would appear that Berolzheimer lead a very contented life. Much later, in a letter of December 28, 1935, to the district office in Garmisch, Melitta would also draw attention to the happy years spent in Untergrainau and her husband's extensive voluntary work before the war.[42]

More detailed information on the Berolzheimer Collection is to be found in the essays by Andrea Bambi (pp. 155–63) and Sven Bruntjen (pp. 165–85), in particular, in Section III of this volume.

WORLD WAR I

In November 1912, a striking natural phenomenon was noticed and reported in the daily paper in Garmisch. It was full moon and "two strips of clouds stretched across the face of the moon and beyond, forming a cross—which superstitious minds equate with the [imminent] danger of war."[43] Two years later, Europe really was at war. On July 28, 1914, World War I broke out, claiming in its course about seventeen million lives and creating the conditions for the rise of National Socialism, and ultimately for World War II.[44]

There was a pronounced sense of patriotism in Germany, and—like virtually everywhere in Europe—many people were keen to fight for their homeland, regardless of their religious or social background. In a letter of December 28, 1935, Melitta also wrote about those times: "My two sons [Waldemar and Robert] were on the front throughout the war, one as a physician until he was wounded in 1917, the other as an artillery officer until he too was wounded in April 1918. They both received a number of decorations, the artillery officer also being given the EK I [Iron Cross, 1st Class] ...."[45]

Melitta made her own personal contribution to the war effort by setting up an office at Hügel am Weg in 1915 (fig. 17). Residents of Untergrainau could bring letters and parcels for soldiers in the field, to whom she would address and dispatch them.[46] She also reputedly established a sort of private field hospital in her house "and made sure that it was occupied by officers and junior ranks in equal number, free of charge."[47] Berolzheimer was also prepared to do his "war service" by working again, as previously mentioned, as an attorney.

The effects of the war, which dragged on so long, very soon became noticeable among the ordinary people. Food, clothing, and fuel were rationed and only handed out against coupons. The food crisis reached its peak in winter 1916/17, which has gone down in history as the "turnip winter," since only root vegetables were available in any quantity.[48] That following summer, the local newspaper appealed to the few guests who still came to Grainau on vacation in spite of the war, to help with the hay harvest.[49] Not only was there a lack of food, there was

fig. 17 A notice in the local newspaper, the Loisachboote, dated March 9, 1915, announcing that "Mrs. Court Counselor Dr. Berolzheimer" had opened a writing room at her house and that mail could be sent to soldiers in the field free of charge

Bekanntmachung.

Unterfertigte Gemeindeverwaltung bringt hiemit zur Kenntnisnahme, daß **Frau Hofrat Dr. Berolzheimer** in ihrer Villa eine Schreibstube errichtet hat, in der die Einwohner von Untergrainau unentgeltlich Feldadressen adressieren sowie die Feldpostpakete verpacken lassen können. Papier sowie Schnüre zum Verpacken werden dortselbst unentgeltlich abgegeben. Ebenso kann dort über Adressen von Gefangenen oder in Lazaretten befindlichen Soldaten Auskunft erholt werden.

Beginn Dienstag, den 9. März täglich von 9 bis 10 Uhr vormittags und von halb 3 bis halb 4 Uhr nachmittags.

Gemeinde-Verwaltung Untergrainau
J. V.
Reiser, Bürgermeister.

also a dire shortage of coins—regular copper and nickel coins had been withdrawn, as the metal was needed for munitions. The villages of Obergrainau and Untergrainau issued emergency coins to the value of 10, 20, and 50 Pfennigs.[50]

At those gloomy times, the Berolzheimer family invited especially needy children from Untergrainau to Hügel am Weg in the Christmas period and gave them presents, mostly clothing and shoes, but also money to be able to buy bread. Every summer, the shoemaker Jakob Schäffler of Untergrainau was commissioned by Michael Berolzheimer to make several pairs of children's shoes. These generous acts continued until the 1930s. Anton Reindl, who was born in 1929, remembers the clothes were not liked very much by the children: "They were mostly city clothes which weren't worn here and children were embarrassed to wear them. But a few times down the hillside on the seat of your pants and they were ruined. After that you didn't have to wear them anymore." Nevertheless, the children were urged by their parents to thank the Berolzheimers personally with a gift. And so a number of bouquets of wild flowers or freshly picked strawberries found their way to Hügel am Weg in the summer (*fig. 18*).[51]

fig. 18 Children with posies of flowers for Melitta Berolzheimer, c. 1930

fig. 19 The war memorial in Grainau with a Pietà in terracotta by the sculptor Adolf von Hildebrand, 1921

THE WAR MEMORIAL IN GRAINAU

The celebration to welcome the return of 120 soldiers from Grainau took place on January 6, 1919, and a memorial service was held for the twenty-two soldiers from both villages who had fallen. In his sermon, the local Catholic prebendary, Karl Herdegen, suggested building a war memorial to keep their memory alive.[52] The parish councils later asked a number of local residents to help, among them Berolzheimer, who saw no reason not to become involved. Berolzheimer then accompanied the building of the memorial until its official dedication on September 25, 1921. The events leading up to this deserve a brief mention here.[53]

In March 1920, the local councillors from Obergrainau and Untergrainau held a joint meeting and decided to establish a war memorial committee. Court counselor Michael Berolzheimer and publisher Walther Hirth were invited to the second committee meeting. In the minutes of the meeting it was recorded: "The Court Counselor then speaks and emphasizes the dignity of such a memorial, and warns of keeping costs under control and of designing a memorial to suit its surroundings. He suggests setting up a sub-committee to clarify the finer points, which was then formed on the spot ...."

The sub-committee met on October 6, 1920, in Hügel am Weg. Prebendary Karl Herdegen also attended. It was decided to commission the well known Munich architect Carl Sattler (1877–1966). The estimated cost of 36,000 Marks included a terracotta pieta made to a design by the renowned sculptor Adolf von Hildebrand (1847–1921; *fig. 19*). Since such an amount could not be stemmed by the villages alone, a financial committee was formed in February 1921, and Berolzheimer was elected chairman.

Hügel am Weg became the venue of the meetings and all correspondence passed over Berolzheimer's desk. Melitta and her son, Robert, also attended these meetings. Special concerts in hotels in Grainau and collections—to which "besides Mayor Bader and Walther Hirth, the Court Counselor's wife also personally contributed"—helped finance the project.

At the final meeting on August 31, 1921, the mayor of Obergrainau, Johann Bader, thanked Berolzheimer on behalf of both villages. As recorded in the minutes of the last committee meeting, his work had been excellent and this would never be forgotten. In November 1921, Robert Schweisheimer published an essay in the highly regarded cultural magazine "Das Bayernland" entitled: "Dedication of war memorial in Grainau near Garmisch." (*fig. 20*)[54]

TAXES AND RATES IN UNTERGRAINAU

On October 1, 1919, the Berolzheimer family officially registered their change of address from Munich to Untergrainau, and declared their country house to be their principal residence.[55] The move from Munich may also have been precipitated by the turbulent and unpredicable circumstances in the state capital. Untergrainau at any rate would have seemed a safe hideaway.[56]

The small community had considerable difficulties at that time balancing its annual budget. In 1909, the parish introduced a so-called "supplementary beer tax." This tax financed part of the parish's budget. Due to the poor economic situation towards the end of the war, income from this tax however became less and less, while expenses exploded rapidly. In 1918, the village was forced to ask court counselor Berolzheimer for a loan of 4500 marks.[57] Around 1928, when the village again had financial difficulties as a result of work on the Krepbach stream (*fig. 21*), Berolzheimer waived the repayment of this loan.[58]

Besides the beer tax, water rates and a property-related tax were other vital sources of income for the parish. The amount payable was calculated according to the land owned. The Berolzheimers' was one of the three most heavily taxed properties in Untergrainau.[59]

fig. 20 The inauguration of the war memorial in Grainau on September 25, 1921

The relation between Berolzheimer and Untergrainau council was not always without friction. The construction of a new footpath from the village to the station along Krepbach, planned by Untergrainau council in 1927, for example, effected a parcel of land owned by Berolzheimer. Nearly all other owners were prepared to surrender the necessary strips of land free of charge. Berolzheimer however caused a certain amount of difficulty by demanding a tract of grazing land behind his property as compensation, as recorded in the minutes of a meeting held on September 14, 1927, following a site visit by the council. Berolzheimer was obviously not prepared to relinquish his land for nothing. However, the holders of grazing rights and the council itself objected to handing over these meadows and the path was built nevertheless.[60] The matter dragged on for years, and it was not until 1934—perhaps in acknowledgment of the "new times"—that Berolzheimer agreed to surrender the land required without compensation.[61]

The council and Berolzheimer also had different opinions about how the parcels of land around his country house should be assessed. They were not considered to be for agricultural use and were taxed accordingly as building land as "they were bought in order that no new properties could be built around the house, and their agricultural use is just a secondary aim." Berolzheimer's objection against this decision at the beginning of 1933 was turned down and no further appeals were permitted in those days.[62]

TIMES OF UNREST

fig. 21 Work on regulating the Krepbach stream near Untergrainau, 1928

At the end of World War I, the monarchy in Bavaria came to an end. On November 8, 1918, a Free State was proclaimed in Munich. The Treaty of Versailles, negotiated in May 1919, formally ended World War I. Due to its seemingly harsh conditions, the Treaty was considered illegal and humiliating by the majority of Germans.[63] It resulted in the hatred of everything "foreign," especially everything French, and also led to anti-French campaigns in the press, startlingly similar to the anti-Semitic hate paroles in years to come.[64] The Treaty of Versailles, "the root of all adversity and all misery" as the local newspaper, the "Loisachbote," put it,[65] provided the breeding ground for marginal groups lioke the German National Socialist Workers' Party in Munich.

Adolf Hitler gave two speeches in the Garmisch-Partenkirchen region—on March 18, 1923, in the Rassensaal (Hall of Races) in Partenkirchen, and on May 6, 1923, in the sports hall in the nearby town of Murnau.[66] The voice of the Party was soon to be heard in the immediate vicinity, namely in Villa Schönbichl in Untergrainau, barely 200 yards from Hügel am Weg. A large advertisement placed in the "Loisachbote" by someone by the name of Frankl, about whom nothing else is known, appealed for recruits to join the mounted division of the "Sturm-abteilung" (the Brownshirts or SA), the paramilitary wing of the Nazi Party.[67]

In Untergrainau, the political situation in 1923 would probably only have been seen as a storm brewing on the horizon, as everyday life carried on as usual.

AT HOME WITH THE BEROLZHEIMERS

A staff of three or four—a cook, a housemaid, a custodian, and a gardener—was usually employed for work around the house and garden. Many of the household staff came from Grainau, and some of the girls from further away later found a husband in the area, such as Emilie Auer (*fig. 22*), who worked as a housemaid and cook from 1917 through 1920 and who married into an old Untergrainau family. Or Therese Heigl, employed from 1929 onward, who also married and settled in Untergrainau. The list of staff in the Untergrainau village registry recording the names of those working in the Berolzheimer household has virtually no breaks in it between 1910 and 1930. It can therefore be assumed that the Berolzheimers were virtually continuously present at Hügel am Weg during this period.[68]

In 1926, Anton Reindl of Untergrainau (*fig. 23*) was taken on as full-time gardener and custodian, and Ferdinand Koller was hired in 1929 as chauffeur for the new Horch automobile. Over the years, Berolzheimer and Reindl developed an almost friendly relationship and are even said to have addressed each other using the familiar "Du" form, as opposed to the more distancing "Sie."[69] Koller was also a faithful member of staff and very loyal to his employer. After the Berolzheimers fled Germany, they were to acknowledge their gratitude to both Reindl and Koller in a special way.

From 1919 onward, a number of chickens, which had a pen next to the greenhouse,[70] and two dogs—a German shepherd and a dachshund (*fig. 24*)—were also part of the household. Every year, the dog license had to be paid; one dog cost five Marks and the second twenty. This was later raised to fifteen and fifty Marks.[71] Melitta in particular loved the dogs and was never seen without them in the garden.[72]

fig. 22 Emilie Auer (*left*) who worked for the Berolzheimers from 1917–20

fig. 23 Anton Reindl with suitcases on a cart

fig. 24 Lilly, Robert Schweisheimer's wife, with the Berolzheimers' dogs in the garden

Melitta, who ran the household strictly, was always elegantly and colorfully dressed, with a hairdresser from Untergrainau visiting every morning. Although polite toward the staff, she—as well as her daughter Nelly—were said to have been somewhat condescending and always kept a distance between themselves and the staff.[73] In 1942, Melitta's son Waldemar Schweisheimer reminisced: "Mama had to suffer a lot with the servants, and so did they with her."[74] Melitta placed great importance on good cooking, serving down-to-earth, traditional dishes. One of Berolzheimer's favorite dishes was Franconian pork sausages with spinach and fried potatoes, and sour-cherry cake for dessert.[75] They liked to drink wine from Traben-Trarbach in the Mosel wine-producing area.[76]

Melitta's grand-daughter, Suzanne Schiessel (b. 1921), Nelly Friedberg's daughter, often stayed at her grandparents' in Untergrainau (*fig. 26*) when she was a child, and has vivid memories of these visits: "Michael had a beautiful study, completely panelled in wood. He was always studying. Michael was very kind to Melitta. She was educated, asked intelligent questions, and was also very nice to him. Melitta had white hair, dyed slightly brown at the front. She had lived in England as a young woman, and ever since then loved cucumber sandwiches and afternoon tea. She liked to go rowing on Eibsee with Michael or to take the little train up the mountain (*fig. 25*). Michael was one of the first to have a car. With it came the chauffeur and the stable became the garage. Most of the time, we children played in the large garden and secretly slipped into the kitchen to get some treats from the cook. There was a stove with lots of electric hotplates in the large kitchen. As it was on the lower floor, the food was sent up to the dining room in a small elevator. There was a large *Kachelofen* in the living room, with a bench around it. Large stacks of logs were all around the outside of the house."

Suzanne's brother Max (b. 1922) recalls the atmosphere at table as being quite formal. At a young age, the children were expected to have good table manners. Michael was considered quite stern. "When our mother and stepfather

had dinner quests, we were banished to the kitchen, which was okay with us." Max also remembers squeezing his younger brother, Ernst (1925–2013), into the dumb-waiter for rides from floor to floor.[77]

The whole family celebrated Pesach together, but it was never very orthodox at all. At New Year, the children were given *Weißwurst* (veal sausages) and mustard. "We children never felt anything anti-Semitic. From 1936 onward, we were at boarding school in Italy and were not here during the Night of Broken Glass ...."[78]

"WELL LIKED AND NEVER POLITICALLY ACTIVE"

Berolzheimer is remembered as a very well liked person—"a good soul," as Maria Schuster, who knew the couple personally, recalled. The Berolzheimers were highly regarded, as were the five other Jewish families in Grainau. They all provided jobs, which were rare in the village and particularly sought after.[79]

On December 30, 1935, the mayor, Anton Bader, stated: "Court Counselor Berolzheimer has been living in the parish of Untergrainau now for about thirty years. During his time here, he has always lived alone with his wife, without giving rise to any complaints whatsoever. He has never been politically active, has always been quiet, and is held in high esteem by the residents of Grainau for his generosity ...."[80]

fig. 25 Inauguration of the mountain railway up the Zugspitze, 1928

fig. 26 Michael and Melitta with Michael's step-daughter,
Nelly (r.) and two of her children, Max and Suzanne,
in the garden in Untergrainau, c. 1930

During their daily walk to the post office in Obergrainau (*figs 27, 28*), the Berolzheimers were always greeted warmly "by the locals."[81] This walk was not just to further communication or for the good of their health, but was also so that Berolzheimer could mail the countless letters he wrote to all corners of the world.

EXTENSIVE CORRESPONDENCE

Berolzheimer kept up an intense exchange of letters,[82] mostly in connection with his genealogical research into Jewish families in Bavaria (*see also pp. 137–41*). Through his work on the history of his own family and the small parish of Markt Berolzheim in Middle Franconia, he had became a recognized expert on Jewish family research. His advice was frequently sought when questions arose to do with inheritance, bequests or family trees. In 1932, he had planned to publish his work on Jewish families and place names in Franconia, but he did not have enough time.

Two examples show quite clearly that not only research but also friendship motivated his correspondence. Berolzheimer enjoyed an intensive exchange of letters with Dr. Max Freudenthal for many years. On Freudenthal's sixtieth birthday, he was given a "wonderful and precious gift" by the court counselor.

fig. 27 The post office in Grainau (r.) with the airship "Graf Zeppelin" LZ 123 flying overhead, 1928

fig. 28 Michael Berolzheimer by a wayside cross

A trip was planned that coming winter (1928/29) to the Bavarian mountains and of course a visit to Hügel am Weg, "which always holds a special attraction for me." After Freudenthal's death in 1937, the Berolzheimers kept in touch with his widow, Else. One of her postcards, sent from Munich, bears a postmark which advertized "Sincere greetings overseas through reduced rate telegrams"—a macabre slogan for all Jewish emigrants. Else wrote her last letter on January 22, 1939, from Norrköping in Sweden, to where she had emigrated. The letter was forwarded to Berolzheimer, who by that time was already in New York.

Many letters were also exchanged with Theodor Harburger from 1928 onward in which they shared findings from their genealogical research into their own family histories. However, that was not their only contact. The two met in Munich on several ocassions and Harburger also visited Hügel am Weg.

On June 30, 1930, a "Bavarian Society for Jewish Museums and the Care of Works of Art" was founded by the "Verband Bayerischer Israelitischer Gemeinden" (Association of Bavarian Israelite Congregations). Harburger invited Berolzheimer to support this new society and to help with establishing a principal museum in Bavaria (*see p. 123*). Berolzheimer immediately took an active part in this, and told Harburger about some special artworks and rare items, which would be suitable for the museum planned. Political circumstances however prevented this project too from being realized.[83]

All Harburger's activities came to a sudden end when the National Socialists seized power. He moved to Tiberias in Palestine in October 1933, but the exchange of letters did not stop. In a letter written to Harburger in November 1934, Berolzheimer enthused about his own trip to the Holy Land some twenty years earlier. The letter sheds a unique light on himself, his cultural interests, and his joy of traveling:

"I was extremely pleased to receive your letter of October 29. Your wife has resolutely taken to her work as the owner of a guesthouse, and I believe Tiberias is a very suitable place. Firstly, it has a very mild climate and is therefore very suitable for winter guests; secondly, the area is particularly beautiful; and, thirdly, if I remember correctly, it has an inn where we stayed which did not meet even modest requirements for cleanliness and quality, so it will not be at all difficult for your wife to provide better quality than the competition. On top of that, there are good fish in the Sea of Kinnereth, making it possible for "Pension Kinnereth" to become a renowned guesthouse specializing in fish dishes, served with excellent wines from Palestine ....

From your house you can probably see the black basalt walls of the city, possibly built by Emperor Barbarossa. And the same stone can also be found on the slopes around the old burial place, where I was particularly moved by the Tomb of Maimonides, that great intellectual, who influenced European culture to such an extent, without the Europeans even having the slightest notion of this. Whether we will ever be able to return to the Holy Land? I would love to ...."

However, first of all, there was still a lot of work to be done at home.

REMODELING THE HOUSE

In 1929, Hügel am Weg was enlarged and modernized. An extension was added on the west side, housing a boiler room and coal cellar on the lower floor, a veranda on the ground floor next to the new front door, and another bedroom upstairs.[84] "We're as warm as toast here," Berolzheimer wrote on a Christmas card of December 20, 1932, enthusing about his new heating system to the architect Carl Sattler of Munich, who had drafted the plans for remodeling the house. [85]

The garage was revamped for the new Horch, and a small apartment added to it for the chauffeur, Ferdinand Koller.[86] This small building by Sattler still exists today, unchanged on the outside (*fig. 29*). Sattler left a number of architectural landmarks in the Garmisch-Partenkirchen area, especially famous Schloss Elmau near Klais, which was built to his plans between 1914 and 1916.[87]

While Hügel am Weg was being remodeled, the Berolzheimers continued to take an active role in parish life. Up until 1928, the two villages had received their electricity from a private supplier; now they were about to be connected to the national "Isarwerke" electricity network. The copious paperwork concerning the electricity supply was checked and corrected by Berolzheimer in his capacity as attorney, and then presented to both parish councils.[88]

Melitta and Michael Berolzheimer felt very much at home in Untergrainau. They did not merely live there, but felt closely tied to the village and were well respected.

fig. 29 The garage building with adjoining apartment for the chauffeur and his family, designed by the architect Carl Sattler in 1929. Photograph taken in 2011

THE ARRIVAL OF THE NAZIS

fig. 30 The omnipresent swastika banner
in the village

fig. 31 Waxensteinstrasse between Obergrainau
and Untergrainau in the 1930s

"We have not migrated here, we were born here, and because of that, we have no claim to be at home anywhere else; either we are Germans or we are without a home."[89] These words, written by Gabriel Riesser (1806–63), a Jewish lawyer, journalist, and politician, however, no longer held true following the rise of the National Socialists.

The changes which swept across the nation after Adolf Hitler seized power on January 30, 1933, soon had an effect on Grainau too (*fig. 30*). Of the eight men who sat on Untergrainau local council, six had become members of the NSDAP (Nazi Party) by April 1933; in Obergrainau all eight had joined the "Brown Party."[90]

   Head teacher Otto Pentenrieder was elected the new mayor of Obergrainau, "the first National Socialist mayor of the village to be sworn in," as ceremoniously announced at the pompous reception at Hotel Post in Obergrainau.[91] Pentenrieder was appointed mayor of the new local authority of Grainau, following the forced amalgamation of the two villages on October 1, 1937.[92]

   The sight of swastika banners everywhere was by now part of the everyday village scene (*figs 31, 32*), as was the "Hitlerheim"—a building used by the HJ, the Hitler Youth organization, and the local SA. Garmisch-Partenkirchen and the Zugspitze witnessed repeated visits by "big Nazi names." Hitler had appeared in the area eight times by 1936, three of which were during the 1936 Olympic Games in Garmisch-Partenkirchen. The "Führer" made a brief visit to the local lake, the Eibsee, on April 14, 1936, and had to pass Hügel am Weg to get there.[93]

Heinrich Himmler, Hermann Göring, Rudolf Heß, Martin Bormann, Adolf Wagner, and Baldur von Schirach also visited the region.

Anti-Jewish propaganda (*fig. 33*) and jeering at NSDAP meetings in the area became increasingly threatening. Even as early as in 1930, on February 23 in fact, in Wallgau—some 8 miles to the east of Garmisch—residents were called upon "to fight Judaism." "Ordinary people have become slaves to the Jews' interest policies, and will be ruined without the NSDAP," was to be heard on January 18, 1931, in Garmisch. In the nearby village of Eschenlohe, rantings on June 21, 1931, were directed "against Jews in particular"; on February 24, 1932, "the stinking East Galicians" were derided in Garmisch, "these people, who have no right to be in this State." One speaker on March 12, 1932, proposed that "all Jews should be hanged"—a suggestion that "was received with considerable enthusiasm by the audience." "The National Socialists will send the Jews where they belong,"[94] was to be heard in Ohlstadt, a village bordering Eschenlohe to the north, on October 10, 1932.

FLEEING FOR THE FIRST TIME

In summer 1933, the political pressure obviously became too much for the Berolzheimer family. Therese Geiger of Untergrainau, who was working at the time as a housemaid at Hügel am Weg (*fig. 34*), recalled that day in July 1933: "In the morning, the plan for the day's meals was suddenly cancelled; none of the four members of staff knew the reason. Robert, Michael's stepson and Nelly's brother, arrived out of the blue in the morning, and the whole family withdrew upstairs to discuss things. Nobody knew why. One of the staff thought there must be 'trouble up there.' Suddenly, the family departed in the seven-seater Horch, without any comment, without telling us staff why or where they were going. Mrs. Berolzheimer only had a tiny bag with her; normally they traveled

fig. 32 Höllentalklamm Hotel with the swastika banner

fig. 33 Propaganda slogan stating "Jews not wanted here"

fig. 34 Two members of the Berolzheimers' staff outside the house, with Therese Geiger on the left, c. 1933

with wardrobe trunks. We just sat around for the rest of the day. Then, in the evening, a phone call came from Switzerland: the money for the staff's salaries—65 Reichsmarks for the cook, 55 Reichsmarks for the housemaids—was to be collected from a bank in Garmisch. The Berolzheimer family, it would seem, had left by car without a penny, and lived for the first day from the money the chauffeur, Ferdinand Koller, had with him. One day, I don't know exactly when any more, perhaps at the beginning of August, the Berolzheimers came back to Grainau again."[95]

Maria Schuster also remembered when they fled: "Ferdinand Koller was traveling with the Berolzheimers for quite a while, around Switzerland, perhaps also France or the Mediterranean …" (*fig. 35*).[96]

HASTY DEPARTURE FOR SWITZERLAND

The two Nuremberg Laws of September 16, 1935, created a legal basis for the exclusion of Jews from everyday life in Germany, and had become progressively more radical since 1933. The "Reich Citizenship Law" excluded Jews from all public offices and stripped them of their right to vote. The "Law for the Protection of German Blood and German Honor" was to guarantee—to use the Nazi's own terminology—that "German blood remained uncontaminated."[97]

A trip to Switzerland[98] by Melitta and Michael, for which no precise dates are available and which Therese Geiger referred to simply as "the second time they fled," could well have had some connection with the Reich Citizenship Law. Mrs. Geiger recalled: "In about 1935, then—head over heals—they fled for a second time. There was no time to say good-bye then either. That was unusual, since Mrs. Berolzheimer had promised to say good-bye beforehand and she always kept her word very strictly. The Berolzheimers were very rich and had important works of art in the house. I don't know whether they took anything with them at the time …."[99]

EXCLUSION, HARASSMENT, DISCRIMINATION

Paragraph 3 of the "Law for the Protection of German Blood and German Honor"[100] of September 15, 1935, forbade Jews from employing domestic servants "of German or kindred blood" under the age of forty-five. This effected the Berolzheimer household, as "Aryan" staff were continuously employed there. Berolzheimer himself was nearly seventy years old at the time this legislation was brought out, but according to the law he was a "danger" to the two housemaids. On December 28, 1935, Melitta Berolzheimer therefore applied to the local police station in Untergrainau to be allowed to keep the two members of staff from Untergrainau in her service. Melitta tried to make as favorable an impression as possible to back her application by listing all the services various members of her family had provided for the good of the community, as well as for "the Fatherland" during World War I. The two women from Untergrainau, both called Maria, had been employed for many years in the house and were only needed on an alternating

fig. 35 Melitta and Michael Berolzheimer, possibly taken in Switzerland, 1933

basis for a few days a week to do the cleaning and laundry. They received lunch in addition to their pay; an overnight stay in the house was out of the question.

On December 30, 1935, the mayor of Untergrainau, Anton Bader, wrote a very positive reference for Berolzheimer, emphasizing his "moral and political" integrity. Even the National Socialist mayor of Obergrainau, Otto Pentenrieder, gave a favorable report. The application was passed on to the district office in Garmisch, were it was also supported by the district clerk, Dr. Wiesend, who issued a statement on January 2, 1936, that read: "Given the age of the house owner and the circumstance that no other Jewish males live in the household, it would seem that a threat to German blood can be ruled out."[101]

The Reich and Prussian Minister of the Interior in Berlin, however, saw things differently and simply stated in a brief note of January 9, 1936, that the application to continue employing Maria Schuster on the household staff could not be granted. On February 12, 1936, the district clerk added that "standard enquiries have revealed that the continued employment of Maria L. is also not admissible either."[102] It is not known how Melitta later coped with the prohibition or organized her household.

Another change was also to have an impact on Berolzheimer. From around 1937 onward, all things "Jewish" disappeared from official address books. In the first book for Grainau in 1938, listing the addresses of the two villages combined, house number 47¹/₆ had disappeared. The name Michael Berolzheimer, as the owner of the house and as listed in all previous address books since 1912, was no longer mentioned.[103]

There is no mention of the Berolzheimers in the Grainau registry either, even though the family had made Grainau their official place of abode in 1919. This can only be explained by a "purging of the files." When that might have taken place is however not clear.[104] During restitution proceedings in 1953, the mayor of Grainau at that time, Hans Schwägele, complained that it was not possible to confirm the Berolzheimers' place of residence in any detail since all the corresponding documents were missing.[105]

The Winter Olympic Games in Garmisch-Partenkirchen from February 6 through 16, 1936, would have been a cause for further alarm as well. The initial exclusion of Jewish athletes from Germany created a furor worldwide and would not have gone unnoticed by Berolzheimer either. After a movement started to grow in the USA to boycott the games as a result, and since the propaganda value of the games would be vastly reduced without America's participation, Berlin reacted swiftly and ordered all anti-Semitic activities to be stopped in public. For a short time, even the signs that had been put up everywhere saying "Jews not wanted here" were removed. But it was just a temporary lull in anti-Jewish hostilities, which restarted immediately after the end of the Summer Games in Berlin, which ran from August 1 through 16.[106]

In spite of all the harassment and discrimination from official bodies, the behavior of most local villagers toward Jewish families reputedly changed little—people were merely "just a little more cautious."[107] Only the girls and boys, some of whom may well have been given presents from the Berolzheimers not long before, could now been seen marching past Hügel am Weg. Organized into the HJ (Hitler Youth) or the BDM (League of German Girls) movements, and goaded by their leader, they strode along singing "particularly loudly, even screaming out their anti-Semitic hate songs."[108]

This change of allegiance even threw a new light on past events within the community. The village clerk in Obergrainau, Heinz Holzner, had kept the minutes at all village committee and financial committee meetings back in 1921 which were held in connection with the building of the war memorial, and at the time had recorded the mayor, Johann Bader's "warmest gratitude" toward Michael Berolzheimer's for the latter's "exemplary work." Holzner joined the NSDAP on May 1, 1933,[109] and became an avid supporter.

In 1936, under the new mayor, Otto Pentenrieder, Holzner "suddenly remembered" events at that time as follows: "Apart from Walther Hirth, court counselor Dr. Michael Berolzheimer was also called to the meeting on October 3, 1920. Through the demands imposed by the latter and the cooperation of other such patriots, the history of setting up a memorial took on a bitter taste. It was a sign of the times that Jews, even here in our small community, wanted to earn a position of 'merit.' As treasurer and member of the sub-committee, Berolzheimer influenced the matter to no small degree ...." And in reference to a later meeting, Holzner noted: "In the committee meeting of February 20, 1921, a financial sub-committee was formed. The Jew also elbowed his way into that sub-committee too ...."[110]

fig. 36 Portrait of Michael Berolzheimer's brother, Philip

TRIPS TO THE UNITED STATES

Melitta and Michael Berolzheimer left their home in Grainau on two occasions to visit relatives in the USA. From December 2, 1933, through January 2, 1934, they stayed with Michael's brother, Philip (fig. 36), and his wife, Clara, on Little St. Simons Island on the Atlantic coast.[111] The island covers 10,000 acres and is located off the coast of Georgia. It was purchased in 1908 by the Eagle Pencil Company for its abundance of red cedars, intended to be used in the production of pencils. However, it transpired that the wood was not suitable due to the effects of wind and salt, and Philip bought the island from the company. A hunting lodge, built in 1917, became a favorite destination for vacations by members of the Berolzheimer family.[112]

In early 1937, Michael and Melitta departed on the second of their two trips to the USA. At the beginning of February they boarded the steamship Washington in Le Havre and reached the United States on February 5. They stayed on the island again, this time occupying "Michael Cottage," which Philip had built especially for them. The decision to leave Germany was most probably made at around this time. At the end of March 1937, they returned to Untergrainau one last time.[113]

Melitta celebrated her seventieth birthday on October 21, 1937, in Untergrainau, with members of her family. Her children, Robert and Nelly, who were still living in Germany, gave their mother a photo album recording life at Hügel am Weg, which she later took with her to the USA. Looking at the pictures of the elderly Berolzheimers, it is difficult to imagine that they would soon be leaving for the New World (fig. 37).[114]

THE FINAL MONTHS IN UNTERGRAINAU

On March 12, 1938, the Wehrmacht—the unified armed forces of Germany—
and SS divisions marched into Austria and forced its annexation to the German
Reich. For German and Austrian National Socialists this was another opportunity for riots targeting the Jewish population. Countless Jews were publicly
humiliated—often cheered on by local residents. People from all over Austria fled
by the thousand to Switzerland through the westernmost state of Vorarlberg.[115]
Berolzheimer would certainly have known about this development.

  In spring 1938, Berolzheimer suffered severe health problems again—most
probably heart failure—from which he had still not recovered by April. "He simply

fig. 37 Michael and Melitta in front of the house

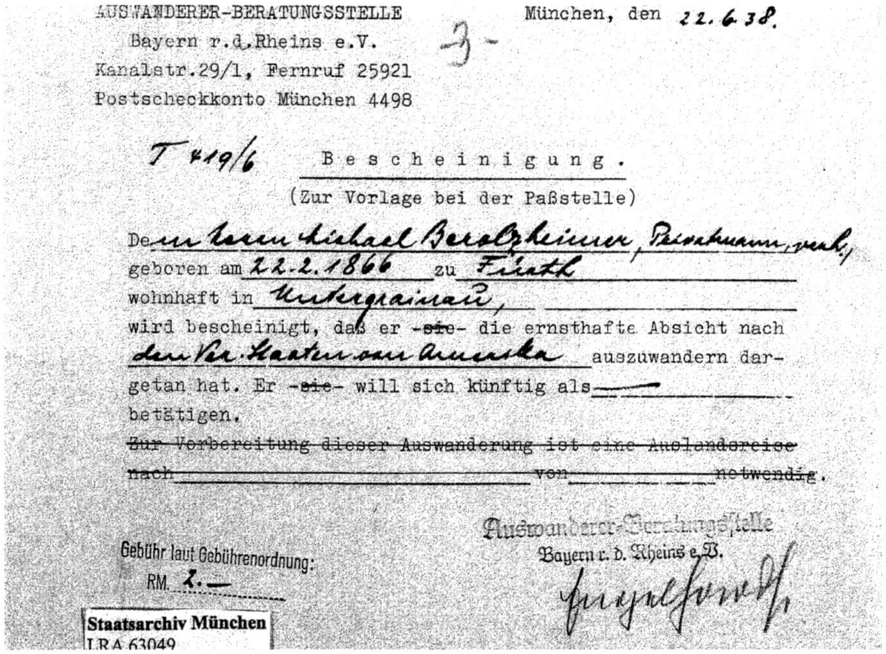

AUSWANDERER-BERATUNGSSTELLE   München, den *22.6.38.*
   Bayern r.d.Rheins e.V.
   Kanalstr.29/1, Fernruf 25921
   Postscheckkonto München 4498

         T 419/6   B e s c h e i n i g u n g .
                     (Zur Vorlage bei der Paßstelle)

   De*m Herrn Michael Berolzheimer, Privatmann, verh.,*
   geboren am *22.2.1866*   zu *Fürth*
   wohnhaft in *Untergrainau,*
   wird bescheinigt, daß er -sie- die ernsthafte Absicht nach
   den Ver.Staaten von Amerika auszuwandern dar-
   getan hat. Er -sie- will sich künftig als————————— .
   betätigen.
   Zur Vorbereitung dieser Auswanderung ist eine Auslandsreise
   nach———————————————— von —————————notwendig.

   Gebühr laut Gebührenordnung:
       RM *2.—*

   Staatsarchiv München
   LRA 63049

had no zest for life anymore," is how Anton Reindl described Berolzheimer's physical and mental state in early summer 1938.[116] The time had now arrived, however, to start emigration proceedings.

An affidavit, the attested surety of an American citizen—one of the prerequisites for immigration[117]—had already been received from Berolzheimer's brother, Philip. From June 11 through 18, 1938, Berolzheimer sold all the securities he held at the Vereinsbank Garmisch-Partenkirchen.[118]

PREPARATIONS

On June 2, 1938, attorney Robert Held of Munich wrote to the district office in Garmisch-Partenkirchen about Melitta and Michael Berolzheimer's intention to emigrate to the United States and requested information as to what documents had to be submitted. Dr. Wiesend from the district office answered, in a not unfriendly tone, on June 28, 1938, saying emigration was indeed admissible. It was, however, only possible to open proceedings once "the seriousness of the intention" had been certified by the Jewish emigration advisory office in Munich. A little later, the attorney handed in all the necessary attestations he had gathered (*fig. 38*). Emigration proceedings at the district office were opened on July 4, 1938.

A plethora of authorities and institutions had to give their approval because of "suspected tax evasion and capital flight"—these included the mayor of Grainau, Otto Pentenrieder, the State Police in Munich, the Customs Investigation Office, the Reichsbankanstalt in Munich, the foreign currency bureau at the State Tax Office in Munich, the President of the State Tax Office in Berlin, and the District Attorney at the District Court in Munich. Robert Held put all the necessary papers

fig. 38 Confirmation of Michael Berolzheimers' "intention to emigrate," dated June 22, 1938

together meticulously and—without any qualms—submitted them, together with the Berolzheimers' passports, to the district office. On July 14, 1938, the couple received their foreign travel papers.[119]

Then the packing began in Untergrainau. Wardrobe trunks, boxes, suitcases, and bags were squeezed into the Buick which had replaced the Horch. The big bronze sculpture in the garden, *Saint Jean-Baptiste,* was carefully packed in a specially made crate and sent on its way from Untergrainau station, together with other boxes, packages, and some of the furniture.[120] All of these items later arrived safely in the port of New York in a transport container, a so-called "lift." Even the Buick was taken to America, albeit without the chauffeur.[121]

The police record, required by the American consulate, arrived at Robert Held's office on July 20, 1938. The Berolzheimers' departure seemed assured. On July 25, they left Untergrainau, most likely for Munich to pick up their daughter-in-law, Lilly Schweisheimer. The next day, Ferdinand Koller drove the three of them to Stuttgart, where the Berolzheimers were given their immigration visas, numbered QIV 3672 and QIV 3673, from the US consulate. "Fortunately, my fear that my deafness and poor heart condition could be a hindrance in receiving our papers, did not come to anything. And when we finally had the possibility to leave Germany, nothing held us back any more .... One hour after being given our American papers, we left Stuttgart again."[122]

On the same day, July 26, 1938, they crossed the border into Switzerland where they remained before traveling to Le Havre on the north coast of France in September, bound for America. For them, this was a stroke of luck, for just two days later, on July 28, 1938, the tax office in Garmisch-Partenkirchen asked the district office to withhold the Berolzheimers' passports (*figs 39, 40*), stating that there was "still something not clarified concerning foreign currency." A telegram from the district office ordered the police in Grainau to confiscate the passports straight away and return them to the district office. The reply they received read: "Unfortunately the order has arrived too late."

LOYALTY REWARDED

Berolzheimer did not know what fate would befall Hügel am Weg and his other property in Grainau, but he wanted to make sure that one matter in particular was settled, which he had not been able to take care of himself due to the lack of time. Shortly before his departure, on July 23, 1938, he gave his stepson, Robert Schweisheimer (*fig. 41*), a general power of attorney. With this authorization, Robert signed two deeds of transfer in October 1938 at a notary's in Garmisch, which gratuitously gifted two parcels of land owned by Berolzheimer, one to each of his two employees, Anton Reindl and Ferdinand Koller, who had been faithful to the end. Koller was given the "Engelt-Eggart" in Untergrainau Feld; Reindl the "Hassaraut."[123] As neither of them belonged to any National Socialist organization, they had to suffer some locals reviling them as "slaves to the Jews."[124]

fig. 39 Michael Berolzheimer's passport photo

fig. 40 Melitta's passport photo

PASSAGE TO AMERICA

On September 8, 1938, the Berolzheimers boarded the SS Washington in Le Havre. They traveled first class on the liner, operated by the United States Line, on which they had already crossed to America on a previous occasion.[125] They reached New York on September 15, 1938, where they were met by Melitta's son, Waldemar Schweisheimer.

EMIGRATION COSTS

After the Berolzheimers' had emigrated, Georg Keller of Munich was appointed trustee of the Berolzheimers' assets by the district court in Garmisch-Parten-kirchen. From that time onward, all financial matters were handled by him.[126]

To provide some idea of the value in real terms of the amounts given here and elsewhere in this volume in Reichsmarks, and some approximate equivalent of these sums in US dollars today, please see Appendix.

a) "Special payments"

At the time of emigration, Berolzheimer's wealth, estimated by the tax offices in Garmisch-Partenkirchen and Berlin-Moabit, where the paperwork was dealt with, was around 403,000 Reichsmarks (RM). "Reichsfluchtsteuer" (Reich flight tax) was due upon leaving the country, as stipulated in §5 of the Reichs flight tax law. This amounted to 25% of a person's assets, i.e. RM 101,000.[127]

The "export funding payment," enabling owners to take their possessions abroad—a "payment to the Deutsche Golddiskontbank in Berlin-Grunewald," known as a "Dego" payment for short—was set at RM 72,900, and was paid by the trustee in two installments in September 1938 and in early 1939.[128]

Following the destruction caused during the "Night of Broken Glass" (Reichskristallnacht) on November 9, 1938, a by-law was passed on November 21, 1938, which could not possibly have been any more cynical. It was called the "Durchführungsverordnung über die Sühneleistung der Juden" (legislation on reparations to be paid by Jews) or "Judenvermögens-abgabe" (tax on Jewish assets)—"Juva" for short. The victims of the pogrom, namely the Jews themselves, had to pay for damage done to property. On December 10, 1940, the tax office in Berlin-Moabit set the sum payable by Berolzheimer at RM 55,250.[129]

In order to meet some of these "special payments" at all, Berolzheimer had to seek help from his brother, Philip, in New York, who provided a not insignificant loan of RM 94,593.[130]

b) Financial losses[131]

On June 9, 1941, the probate court in Garmisch-Partenkirchen awarded the trustee, Georg Keller, a handling fee of RM 10,950.

In addition, the government of Upper Bavaria appointed a trustee from the Nazi "Gauleitung" authorities to supervise the sale of land in Berolzheimer's possession. This trustee received a payment of RM 7,710 for his admin-istrative work and providing the necessary authorization.

Last of all, fees amounting to RM 2,610 had to be paid to a real estate agent from Grainau for handling the sale of the parcels of land.

c) Cost of emigrating to New York

These costs, amounting to RM 6,515, include the price of the crossing by ship, US head tax (RM 1,440), on-board expenses (RM 300), transport costs and customs duty for the Buick (RM 275), and costs for transporting the furniture to the USA (RM 4,500).[132]

d) Taxes and other duty liable after July 25, 1938

The tax office in Garmisch-Partenkirchen demanded the payment in arrears of income tax and church tax for the first six months of 1938 amounting to RM 57.24.[133] For 1939, a currency devaluation payment was set at RM 142.50,[134] and in 1941, RM 681 was paid for the collection of unpaid tax debts by "the Jew Michael Israel Berolzheimer."[135] Finally, a residual capital tax payment of RM 106.75 was levied for 1942, which "given the present war-time situation and the considerable need for money by the Reich," had to be paid immediately.[136]

The sum of payments made is summarized in Table 3 below.[137]

	Due date	Sum in RM
a) Special payments		
Reich flight tax	in July 1938 upon emigrating	101,000
Export funding payment	in July 1938 upon emigrating	72,900
Tax on Jewish assets	21.11.1938 as "reparations"	55,200
b) Financial losses		
Remuneration of trustee	1941 after court order	10,950
Remuneration of trustee appointed by government	1941 after enactment of law	7,710
Real estate agent's fee	c. 1941	2,610
c) Emigration Costs		
Fare and on-board expenses	8.9.1938	1,740
Transport costs for automobile and furniture	8.9.1938	4,775
Total amount*		**256,885**
d) Taxes and duties	after 25.7.1938	c. 1,400

* Compensation as part of reparations was paid on September 22, 1961[138]

Table 3: Summary of emigration expenses

Even after Berolzheimer's death, the tax office demanded a capital tax payment of RM 415 "from the moneyed pensioner Dr. jur. Michael Israel Berolzheimer of New York for the last quarter of 1942 and for 1943." This claim however was dropped on January 3, 1944, as a "foreclosure against the debtor [was] futile."[139]

On November 27, 1941, the real estate value of the country house and other property, excluding the gifted parcels of land, was estimated by the regional tax office in Munich to be RM 257,000.[140] This is almost exactly the same as the sum of the taxes and other duties which Berolzheimer had had to pay to the German state when he emigrated.

MELITTA'S CHILDREN

All three of Melitta's children managed to leave Germany with their families (*fig. 42*). Waldemar Schweisheimer left Munich on June 21, 1936, and reached New York on July 9, 1936. Nelly Friedberg sent her four children to boarding school in Italy in January 1936, from where they were taken to England before traveling to New Zealand in 1939, where they had been given refugee status. That same year, Nelly fled with her husband, Leopold Friedberg, to France on the last train leaving Karlsruhe, which Jews were allowed to take. From France, they traveled on to England. On June 21, 1947, they emigrated to New Zealand to join their children.

After his mother and step-father had emigrated, Robert Schweisheimer dealt with the transfer of deeds for the two parcels of land and artworks still in the house in Untergrainau.[141] He fled immediately after the "Night of Broken Glass" on November 10, 1938, with his wife, Lilly, to Switzerland, and from there carried on alone to London. He reached the United States on February 19, 1940, and changed his name to Robert Sheridan. Lilly Schweisheimer-Klöckner remained in Germany, and for her own safety divorced Robert on February 23, 1939. She was arrested in April 1939 because of her divorced husband's escape and remanded in custody until July 1939. After the war, Lilly and Robert re-married in London.[142]

THE LATER FATE OF HÜGEL AM WEG

Most of the contents of Hügel am Weg were taken to America with the Berolzheimers (*fig. 43*) and, after the sale of the remaining items, the house stood virtually empty. Only the "Dutch Room" remained untouched.[143] The house was still unoccupied in early 1940, as Lilly Klöckner stated in a letter to Michael: "The house suffers from being empty, and taking everything into consideration the best thing would be to sell it. To do that, I would need a general power of attorney .... I would take great care [with the sale] as I did with your move!" As she feared her letter would probably be censored, she added in veiled terms: "Dear Uncle Michael, don't worry about details, which I can't put down the way you would perhaps. I mean it plainly and simply, just as you have always known me all these years."[144]

fig. 42 Melitta with two of her grandchildren, Elsieliese and Peter, and Michael, 1928

fig. 43 The Berolzheimers in their garden

Klöckner already knew of a possible buyer, Count Hermann von Arnim, the owner of Schloss Muskau in Upper Lusatia and a neighbor in Untergrainau to the west (house no. 47½, now Loisachstrasse 47), who was recommended to her by friends as being "absolutely anti-Nazi."[145] Berolzheimer, however, did not want to hear anything about a sale, "since the money would be credited to a frozen account, which I cannot access, and I would need the money here in America in dollars." This letter from the USA was opened by the Supreme Command of the German Armed Forces before delivery, as shown by an official stamp.[146]

As the sale of the house was not possible (at that time) without Berolzheimer's authorization, the trustee, Georg Keller, was appointed absentee caretaker in October 1940 at his request.[147] Through this round about way, he gained authorization to negotiate a sale.

On October 10, 1940, Count Arnim bought Hügel am Weg, including the few household effects still in situ and the surrounding land, for RM 170,000[148]— but from whom? From Keller, who was merely absentee caretaker and did not own the house? From Berolzheimer, without his permission? From Klöckner, who had neither the power of attorney nor was she the owner? Or from the German Reich, which only later assumed ownership? This unclear legal situation was to cause Count Arnim huge problems later when the house was returned to the heirs and he asked for the purchase price he had paid in 1940 as compensation.

The name of the new owner was not added to the registry of real estate until March 17, 1942, when all the assets belonging to "the Jew Michael Israel Berolzheimer" had been impounded by the regional tax office in Berlin in accordance with a decree, no. 11, which specified that "the loss of German citizenship through leaving the country [led automatically] to the immediate retention of all assets."[149]

In 1943, Birgitta Nestler, later Wolf (1913–2009) and Albert Nestler (1908–65) moved into Hügel am Weg with their children. Whether it was because she was related to Hermann Göring—she was a niece by marriage—that the family Nestler was able to move into the now "Aryanized" house, cannot be proven. It is more likely that they had known the previous owner, Count Arnim.[150] However they must have sympathized with the Nazi ideology, since after they moved in, "there was always a swastika banner flying in the garden," Maria Schuster recalled.[151]

In spring 1945, up to twenty-four people were living in the house and the former chauffeur's apartment, among them refugees and foreigners. These allegedly included three Jewish women, whom Birgitta Nestler wanted to protect from being caught by the Nazi authorities.[152]

The American military government seized the property on October 1, 1945, and a trustee was appointed. Due of the number of tenants, the house had become quite run down and needed complete renovation. The garden was also in a pitiful state.[153] In a letter from December 28, 1945, which an American officer from Germany took with him to the USA and gave to Waldemar Schweisheimer, Count Arnim offered to return the house to its rightful heirs. As he wrote: "Although he had bought the house according to the law at that time, it would never have come on the market without the immoral pressure of the Nazi regime."[154] This voluntary act of returning property to its rightful owners is a credit to von Arnim, who chose to take this step almost two years before legally required to do so. It was not until November 10, 1947, that compensation legislation was passed, according to which all property that had been seized by the German state between January 30, 1933, through May 8, 1945, had to be restituted.[155]

fig. 44 The Krepbach Meadows looking toward the Wetterstein mountains

In September 1946, Lilly Klöckner—Robert Schweisheimer's wife—took over the house, and with a lot of hard work, made it habitable once again.[156] The house was returned to the Schweisheimer heirs on November 21, 1949.[157] Waldemar Schweisheimer visited Hügel am Weg twice, in summer 1952 and 1954, before the property was acquired in September 1957 by the MIAG company (Mühlen und Industrieanlagen GmbH). Since 1967, the house has belonged to a bank, the Stadtsparkasse München.

SALE OF THE LAND

Of the property owned by the Berolzheimers, only the two parcels of land near the station in Untergrainau (cadastral plot nos. 744, 745½), the meadow in Untergrainau Feld (no. 741½), and the Krepbach Meadows (nos. 305, 306, 307; *fig. 44*) still remained. In accordance with decree no. 11 of November 25, 1941, mentioned above, this land was expropriated and an entry made in the land registry on September 30, 1942, that it was now the property of the Reich Finance Administration.[158]

As early as in January 1939, as well as during the war, the mayor, Otto Pentenrieder, had told the district office of the NSDAP in Garmisch-Partenkirchen of his great interest in acquiring land from the village of Grainau within the parish boundaries, which had formerly been in Jewish ownership.[159] The tax office in Garmisch-Partenkirchen, however, informed the council that a ban had been imposed on the sale of the land.[160] In 1943, the tax office itself showed an interest in the Berolzheimers' plot of land near the station. The site was well suited for building apartments for civil servants, and the trees on the other parcels of land could guarantee the supply of wood to heat the offices for the duration of the war.[161] In September 1944, two sheds were erected on the site for the storage of "valuable army property" from Poland,[162] and the other land was leased for agricultural use.[163] The restitution of the land to the heirs, including compensation for their use, took place on October 25, 1949.[164]

FAREWELL

After collecting their emigration papers, Melitta and Michael Berolzheimer fled to Switzerland, and stayed at the Hotel Schweizerhof in Zurich. From there, in a letter written by Michael to Frances Greenhood, a second cousin of his and childhood friend, on July 27, 1938, Melitta added wistfully:

> *"... and now we have said farewell to the children we have to leave behind, to our friends, who proved to be friends in the best meaning of the word, to our little house, which we have loved so dearly, to the dogs, my steady companions, to the garden in which we planted nearly every single tree ...."*[165]

1 Berolzheimer Family Archives, letter dated 08/03/1908.

2 Hans Holzner, "Die Gemeinde Obergrainau. Ein Rückblick. Herrn Bürgermeister Johann Bader in Dankbarkeit zu seinem 25jährigen Dienstjubiläum gewidmet," unpublished manuscript, Grainau 1931, p. 6.

3 Peter Schwarz, "Kurze Chronik über die Zusammenlegung der beiden Gemeinden Obergrainau und Untergrainau" in: *Groana. Mitteilungsblatt des Grainauer Geschichtsvereins Bär und Lilie,* no. 3, November 1987 pp. 129–30.

4 Peter Schwarz, "Der Kirchensturz in Obergrainau im Jahre 1848" in: ibid., no. 2, June 1987, p. 45.

5 Holzner, op. cit. (note 2), pp. 23–24.

6 Heinrich Bamberger, *Chronik des Amtsgerichts Garmisch-Partenkirchen,* Garmisch-Partenkirchen 1990, p. 47.

7 For 1895: Loisachbote 12/15/1895; for 1910: Book of Addresses 1912, p. 182; for 1925: Book of Addresses 1927, pp. 179, 181; for 1937: Book of Addresses 1939, pp. 176, 178.

8 Staatsarchiv München, Bauplanverzeichnis (planning register) 1848–1914.

9 Loisachbote 09/30/1883.

10 Loisachbote 10/04/1908.

11 Holzner, op. cit. (note 2), pp. 28.

12 Loisachbote 11/27/1910.

13 Josef Bader, "Entwicklung eines Bergbauerndorfes in den Bayerischen Alpen zu einem Fremdenverkehrsdorf, dargestellt am Beispiel von Grainau im Werdenfelser Land," unpublished manuscript, Grainau 1979, pp. 34, 37.

14 Michael G. Berolzheimer, "Overview of Dr. Michael Berolzheimer's Life (1866–1942)," unpublished manuscript dated December 2011, p. 2.

15 http://de.wikipedia.org/wiki/Heinrich_Berolzheimer 8.8.2011; Leo Baeck Institute, Center for Jewish History, New York, Michael Berolzheimer Collection 1325–1942, Nürnberger Zeitung of 04/14/1931.

16 Bayerisches Hauptstaatsarchiv, Munich, Justice Dept. 20380, qualification 1894, Berolzheimer, op. cit. (note 14), p. 8.

17 All details about Michael Berolzheimer's career as an attorney are from the Bayerisches Hauptstaatsarchiv, Munich, Justice Dept. 20380.

18 Hof- und Staatshandbuch (court and state index) 1894, p. 237, through 1914, p. 219 (last volume published).

19 Horst Kessler/Vanessa provenance research, final report (unpublished), 2011 p. 4.

20 Information kindly provided by Maria Schuster (b. 1920), in interviews with the present author on 05/23/2011 and 07/07/2011.

21 Berolzheimer, op. cit. (note 14), p. 2.

22 R. Bruce Livie, "Foreword" in: *29 Drawings from the Michael Berolzheimer Collection, restituted by the Albertina Vienna, 2010,* Arnoldi-Livie Catalogue 27, Munich 2011.

23 Berolzheimer Family Archives (Timetable rev. 5).

24 Staatsarchiv München, construction plans, Garmisch 1906/79, new build/Berolzheimer.

25 Ibid., 1907/75, amendment to plans.

26 Parish of Grainau, minutes of local council meeting, Untergrainau, decision passed on 06/19/1907.

27 Stefan Hirsch, "Von Heimat und Heimatstil" in: *Charivari* 1996, from no. 10, three issues; Dieter Schwaiger, "Vom 'Werden-felser Haus' zum 'Haus Werdenfels'" in: *Schönere Heimat* 2011, issue 4, pp. 289–93.

28 Book of Addresses 1912. After the introduction of street names in 1949, the former house number 471/6 became Loisachstrasse 33 (register 1949, p. 12). Following renumbering in 1993 it became Loisachstrasse 55 (Grainau, Straßen- und Hausnummernänderungen 1993). Note: Addresses with fractions are the result of the division of cadastral plots. Houses erected on a sub-divided plot kept the original number of the plot with the additon of a fraction, relating to the size of the new sub-plot. This system can still be found in several towns and villages in the foothills of the Alps even today.

29 http://de.wikipedia.org/wiki/Paul_Roloff, 02/29/2012.

30 The first mention of the Delft tiles is in the plan for changing the hot-water system in 1929: "Die Delfter Verplättelung im Wohnzimmer darf nicht beschädigt werden" (The Delft tiling in the living room is not to be damaged), Architekturmuseum der Technischen Universität, Munich: sat-285-1, Carl Sattler, Haus Berolzheimer Untergrainau 1921–31.

31 www.delfttiles.com, 03/17/2012, dating based on www.delfter-fliese.de, 03/17/2012.

32 Staatsarchiv München, tax office 16852, summary of property 1942; Staatsarchiv München, Oberfinanzdirektion München 10181, correspondence dated 11/20/1946; Staatsarchiv München, restitution files: Ia 466, excerpt from land register from 09/05/1949; Parish of Grainau, contract for the sale of land, 1963.

33 Information kindly provided by Anton Reindl (b. 1929), in an interview with the present author on 05/23/2011.

34 Leo Baeck Institute, Center for Jewish History, New York, correspondence with rabbi Max Freudenthal and Theo Harburger, 1928–37.

35 Berolzheimer Family Archives, guestbook.

36 Livie, op. cit. (note 22).

37 J.A. Schmoll gen. Eisenwerth, *August Rodin and Camille Claudel,* Munich 2000 (2011), p. 21.

38 Berolzheimer Family Archives, letter from August Rodin of 07/07/1912.

39 Ibid., letter from Waldemar Schweisheimer of 11/01/1945.

40 Ibid., 01/09/1947.

41 Ibid., 08/24/1955.

42 Staatsarchiv München, Landratsamt Garmisch-Partenkirchen (LRA GAP) 63212, letter from Melitta Berolzheimer of 12/28/1935.

43 Loisachbote 11/26/1912.

44 http://de.wikipedia.org/wiki/Erster_Weltkrieg. 02/20/2012.

45 Staatsarchiv München, LRA GAP 63212, letter from Melitta Berolzheimer of 12/28/1935.

46 Loisachbote 03/09/1915.

47 Staatsarchiv München, LRA GAP 63212, letter of 12/28/1935.

48 http://de.wikipedia.org/wiki/Deutsche_Wirtschaftsge-schichte_im_Ersten_Weltkrieg, 02/20/2012.

49 Loisachbote 07/03/1917.

50 Hubert Riesch, "Grainauer Notgeld" in: *Groana. Mitteilungsblatt des Grainauer Geschichtsvereins Bär und Lilie,* no. 18, July 2003, p. 1093.

51 Information kindly provided by Anton Reindl and Maria Schuster on 05/23/2011, and Johannes Schäffler on 07/07/2011.

52 Loisachbote 01/12/1919.

53 All details in "The war memorial in Grainau" have been taken from: Parish of Grainau, "Errichtung eines Kriegerdenkmals 1919–21," and Andreas Hildebrandt, "80 Jahre Kriegerdenk-mal an der Kirche St. Johannes d. Täufer" in: *Pfarrkirche St. Johannes d. Täufer, Grainau 1927–2002. Festschrift zum 75jährigen Jubiläum,* Grainau 2002, pp. 69–77.

54 Robert Schweisheimer, "Kriegerdenkmaleinweihung in Grainau bei Garmisch" in: Zeitschrift Bayerland, year 23, November 1 issue, 1921, p. 63.

55 Stadtarchiv München, directory of residents, PMB B 22.

56 Livie, op. cit. (note 22).

57 Parish of Grainau, minutes of local council meeting, Untergrainau, decision passed on 05/09/1920.

58 Staatsarchiv München, LRA GAP 63212, letter from the mayor, Anton Bader, of 12/30/1935.

59 Parish of Grainau, minutes of local council meeting, Untergrainau, decisions passed on 04/14/1920 and 07/25/1924.

60 Staatsarchiv München, LRA GAP 107181, site inspection on 09/14/1927.

61 Parish of Grainau, minutes of local council meeting, Untergrainau, 05/25/1934. The local council "acknowledged the transfer of the land without compensation."

62 Parish of Grainau, minutes of local council meeting, Obergrainau, decision passed on 03/10/1933.

63 http://de.wikipedia.org/wiki/Friedensvertrag_von_Versailles, 02/20/2012.

64 Loisachbote 01/28/1923.

65 Loisachbote 04/09/1922.

66 Loisachbote 03/18/1923 and 05/06/1923.

67 Loisachbote 10/25/1923.

68 Grainau, register of household staff in Untergrainau, 1910/11–1929.

69 Reindl, op. cit. (note 51).

70 Schuster, op. cit. (note 51).

71 Dog tax register, Parish of Untergrainau, 1918–33.

72 Berolzheimer Family Archives, letter from Melitta Berolzheimer of 07/27/1938.

73 Schuster, op. cit. (note 51).

74 Berolzheimer Family Archives, letter from Waldemar Schweisheimer of 06/08/1942.

75 Ibid., 03/13/1942.

76 Leo Baeck Institute, Center for Jewish History, New York, Michael Berolzheimer Collection 1325–1942, wine offer of 02/01/1929.

77 Interview with Michael G. Berolzheimer, 2013.

78 Suzanne Schiessel (b. 1921), interview with her daughter, Linda Radich, March 2011.

79 Schuster, op. cit. (note 51); Schäffler, op. cit. (note 51). In 1938, four Jewish families had a holiday house in Untergrainau: Max Lehmann of Augsburg (house no. 39½), Martin Rosenthal of Munich (no. 46½), Gerhard Ollendorf of Berlin (no. 48b), and Albert Zuntz of Bonn (no 423/4); in Obergrainau: Nelly Hartmann of Augsburg (no. 24¼). Source: Staatsarchiv München LRA GAP 61664, LRA GAP 61665, LRA GAP 61668.

80 Staatsarchiv München, LRA GAP 63212, letter from the mayor, Anton Bader, of 12/30/1935.

81 Schuster op. cit. (note 51).

82 The section "Extensive correspondence" has been compiled from correspondence at the Leo Baeck Institute, Center for Jewish History, New York (Michael Berolzheimer Collection).

83 Barbara Staudinger, *From Bavaria to Eretz Israel—Tracing Jewish Folk Art,* Jewish Museum Munich, Collecting Images, vol. 04, Munich 2007, pp. 16–32.

84 Staatsarchiv München, construction plans, Garmisch 1929/125, extension and alterations to the Berolzheimers' property.

85 Architekturmuseum der Technischen Universität, Munich, Carl Sattler Photo Collection, "Various Small Buildings."

86 Ibid., sat-285-1; Benedikt Maria Scherer, *Der Architekt Carl Sattler. Leben und Werk (1877–1966),* vol. 2, catalogue of works, Munich 2007, p. 338.

87 Ibid. (Scherer), vol. 1 (Life & Work), pp. 138–53; Peter Schwarz, "Carl Sattler. Der Architekt der Grainauer Kirche" in: *Pfarrkirche St. Johannes d. Täufer, Grainau 1927–2002. Festschrift zum 75jährigen Jubiläum,* Grainau 2002, pp. 39–43.

88 Archiv der Isar-Amper-Werke, contracts between the villages of Obergrainau and Untergrainau, 1928; Benno Glatz, "Die Elektrifizierung von Grainau" in: *Groana. Mitteilungsblatt des Vereins Bär und Lilie,* June 10, 1992, p. 539.

89 http://de.wikipedia.org/wiki/Gabriel_Riesser, 02/20/2012.

90 Garmisch-Partenkirchner Tagblatt 04/25/1933.

91 Ibid. 11/11/1933.

92 Staatsarchiv München LRA GAP 61636, minutes from 10/01/1937; Schwarz, op. cit. (note 3), p. 130.

93 Garmisch-Partenkirchner Tagblatt 04/15/1936.

94 http://members.gaponline.de/alois.schwarzmueller/juden_in_gap_index/index_juedischer_buerger.htm; Alois Schwarzmüller, "'Juden sind hier nicht erwünscht!' Zur Geschichte der jüdischen Bürger in Garmisch-Partenkirchen von 1933 bis 1945" in: Verein für Geschichte, Kunst und Kulturgeschichte im Landkreis Garmisch-Partenkirchen (ed.), *Mohr-Löwe-Raute. Beiträge zur Geschichte des Landkreises Garmisch-Partenkirchen,* vol. 3, 1995, pp. 184–232.

95 Information kindly provided by Therese Geiger (1910–2003) in an interview with the present author on 01/12/2001.

96 Schuster, op. cit. (note 51).

97 *Die tödliche Utopie. Dokumentation Obersalzberg,* edited by the Institut für Zeitgeschichte, Munich, 5th edition, Munich 2008, p. 375; http://en.wikipedia.org/wiki/Nuremberg_Laws

98 Berolzheimer Family Archives, photo albums.

99 Geiger, op. cit. (note 95).

100 Law for the Protection of German Blood and German Honor, (September 15, 1935), Paragraph 3, "Jews will not be permitted to employ female citizens of German or kindred blood as domestic servants"; www.jewishvirtuallibrary.org/jsource/Holocaust/nurmlaw2.html (02/25/2013).

101 Information based on documents in the Staatsarchiv München LRA GAP 63212.

102 Ibid.; Schwarzmüller, op. cit. (note 94), pp. 199–201.

103 Book of Addresses 1939.

104 Hildebrandt, op. cit. (note 53).

105 Bayerisches Hauptstaatsarchiv, Munich, Landesentschädigungsakten (LEA) 408, Hofrat Dr. Michael Berolzheimer, 1938–65, letter from Grainau council of 07/08/1953.

106 "Die Kehrseite der Medaille. IV. Olympische Winterspiele Garmisch-Partenkirchen 1936," exh., Kurhaus Garmisch, 2011, unpublished manuscript, 2010; Alexander Emmerich, Olympia 1936, Cologne 2011, pp. 93–97.

107 Schäffler, op. cit. (note 51).

108 Schuster, op. cit. (note 51).

109 Alois Schwarzmüller collection, CIC files, list of members in local NSDAP group, Grainau.

110 Verein Bär und Lilie archives, Grainau.

111 Berolzheimer, op. cit. (note 14), p. 12.

112 http://www.nycago.org/Organs/NYC/html/ResBerolzheimerPC.html

113 Leo Baeck Institute, Center for Jewish History, New York, Michael Berolzheimer Collection, letter of 02/08/1937.

114 Berolzheimer Family Archives, photo album.

115 Die tödliche Utopie, op. cit. (see note 97), p. 376; Hanno Loewy/Gerhard Milchram (eds.), Hast du meine Alpen gesehen? Eine jüdische Beziehungsgeschichte, exh. cat., Hohenems/Vienna 2009, p. 357.

116 Leo Baeck Institute, Center for Jewish History, New York, Michael Berolzheimer Collection 1325–1942, letter of 04/28/1938; Anton Reindl. op. cit. (note 51).

117 Margot Hamm, et al., Good Bye Bayern Grüß Gott America. Auswanderung aus Bayern nach Amerika, edited by the Haus der Bayerischen Geschichte, Augsburg 2004, p. 47.

118 Bayerisches Hauptstaatsarchiv, Munich, LEA 408, statement of securities held, 01/01/1938.

119 Compiled from "Preparations," Staatsarchiv München 63049; Schwarzmüller, op. cit. (note 94), pp. 199–201.

120 Anton Reindl, op. cit. (note 51).

121 Precise details of these crates and their contents are missing. In general, wooden crates were used that were transported to the ports on trailers, see Hamm, op. cit. (note 117), pp. 49, 190.

122 Berolzheimer Family Archives, letter from Michael Berolzheimer of 07/27/1938 from Zurich.

123 Berolzheimer Family Archives, doc. nos. 1200, 1201, Notar Dr. Richard Daimer, Garmisch-Partenkirchen; letter of 02/22/1948; entry in deeds register on 03/13/1941 for Ferdinand Koller and on 04/23/1941 for Anton Reindl; Staatsarchiv München, tax office 16852, letter from Garmisch-Partenkirchen tax office of 09/02/1942.

124 Berolzheimer Family Archives, letter from Peter Schweisheimer of 11/17/1945.

125 Bayerisches Hauptstaatsarchiv, Munich, LEA 408, booking confirmation, 09/08/1938.

126 Berolzheimer Family Archives, letters from Georg Keller to the Amtsgericht Garmisch-Partenkirchen (10/04/1940) and the Landesamt for Widergutmachung (03/07/1947).

127 Bayerisches Hauptstaatsarchiv, Munich, LEA 408, list of assets, 11/25/1957 [1], summary 07/17/1961 [2], and confirmation of compensation 09/22/1961 [3].

128 Bayerisches Hauptstaatsarchiv, Munich, LEA 408, letter of 08/24/1953 and [1], [2] and [3].

129 Bayerisches Hauptstaatsarchiv, Munich, LEA 408, notification of 12/10/1940 as well as [1], [2] and [3].

130 Bundesarchiv Berlin R2107/KAV 720722, Landesfinanzamt/Oberfinanzpräsident, Außenstelle für feindliches Vermögen, Berolzheimer Michael, 1941, registration form from the München Nord tax office of 11/11/1941.

131 Bayerisches Hauptstaatsarchiv, Munich, LEA 408, [1], [2], and [3].

132 Ibid., summary, 01/28/1958, as well as [1] and [3].

133 Staatsarchiv München, Finanzamt 16853, notification from the Garmisch-Partenkirchen tax office of 01/17/1941.

134 Ibid., 04/24/1940.

135 Ibid., attachment order from the Garmisch-Partenkirchen tax office of 01/22/1941.

136 Ibid., 04/28/1943.

137 Emigration costs a) to c) based on Bayerisches Hauptstaatsarchiv, Munich, LEA 408, taxes and duties d) based on Staatsarchiv München, Finanzamt 16853.

138 Bayerisches Hauptstaatsarchiv, Munich, LEA 408, confirmation of compensation of 09/22/1961.

139 Staatsarchiv München, tax office 16853, letter of 12/15/1943 as well as Niederschlagungsverfügung of 01/03/1944.

140 Staatsarchiv München, Oberfinanzdirektion München 10181, summary of assets, September 1944, for 11/27/1941.

141 Bundesarchiv Koblenz B 323/360, Treuhandverwaltung von Kulturgut, Michael Berolzheimer 1948–53, appeal of 06/08/1953.

142 Berolzheimer Family Archives, timetable rev. 5.

143 Berolzheimer Family Archives, letter from Georg Keller of 03/07/1947.

144 Berolzheimer Family Archives, letter from Lilly Klöckner of 01/03/1940.

145 Berolzheimer Family Archives, letter from Lilly Klöckner of 11/25/1945.

146 Berolzheimer Family Archives, letter from Michael Berolzheimer of 02/20/1940.

147 Berolzheimer Family Archives, letter from Georg Keller of 10/04/1940.

148 Staatsarchiv München, tax office 16852, summary of assets, 09/02/1942, and letter of 01/31/1957; Staatsarchiv München, restitution file WB Ia 465, Schweisheimer vs. Arnim, 1948–57, decision made by the restitution authority of 01/31/1957.

149 Ibid., Staatsarchiv München WB Ia 465, letter from attorney Robert Held in New York of 07/02/1948; Bayerisches Hauptstaatsarchiv, Munich, LEA 408, note of 07/05/1961.

150 Monica von Rosen, Brigitta Wolf's daughter, 08/15/2011.

151 Maria Schuster, op. cit. (note 51).

152 Brigitta Wolf (1913–2009), May 1994.

153 Berolzheimer Family Archives, letter from trustee Dr. Grete Lanz of 09/21/1946.

154 Berolzheimer Family Archives, letter from Count Arnim of 12/28/1945.

155 Tobias Winstel, "Verordnete 'Ehrenpflicht' – Wiedergutmachung für jüdische Opfer" in: München arisiert. Entrechtung und Enteignung der Juden in der NS-Zeit, Munich 2004, pp. 218–36.

156 Berolzheimer Family Archives, letter from Robert Sheridan of 12/30/1956.

157 Staatsarchiv München, restitution file WB Ia 465, from the restitution authority of 11/21/1949.

158 Staatsarchiv München, tax office 16852, letter from the Garmisch-Partenkirchen tax office of 08/25/1943.

159 Parish of Grainau, Rosenthal Restitution file, letter of 01/21/1939.

160 Staatsarchiv München, tax office 16852, letter of 02/21/1945.

161 Staatsarchiv München, tax office 16852, letter from the Garmisch-Partenkirchen tax office of 05/08/1943.

162 Staatsarchiv München, tax office 16852, letter from the army base authorities of 09/23/1944.

163 Staatsarchiv München, Oberfinanzdirektion 10181, letter of 01/08/1946.

164 Staatsarchiv München, restitution file WB Ia 466, letter from the restitution authority of 10/25/1949.

165 Berolzheimer Family Archives, letter from Michael and Melitta Berolzheimer dated 27.7.1938 from Zurich.

MELITTA

The most influential woman in Michael Berolzheimer's adult life was without doubt his wife, Melitta (*fig. 1*), considered a beautiful woman and a charming host with great taste. She proved to be a very caring, supportive, and loving companion for her husband, organizing his domestic and social life in Munich and Untergrainau, accompanying him on the trips they undertook around Europe and to America, and staunchly supporting him through the difficulties and uncertainties connected with their emigration.

CHILDHOOD AND MARRIAGE

Melitta was born on October 21, 1867, in Munich, the daughter of Sigmund and Doris Dispeker, née Lehmeier. She was the second child and eldest daughter; her brother Siegfried was born on January 5, 1865, and her younger sister, Marie, on February 2, 1870.

In fall and winter 1873/74, a cholera epidemic swept through Munich, to which her father succumbed on January 19, 1874, just after his thirty-sixth birthday. Melitta was barely six years old, but her memory of the terrible consequences of this disease—striking healthy people and killing them often within hours—was to mark her young life. After her father's sudden death, the family moved to Leipzig to live with Melitta's widowed grandfather. When he passed away twelve years later in spring 1886, Melitta, her sister, and their mother, moved back to Munich to be nearer her brother, who by that time was studying law at the university.

Melitta first married on March 26, 1887, when she was just nineteen years old. Her husband, Eugen Schweisheimer was nine years her senior. He was a banker in Munich, where he had established a business in 1885 with Melitta's uncle, Simon Dispeker. After the death of her father and grandfather, Melitta may well have looked for support and leadership in her marriage to Eugen. Society, as well as her mother—who still had to arrange the marriage of her younger daughter, Marie—will also have expected her to marry. It is left to the imagination how much Melitta may have overestimated her needs as a fatherless

fig. 1   Melitta, photographed in 1900

young woman in the second half of the nineteenth century. Her divorce and subsequent marriage to Michael Berolzheimer, however, speaks of her strong mind and emerging independence.

Melitta's mother died in summer 1894 when the twenty-seven year old Melitta was six months pregnant with her third child and youngest son, Robert, who was born on November 8, 1894. She reportedly had already known Berolzheimer at that time, perhaps introduced to him by her brother, a fellow law student who was one year older than Berolzheimer. Or they might have met in Munich's art circles through her sister, Marie, who had married Julius Drey in 1889, a local important classical art dealer.

Divorcing Eugen will certainly not have been a quick or easy decision, his business partnership with Melitta's uncle, Simon, presenting additional problems. That partnership was dissolved in 1893, with Eugen taking on his younger brother, Julius (1863–1942) as a new partner.[1]

The marriage between Michael and Melitta was incidentally not the first connection between the Berolzheimers and the Dispeckers. In the family history compiled by Berolzheimer, he wrote that Baruch Berolzheimer, his great-grandfather Emmanuel's brother, had paid a relative in Hechingen, southern Germany, a monthly stipend through a Rabbi Dispe[c]ker sometime before 1832. This rabbi was Melitta's great-grandfather, Simon ben David Dispecker, formerly rabbi in Hechingen, and assistant rabbi in Fürth from 1820–34. The spelling Dispecker was changed to Dispeker by Melitta's father.

Melitta had to renounce the care of her young children to Eugen upon her marriage to Berolzheimer. However, since they all lived in Munich for the first few years after she remarried, Melitta and Berolzheimer often saw the children. Later, her son Robert and his wife Lilly, who continued to live in Munich, were the most frequent guests in Untergrainau. Daughter Nelly had moved to Karlsruhe after her marriage to lawyer Leopold Friedberg. Leopold, however, was a great outdoor enthusiast and loved hiking and skiing in the mountains around Untergrainau. Family photos as well as Leopold's memoirs, preserved in the Leo Baeck Institute in New York, bear witness to happy holidays with their children, in summer as well as in winter.

FROM "UNDESIRABLE" TO "TRULY HOSPITABLE"

A family rift, which took a few years to heal, was brought about by Berolzheimer's marriage to Melitta in 1903. She was a divorced woman and considered by some as socially "undesirable."[2] The details of Melitta's divorce from Eugen Schweisheimer are not known. Eugen never remarried. On his official asset declaration in 1941, his marital status is given as "getrennt" (separated). It is not clear how the law was satisfied to make Berolzheimer's marriage to Melitta possible, but it is significant that they were married under British law in London, and not within their family circles in Bavaria.

It is not known when Berolzheimer introduced Melitta to his parents, or whether his mother, who died in August 1901, ever met her. Berolzheimer's brother, Emil, was introduced to Melitta during his visit to Germany in 1905 and he seems to have accepted Berolzheimer's choice of spouse earlier than his brother,

fig. 2 A photograph of Melitta included in the photo album her children gave her on her 70th birthday

Uncle Michal of Mama
Febr. 22, 1936
Untergrainau

fig. 3   Melitta and Michael outside their house

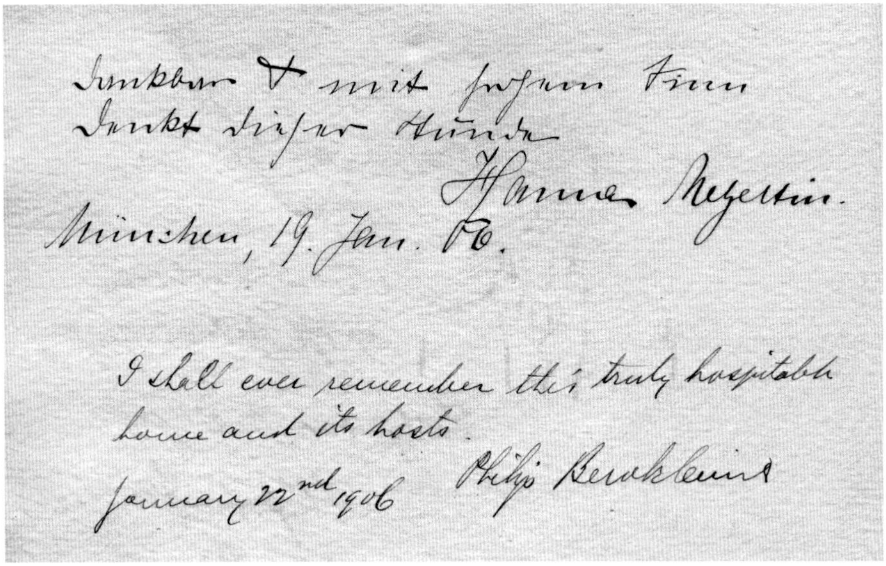

Philip. Philip took until January 1906—when he returned to Germany, concerned about his father's health—to break his silence towards his brother.

Since both sons wanted to please their dying father who had urged them to reconcile, Philip accepted an invitation to visit Berolzheimer and Melitta in their Munich apartment. He signed their guestbook: "I shall ever remember this truly hospitable home and its hosts," making it clear—by writing in English and not in his mother tongue—that he came as an "American" guest (*fig. 4*).

Philip wrote to his wife, Clara, about this visit and asked her to make an effort to communicate with Melitta "as if she were your dear sister-in-law for the past twenty years," raving in his letter about the "most beautifully and tastefully furnished apartment I have ever seen."[3] Philip and Clara finally did accept Melitta into the family and eventually established a very cordial relationship. Melitta's warmth, charm, and caring had won the family over.

THE GUESTBOOK

The guestbook provides a glimpse into the social life of the Berolzheimers and their often prominent guests, including Prince Rupprecht of Bavaria, art dealers and collectors, dancers, musicians, lawyers, politicians, and of course friends and relatives. With Melitta's birthday falling on October 21, her children Robert's and Waldemar's on November 8 and 9 respectively, and Berolzheimer's on February 22, there was a tendency to socialise during the cold winter months in Munich, only to leave the city as soon as possible in the spring to travel or to move out to Hügel am Weg in Untergrainau as soon as the snow had melted. On its opening page the book carries a poetic dedication to all future guests, be they poets, painters, family or friends, and is dated September 26, 1904. Melitta will have looked forward to her first social winter season in Munich as the official Mrs. Michael Berolzheimer, and a guestbook would therefore have been a

fig. 4 Philip Berolzheimer's entry in Michael and Melitta's guestbook

necessity. Unfortunately only certain pages have survived. Nevertheless, these guestbook entries, which span a decade, give a fascinating insight into the Berolzheimers' connections to the political and artistic community.

The Berolzheimers had cultivated their contact with the Munich art scene over a number of years (*fig. 5*). One of the undated guestbook entries is that of Adriaan Jacob Domela Nieuwenhuis of Amsterdam. He settled in Munich in 1891 and started building up an art collection of works on paper with the help of the art dealer and auctioneer Hugo Helbing, the same prominent Munich art dealer who had a major influence on Berolzheimer's art collection. Helbing was also introduced to Philip who bought a small painting, *The Turk* by Carl Spitzweg, from him in 1906. Helbing and his first wife, Sofie, signed the Berolzheimer guestbook on March 8, 1906, undoubtedly not the last of Helbing's visits.

On October 12, 1905, Franz Langheinrich and his wife, Anna, dedicated their entry in the guestbook to the "home of the arts." Langheinrich was a picture editor for the Munich-based magazine "Jugend" and a colleague of Arthur Hirth, an illustrator and son of the magazine's founder, Georg Hirth. Arthur graced the Berolzheimer guestbook on January 21, 1906 with an invitation for coffee and a lovely Jugendstil drawing of a lady with an umbrella, a motif he had improved on since it first appeared on the title page of "Jugend" in 1896 (*fig. 6*). This cultural weekly publication, an avant-garde magazine and trend-setting icon, was so influential at the time that it even gave its name to a whole new art

fig. 5 Watercolor in the guestbook by an unknown artist, 1905

style—Jugendstil—the German equivalent of Art Nouveau. The Berolzheimers and Hirths were later to be neighbors in Untergrainau.

Max Lehrs, a German art historian and long-time director of the Dresden Kupferstichkabinett with a special interest in fifteenth-century prints, also became a personal friend of the Berolzheimers and visited when in Munich. Lehrs and his wife were well known for their great hospitality toward artists. Their son, Philipp, became a welcome summer visitor in Untergrainau.

On November 6, 1905, the painter Leo Samberger, famous for his portraits of Munich high society, visited together with Hermann Hahn, a sculptor and professor at the Munich Academy of Fine Arts. Samberger's portrait of Heinrich Berolzheimer (*fig. 8*) as an honorary citizen of Nuremberg, remained unfinished due to Heinrich's death, and was given by Samberger to the city of Nuremberg at Michael's request, most probably in 1906. Hahn shared many interests with Berolzheimer, having made trips to England, France, and Greece, with a long sojourn in Italy to study Italian early Renaissance artists. He may have encouraged Berolzheimer to take an interest in Auguste Rodin's work, since less than two years later, on a trip to France in 1907, Berolzheimer bought not only the larger than life-sized statue *Saint Jean Baptiste*, but also the bust *L'homme au nez cassé* directly from Rodin himself.

Not all guests were necessarily so serious in their pursuits, judging by their entries in the guestbook (*fig. 9*). There are also entries with songs for the then popular lute (*fig. 10*)—texted, composed, and entered in the guestbook after happy and carefree evenings. One entry by Robert Kothe dates from November

fig. 6   Arthur Hirth, 1906, drawing of a lady with an umbrella

fig. 7   A drawing by Gerhard Herms

fig. 8   Leo Samberger, *Portrait of Heinrich Berolzheimer*, 1905

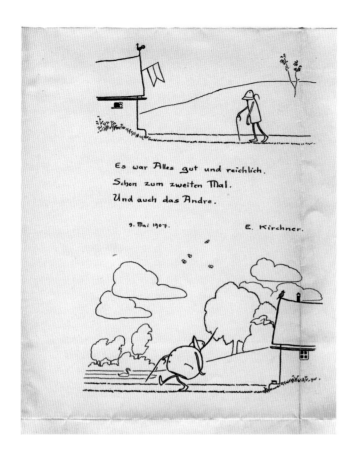

12, 1904. Kothe was a lawyer, composer, poet, violinist, actor, and co-founder of "Die Elf Scharfrichter" (The Eleven Executioners), Germany's first political cabaret. A little later, musician Heinrich Scherrer picked up the challenge and wrote his composition "For the lute." Scherrer became the foremost German teacher of the lute and guitar, writing books teaching how to play these two instruments, rediscovering German folksongs, and leading to their greater popularity. The German folksong booklet *Zupfgeigenhansl* with Scherrer's guitar annotations is still a favourite among guitar players today.

In this context, the terracotta relief at Hügel am Weg on the west wall next to the front door, which still greets visitors after almost a hundred years, is both charming and appropriate (*fig. 11*). The relief depicts a winged muse touching the shoulders of a lute player and has been tentatively attributed to the Munich artist Adolf von Hildebrand. Hildebrand's niece, Bertha Voigtlaender-Hildebrand visited the Berolzheimers in November 1912, together with Albert Voigtländer-Tetzner. One year previously, Voigtländer-Tetzner had bought the Galerie F.A.C. Prestel, an art auction house in Frankfurt and founded the Prestel Society in 1912, which regularly published portfolios comprising facsimiles of works by famous artists. Discussions between the hosts and visitors that November day may well have focussed on the artists in whom they were most interested.

The well-known Munich architect Carl Sattler was also part of this group of acquaintances. He was commissioned to carry out renovations at Voigtländer-Tetzner's country house in 1921–22, was the architect of the war memorial erected in Grainau in 1921 to a design by Adolf von Hildebrand, and later converted the

fig. 9 Cartoon by E. Kirchner, showing a tired, hungry man arriving and a happy, sated man leaving, also stating that is was not the first time. An obvious compliment to his hostess

fig. 10 Heinrich Scherrer's composition "For the lute"

garage at Hügel am Weg (*see also p. 66*). Sattler was also the architect for Robert Schweisheimer's house in Munich, built in 1924 (*see p. 114*), and Schloss Elmau which was started ten years earlier (*fig. 12*).

The last signatures in the guestbook in its present form, dated February 28, 1913, are those of the sisters Elsa Huber-Wiesenthal and Berta Wiesenthal of Vienna. Classically trained dancers with the Viennese Court Opera Ballet, they felt restricted by academic dance culture and founded their own ballet school in Vienna with their sister, Grete, in 1908. Their performances of a modern dance style marked by individualism and freely flowing movements met with great acclaim and reflected the trends in contemporary dance of other famous dancers such as Isadora Duncan and Rudolf Laban. Two years later, Grete left to become an independant, internationally renowned dancer, choreographer, actress, and dance teacher with her own dance school in Vienna. Melitta will no doubt have been delighted to have entertained them as guests in her home.

fig. 11 Adolf von Hildebrand (attrib.), terracotta relief, Hügel am Weg

fig. 12 Schloss Elmau, on the northern side of the Wetterstein range, was also designed by the architect Carl Sattler, c. 1930

The Berolzheimers led a stimulating social life in Munich and a somewhat quieter one in Untergrainau, both households being dictated by Michael's studious interests and supported by Melitta's famed hospitality. She was known to have run her household with a firm but fair hand and working at the "Huegel am Weg" was considered a privilege for local villagers, with an opportunity to be taught by Melitta about the "finer things" in life.

1 The Munich banking firm remained under the name E. & J. Schweisheimer even though Eugen's son Robert replaced Julius as partner in 1924. See also www.alemannia-judaica.de/images/Noerdlingen/FS-SCHWEISHEIMER-EUGEN.pdf. The business was confiscated and dissolved on December 3, 1938, under the "Law to aryanize Jewish property."

2 Eagle Pencil Co. General Manager Sam Kraus in a letter dated February 27, 1905, to Heinrich Berolzheimer: "Emil tells me he met Michael in Nbg, this is better than be estranged on account of a woman even if he married an undesirable lady, he himself still remains what he was before his marriage, they are brothers, it is too bad Michael did not approach Philip & make up with him also."

3 Correspondence dated February 1906.

"TRUE STORIES"

Much later, in 1941, when living in the United States, Melitta wrote several stories for her grandchildren. These anecdotal tales have since been passed down to her great-grandchildren in New Zealand. A transcription of these three stories in their original form reveals another delightful aspect of Melitta's personality.

Clenn, the chauffeur, was a nice man. That does not mean that he was intelligent or good looking. Oh no, not at all. But he was true, honest, economical and not for his own pocket alone but especially – and that was the rare case – for our pocket. He had not necessary to grasp in his own pocket very often, he got almost everything from us: his suit, his coat, his gloves, his cap and he took care of them as a pussy-cat of her youngsters.

One day I saw that his gloves were worn out and I told him: "Clenn, when we shall come to town next week, please buy a pair of new gloves for you." "What's the matter, Ma'am, with my gloves?" he asked. "They look too shaby," I replied, "I can't see them any longer." "Yes Ma'am," was his answer.

The next week we came up to town [Munich]. I had to look for some friends, Clenn went shoping and when I met him again he showed me his hands with the new gloves: fine ones indeed, real kid gloves, brown in color, each with a button.

In the afternoon we started to drive back to our mountain-village [Untergrainau]. It was one of the last days in fall, the leaves on the trees were yellow and red, and the sun sent his last rays to mix up a little gold in the color. I enjoyed the drive very much though it became darker and darker.

Suddenly the car stopped. "Pardon me, Ma'am," Clenn said, "I want to change my gloves. "But what for?" I asked in great surprise.

"Well," he replied quite calmly, "you have told me that you can't see my old gloves any longer as they are too shaby. So I bought the new ones. In ten minutes the sun do set, then you can't see any longer neither the old gloves nor the new ones and I can save the later still a little time."

He was right, I couldn't say any word.

A second story, written in Melitta's same meticulous handwriting, shows her humorous, self-deprecating attitude towards old age:

Mrs. Michael Berolzheimer
Apartment 5-E, Franklin House
300 Hayward Avenue, Fleetwood
Mount Vernon, N.Y.

Grandma was ill, very ill. She had not eaten any food for 5 days and she was very weak.

Her son, a physician, took care of her. He adored his mother, and the care he gave her was excellent. Only so far, she had not been able to eat anything.

The evening of the fifth day he brought her himself a tray with appetizing-looking food and sat it down beside her.

But Grandma shook her head.

Quitly he reminded her that it was important that she take this food, that her body needed it. And he reminded her of the time when he himself had been a little boy and had been sick. And at that time she made him eat his food by eating each spoonful "for somebody he loves; one for Pa, one for Ma, one for sister Nelly, one for brother Robbie" she has said at that time and the little boy had eaten.

And now he was asking her to do the same thing for her grandchildren "one for Elsielies, one for Peter, one for Susan, one for Eric."

The following day the pains were worse and Grandma couldn't eat her soup. Her nurse-maid Cathleen, an intelligent young girl had overheard the conversation of the night before, and she took up the tray now. Gently she placed it on the small nighttable besides her and sat down. "Take at least on [one] spoonful still" she pleaded. But Grandma shook her head "No, I can't, dear" she daid [said] "I am too ill, too weak, not for anybody."

Cathleen was good friend with Grandma and knew many of her thoughts. She smiled quitly and put the spoon into the soup. She stirred it, then she suggested: "Oh, I knew somebody for whom you will do it surely, for – Mr. Roosevelt.

And the old lady took it.

The last story is the most revealing. In it, Melitta tells of her early life and attitudes at the end of the nineteenth century. All three stories were written in English a year before her death, obviously intended as a legacy for her grandchildren. Published here, over seventy years later, they are still delighful and throw a fascinating light on family life at that time.

A True Story of My Life

"Grandma, please, please, tell us a story of your life when you were young. You promised to us you would tell us whether the American girls are different from the German girls."

"Children dear, I do not know the American girls very well, I know only very few of their souls, but it seems to me that American girls know much more of life and of the world than German girls knew in my time. I do not want to tell you how many years have since passed, it is enough to say long, long ago.

We lived in L[eipzig], a city in Saxony of medium size and when I was 17 years old, my grandfather passed away. My mother moved with my younger sister and me to M[unich], one of the most beautiful cities in Germany. My father had died when I was still a little child and mother liked to join my brother who was studying law at the university M[unich]. We had rented a very nice flat and mother was busy in furnishing our apartment. I didn't care about that (I think that is the same with young American girls to-day.) I had to take lessons: piano, English and French and I liked so much to stroll in the streets and to look on the beautiful stores. An aunt of mine accompanied me mostly. She was a funny little woman, stout and well-nourished with folding eye-glasses on her nose and when she got excited, the glasses were trembling and you could hear the noise they made. She was very fond of me and one day she invited me to go with her to the theater. Oh, what happiness for me! Of course I had been in the theater in L[eipzig] sometimes but never in an opera by Richard Wagner and now I should see and listen to "Siegfried".

The evening came and we were in the theater much too early. That was grand, I had time to look around. Some rows in front of us a couple was sitting. The lady and the gentleman looked back and greeted. "Who are this people?" I asked. "The woman is not nice but her husband is good looking." "That is not her husband," Aunt B. answered. "She is an American woman with many dollars and the man on her side is her "Techtelmechtel" [date or affair]. "I can't understand you," I said surprised. "I never heard this word before." I wanted so much to ask still a question, but I looked at the eye-glasses. They were trembling and I heard aunt's voice: "Be silent, little goose."

I was silent and looked around, looked on the balcony. There a woman was sitting wonderful dressed. She had white hair and her dress was of pure pink silk. On her side was sitting a very well dressed gentleman: "Auntie," I asked. "Do you know this lady in the pink dress and her husband? Look, they are sitting in the midst of the balcony." "Yes, child, I know their names. This is Lady S. with her "Gschpusi" [lover]. "With whom?" I asked, "Is that a Bavarian name for husband?" "Be silent, little goose" said Aunt B. and I heard the noise of the trembling glasses. I thought this was my last question to Aunt B.

Suddenly I looked at the box direct beneath the box where the members of the Royal Family were sitting and though I knew it was not right to ask again, I said: "Auntie, please, answer me still one question: who is the woman in the box? Can you see her? She wears a gown of black velvet and she has jewelry, I never saw such pearls and such diamonds. But please Auntie, look at the girl besides her, dressed quite simple in a white mousseline-dress. Isn't she charming? Isn't she lovely? Do you know their names, Auntie?" "Yes, child, everyone knows them, it is Miss K. with her daughter." "Thank you for answering my questions. I always shall remember them, Mrs. K. and her daughter." "I told you, Miss K. with her daughter." "No, Auntie, that is a mistake you are making. Miss K. can't have a daughter, that is not possible." "Be silent, little ...." She couldn't say anymore, the curtain rose.

The opera had finished and on the way to our home Aunt B. said to me: "You looked sweet this night and I observed many gentlemen admiring you." "No, Auntie," I said. "You are wrong, I look awfully in this dress with the red and green flowers, but I have to tell you something: "Siegfried" was singing wonderful on the stage and the marvellous voice and music excited and touched my heart; of the words and the sense of the play I didn't understand anything and I had much time for dreaming. I dreamt, in some years I shall be married – I do hope so – and then I shall ask my husband to give me a white Mousseline dress for a present at my birthday and a gown of pure pink silk for Christmas. Do you think he will do me the favour?" "Surely, little girl, he will do it, but my opinion is that you have not to wait for some years, in one year you will be married."

And Auntie was right. When the Spring came and everywhere there was a beginning of blossom, I was to be married. And the next year I was with child.

In the corner of our street my mother was living and I rushed to her to tell her the good news. I thought, my mother who was my best friend too, would be delighted. But it was not so: "Mother, what is the matter?" I asked. "Are you not happy, you look so sad."

And mother replied: "I shall tell it to you. You yourselve [sic] are still a child and you don't know how many pains and sorrows a little child will bring with. I want not to tell you anything more, but a child never comes without pains and remember: in your bedroom there stands a nice white stove and until it becomes black, your child will not be alive." "Thank you mother dear, I shall wait for the day when my pains begin and when the stove will become black."

And the day came when my pains began. It was awful, I went to bed and looked at the stove – still white. The doctor came, an old woman entered the bedroom, I folded my hands under the counter-pane and prayed quite, quite softly: "Almighty God, please, let the stove become black that my child will come soon." The pains became worse and worse. I couldn't see anything more. Suddenly I heard a little cry. I didn't know what that means, I was so tired, so tired – the stove seemed black to me. After some minutes my husband came in and said: "Darling we have a child, we have a boy."

I couldn't believe it, but it was true. The old woman entered and brought me my child. It was only a little white paket she laid into my arms, and the child, the sweetest child, opened his soft brown eyes, and it was to me, as if I could hear: "Mammy, are you happy now?"

And I had wanted to cry with loud voice: "Yes, my darling, I am happy. I have no wish anymore, neither the white Mousseline dress, nor the pink-pure-silk gown. I have my child, my boy. I am the happiest woman in the world."

THE FINAL YEARS:
EMIGRATION AND LEGACY

On September 8, 1938, Dr. Michael and Melitta Berolzheimer boarded the SS Washington in Le Havre, France, bound for New York (*fig. 1*). The timing of their long-planned emigration was very fortunate indeed. Just two months later, after the "Night of Broken Glass" on November 9, they would no longer have been allowed to emigrate with their household goods, their car, books, papers, and documents, down to Berolzheimer's personalized letterheads, and especially not with parts of his cherished collection of artworks.

PERSECUTION AND PREPARATIONS

Most probably, Michael and Melitta would have lost a lot more than their worldly possessions. They might have had to flee like Berolzheimer's cousin, Michael Prager, and his wife, Pauline (née Sahlmann), who escaped to the Netherlands after Prager was arrested, tortured, and forced to sign over the family home in Nuremberg to the government. Their son, Kurt Adolf, and daughter-in-law, Lisa (née Rau), went with them. The whole family was deported in 1942 from the Westerbork refugee camp and died in 1942 and 1943 in Sobibór and Auschwitz concentration camps. Another cousin, Julius Prager, Michael Prager's brother, emigrated to Czechoslovakia in November 1935 and took his own life in Prague on December 18, 1935 (*see also Appendix*).[1] Melitta's son Robert had to flee to England after defending his house when the SS broke into his garage and set it on fire during the "Night of Broken Glass"; other members of Melitta's family, the Dispekers and Schweisheimers—like so many others—were arrested, deported, and murdered.[2]

It had taken about two years to overcome all the bureaucratic hurdles and obtain the required permits, affidavits, receipts for paid taxes and surcharges, visas, passports—and finally—secure a moving company and passage on a ship at a time when the number of emigrants from Germany was swelling rapidly. Fear gripped the Jewish population that countries would close their borders after complaints by foreign governments about the growing wave of immigrants. Hitler's response was the "Final Solution," reached at the Wannsee Conference

fig. 1   The SS Washington arriving in New York Harbor, 1938

on January 20, 1942, ending all possibility of emigration—all Jews remaining within territories under Hitler's military power, from France, Belgium, and Holland to Germany, Italy, and Eastern Europe, were arrested and deported, either to various concentration camps where they were worked, starved or treated brutally, or straight to death camps where they were murdered on arrival. Few escaped or lived through it to bear witness.

ARRIVAL IN AMERICA

It was not the first time Michael and Melitta Berolzheimer had seen the Statue of Liberty when their steamer pulled into New York Harbor on September 15, 1938. This time, however, they came as legal immigrants sponsored by Berolzheimer's brother, Philip, not as visitors as they had done twice before in 1933 and 1937. Michael and Melitta were seventy-two and seventy years old respectively at the time, and in a much more fortunate position than many other immigrants as they had long-established family and business ties to America.

Waiting at the pier was Melitta's son, Waldemar Schweisheimer (*fig. 2*). Anti-Jewish legislation had robbed Schweisheimer of his livelihood in Germany as a medical doctor and writer. He had emigrated from Germany on July 1, 1936, bound for New York, with his wife, Else, and his children Elsieliese and Peter. Michael Berolzheimer had been able to facilitate Schweisheimer's emigration to America in 1936 by asking his nephews, the three sons of his eldest brother, Emil, to support Schweisheimer and his family financially for a four-year period. Family correspondence shows that Berolzheimer gave several paintings to his nephews as collateral for this support. Emil had died in 1922 and Berolzheimer may have considered the sons to be in the best position to support his stepson since they were the younger generation, wealthy, had a well-established pencil manufacturing business, and were rougly the same age as Schweisheimer. Berolzheimer never knew the degree of misunderstanding that his stepson felt toward his step-cousin's demands for repayment. This only emerged after Berolzheimer's death and is documented in correspondence between Schweisheimer and his brother, Robert.

During Michael and Melitta's visit to the United States in 1937, it is likely that Berolzheimer's simmering plans to emigrate were brought into focus, plans that were openly discussed with his American family. Hitler's annexation of Austria on March 12, 1938, was probably the last straw, finalizing his decision to leave. As listed in the asset declaration required of all Jews in 1938, he owed his brother, Philip, $30,000—a loan, secured by his house in Untergrainau, perhaps used to pay his "exit tax." Berolzheimer could not have predicted how excessively the Nazi regime would eventually tax him, but he must have known that any wealth transfer to America would be more easily accomplished in the form of a collection of artworks rather than a large money transfer. The international transfer of money was strictly regulated, and any such transfers to America would have triggered questions by Nazi government officials.[3]

Michael and Melitta's sea voyage was well planned and they did not have to travel alone. Berolzheimer's niece, Marie Hopf, his sister Frida's daughter, had received emigration visas for herself and her daughter, Lise, from the American Consulate in Stuttgart on July 25, 1938, just one day before her uncle and aunt.

When the Berolzheimers boarded their steamer in Le Havre, Marie and Lise were already on board, having set off from Hamburg the day before.

FAMILY MEMBERS ON THE MOVE

Marie was finally joining her son, Fritz, in America after her husband Ernst Hopf's death in 1935. In 1934, she had taken her seventeen-year-old son to New York, where he was sponsored and financially supported by his great-uncle, Philip Berolzheimer, to finish high school and to go to university in the USA. Hitler's policies severely restricted the public education of Jewish children and Fritz's concerned parents had asked Philip for help. Philip had already been supporting his widowed sister, Frida, since the 1920s with regular payments, and now provided just as generously for her daughter Marie's family, even leaving a bequest for them in his will.

Sadly, Marie's efforts to convince her younger sister, Elisabeth, to emigrate had failed. Elisabeth's first husband, Franz Meussdörffer, was killed in 1918 during World War I. Her second husband, Otto Schwink—a government official— believed he could protect her and pressured her into staying. In a letter to Charles Berolzheimer of December 20, 1940, Marie expressed her worry about her sister who had written in veiled terms about her misery and fear in Germany. A little more than four years later, Elisabeth and her daughter, Ruth, were shot on May 3, 1945, by SS soldiers in the remote Jachenau valley in the far south of Bavaria. According to historical sources, they had approached American troops close-by, in an attempt to prevent fighting in and around Jachenau and to inform them of the SS presence. A painted, wooden commemorative board now marks the spot (*fig. 3*).

fig. 2 Michael and Melitta with Waldemar Schweisheimer in NY

Melitta's family was also on the move. Her sister, Marie Dispeker, had married a Munich art dealer, Julius Drey, and after his death in 1930, emigrated to New York. Melitta's niece, Edith Drey, had emigrated with her husband, Eugen Selz, in 1936 to London, having sent their seventeen-year-old son, Peter, to America. As already mentioned, Melitta's son, Waldemar, emigrated to the United States on July 1, 1936, with his wife and two children. Schweisheimer's cousin, Ruth Kraemer, arrived in New York two months later.

Melitta's daughter, Nelly, and her husband, Leopold Friedberg, had also submitted an application to the German government to emigrate but Nelly hesitated, unwilling to leave her elderly father, Eugen Schweisheimer, behind. However, having been warned by a sympathetic Nazi official in August 1939 of a round-up and deportation of all Jews in Karlsruhe planned for the next day, they hastily left and took the last train from Germany before the borders to France were closed to Jews. They first went to Leopold's sister, Frieda Driesen, whose husband was a banker in Paris.

The Friedbergs eventually made their way to England, where they spent the war years. Their four children, Suzanne, Max, Erika, and Ernst, born in 1921, 1922, 1924, and 1925 respectively, had been at boarding school in Italy since 1936. Frieda collected all four siblings from Italy and, in Genoa, put them on a ship bound for England. They arrived in Southampton on March 10, 1939, and were looked after by Roszika Rothschild[4] and her family until their visas for New Zealand were approved on June 13, 1939. Traveling on two different ships, the children finally arrived in New Zealand on August 9, 1939 after nearly two months at sea, with stopovers in Colombo, Sri Lanka, on July 8, and Fremantle, Western Australia, on July 18.[5] It took until 1947 before Nelly and Leopold[6] were finally allowed to emigrate from England and rejoin their children in New Zealand.

Melitta's son, Robert, had similarly submitted an emigration application for himself and his non-Jewish wife, Lilly (née Klöckner—of the giant steel dynasty; divorced Heimsoeth). Robert and his sister, Nelly, had both tried to convince their father, Eugen Schweisheimer, to leave Germany with them. Eugen, eighty years old in 1938, however refused to abandon his home, banking business, and his fatherland. After the pogrom of November 9, 1938, with detailed lists of Jewish art property declarations in hand, the Munich Gestapo systematically raided Jewish homes. On November 25 that year they also searched Eugen's apartment, "confiscating" a painting in the process. In the spring of 1939, Eugen was arrested and tried on trumped-up charges of financial wrongdoings. He was sentenced to pay a hefty fine and released. His banking business was forced to close and finally deleted from the trade registry on June 6, 1941. Eugen's last letter from his apartment in Munich was written on March 22, 1942; Waldemar Schweisheimer received it on May 3. On June 23, eighty-four-year-old Eugen, his brother Julius, together with many other Jewish citizens from Munich, were deported to Theresienstadt concentration camp. Eugen's brother, Moritz, and his wife, Mathilde, were picked up in another Gestapo sweep in Munich on August 7. The date of Eugen's death was registered a month after his deportation, on July 26, 1942; that of Moritz on November 14, 1942, Mathilde in December 1942, and Julius on November 23, 1942. Eugen's sister, Hina, died in Theresienstadt in 1943. While the three oldest Schweisheimer siblings had died earlier, four Schweisheimer siblings perished in Theresienstadt. Only one of the brothers, Joseph, managed to emigrate to the US and escaped the same fate.[7]

fig. 3   In devout memory of Mrs Elisabeth Schwink and her daughter, Ruth, who lost their lives on this spot on May 3, 1945, as victims of the war. *Forgive us our trespasses, as we forgive those who trespass against us*

ADJUSTMENT

After their arrival, Michael and Melitta first stayed with Waldemar Schweisheimer's family at 238 Eastchester Road in New Rochelle, New York, until their furniture arrived on October 28, 1938. On November 1, they moved into their own two-bedroomed apartment at 300 Hayward Ave. in Mt. Vernon, north of New York City. Philip's wife, Clara, had found the apartment for them, and Philip generously covered the rent for it. The location was well chosen, since it was Schweisheimer, living only a few minutes away by car, who subsequently kept an eye on the health of his mother and stepfather and would visit them often. It was a spacious and bright place and they both liked it. How well it measured up to their memories of their cherished Hügel am Weg, its large garden, and the beautiful surroundings in alpine Bavaria is anyone's guess.

Another change to become accustomed to was transportation. Michael Berolzheimer had owned a car in Germany and employed a chauffeur as a full-time member of the household staff. As one of Melitta's stories reveals, a chauffeur might have been a status symbol, or simply a practicality because Berolzheimer—never a dashing man like stepson Robert—might not have liked driving. The car, conveniently exchanged from a German-built Horch to an American Buick, was shipped to America in a crate with the rest of the household items and was likely intended as a gift to Schweisheimer. Nevertheless, in letters to the family, Michael and Melitta stated their relief and happiness at being in America.

While living in Germany, Berolzheimer had always written in German to his family in America. After his arrival in America, however, he corresponded with his American relatives in English. He was trying to make a conscious break with Germany and a wholehearted effort to accept America as his permanent home. However he continued to use his personal stationary with the printed address of Hügel am Weg in Untergrainau. Although he may simply not have wanted to waste good paper, he knew that this frugality would evoke memories of Germany especially when writing to his nephew, Charles. Interestingly enough, Melitta in her first Christmas letter from America to their former Untergrainau employee, Toni, used a letterhead stamp calling herself "Mrs. Michael Berolzheimer," perhaps her own effort to become integrated in American society. The various letterheads give an indication of their ambivalent sense of identity and belonging.

Berolzheimer apologized to Charles in a letter written on October 26, 1938, for his mistakes in English, explaining he had learned English mostly from written sources and he did not really know how the language "sounded." His first letters in English show his remarkably good vocabulary, but contain clear idiomatic mistakes. As time moved on, and in spite of his bad hearing, his English improved considerably, not only as a result of his English-speaking environment, but through his actively following printed news. His favorite weekly magazine was the London Economist which kept him abreast of events in Europe and around the world. Charles, in his boundless generosity toward his uncle, had placed a subscription for it in his name. News on the radio was not much of an option for him due to his hearing problem, and Melitta most probably briefed him on the day's events. Although commercial television broadcasting was not available until 1947, news of the pogrom in Germany on November 9, 1938, made headlines the very next day in the New York Times. What had happened to families and friends, however, took much longer to filter through the censured mail, and the worry about loved ones left behind in Germany grew. Some families even developed a coded form of communication, informing others of arrests through telegrams by using, for example, the wording "Sigmund and Ernst not at home."

Family gatherings, with everyone speaking German, will have created a comfortable feeling of belonging for Michael and Melitta. Birthdays especially were faithfully celebrated at Schweisheimer's home where his wife, Else (*fig. 4*), excelled at cooking the traditional German way. Berolzheimer's favorite dessert was sour cherry cake; Melitta loved spinach, roast potatoes, and pork sausages. This adherence to familiar German food—and the expectation of German work ethics—gave rise to some bitter clashes between Melitta and her changing American domestic helps, requiring Else to act as a mediator.

Michael's accent would surely have betrayed his German origin, and seamless integration into the established local society in Mt. Vernon will have been difficult at his age. Schweisheimer, on the other hand, had made a point to integrate into mainstream American society as quickly as possible, joining a local community organization and becoming a member of his local Presbyterian Church, to which he also left a bequest in his will. Schweisheimer's son, Peter, went so far as to change his family name from Schweisheimer to Sherwood. When he was sent to Germany with the American occupying forces after the war, it will have served him well that his name did not betray his German roots.

FINANCES

Due to the excessively high emigration penalities, Michael and Melitta's financial situation at the time of their arrival in the US was precarious. Berolzheimer still had nominal possession of their much loved house, Hügel am Weg, but he had had to leave a significant part of his art collection and other valuables behind as a condition for obtaining emigration permits. After their departure, Robert Schweisheimer was forced to send these items to be sold at auction. The proceeds from the auctioned assets fell to the state, Berolzheimer never receiving any payment.

Berolzheimer had, however, taken the most valuable items in his art collection with him, having estimated their value personally, based on pre-war prices. Hyperinflation of the 1920s in Germany will have taught him not to put his trust in monetary assets, and it may have reinforced his long-standing passion of collecting art. Berolzheimer was not poor, he had some American investments and stock, but he had little ready cash, using the interest from his investments and hoping for some profitable art sales. His estimates turned out to be overly optimistic in the depressed American art market of the war years. Nevertheless, with his brother, Philip, covering the rent for his apartment, Berolzheimer would, right up until his death, send monthly payments to support his refugee step-children, Robert and Nelly, finding comfort in still being able to care for "Melitta's and his" children.

However, according to Schweisheimer, Berolzheimer became more cautious, suspicious, and withdrawn, especially with regard to money matters. He will also

have learned that all Jewish property had been forfeited to the government by a decree issued on November 25, 1941. His real estate and bank accounts were confiscated, effective March 18, 1942, which also meant he never received any money from the involuntary sale of Hügel am Weg. Instead, the proceeds went straight into government coffers in Berlin. His distress and worries were well founded.

WORRIES

Although Michael and Melitta described how happy and content they were in America several times in their letters, their final years were overshadowed by health problems and worries about Melitta's children, as well their friends and extended family left behind in Europe. News from Germany became increasingly filled with a sense of doom; reports of anti-Semitic persecution and deportations to concentration camps became the norm, and censorship of mail by the Gestapo increasingly curtailed family news from Germany.

When Berolzheimer emigrated, he knew his sister, Frida, was being well taken care of in the Neu-Friedenheim clinic near Munich, where she had lived since the 1920s due to "mental health problems." He will have learned from Frida's daughters that his sister had been moved to a private care home in Bendorf-Sayn near Koblenz, away from the Nazi hotbed of Munich, where the clinic she had been living in had been closed and sold in 1941 to a government agency that refused to take Jews. Thankfully, he would not have to learn of her deportation to Sobibór death camp on June 15, 1942, ten days after his own death. The date of her death is given as June 30, 1942.

He will however have heard about the death of his Munich art dealer, Hugo Helbing, with whom he had done business for over forty years. Helbing died on November 30, 1938, after being severely beaten by SS soldiers during the night of the pogrom. And he may well have waited in vain for news from his cousin, Michael Prager, and his wife, Paula. Their friendship had lasted from childhood to adulthood and into their married lives; the Pragers were well-loved guests in Untergrainau and often accompanied them on family trips to spas and ski resorts. The Pragers had left on March 11, 1939, for Amsterdam where their son, Kurt Adolf, had moved to in 1935 after losing his position as a judge. They were all hoping for safety there, but with the German troops' invasion of the Netherlands, they, too, were deported and murdered. Kurt died on August 17, 1942, his wife, Lisa, two days later, in Auschwitz. Michael and Paula were deported to the Sobibór death camp on April 2, 1943 (*see also Appendix*).

Together with Melitta, he will have quietly worried how his house and the faithful employees were faring. And they will have followed with much concern the failing health of Berolzheimer's brother, Philip, who died on May 22, 1942, just two weeks before Berolzheimer's own death. In all their worries, they will have felt a certain resignation over their own age and failing health, accepting that their life had changed forever.

HEALTH

In their quest for a safe haven in a new country, free from persecution, it did not matter that Berolzheimer had suffered from heart problems since early adulthood, that he had become quite deaf, and that Melitta suffered from diabetes and a heart condition. In his first letter after leaving Germany, dated July 27, 1938, written from the safety of the Hotel Schweizerhof in Zurich, Switzerland, to his second-cousin, Frankie Greenhood, Berolzheimer told of his worries that their health might be an impediment in being granted visas; to his great relief these fears were unfounded.

Their health issues, however, stayed with them. On March 31, 1942, Schweisheimer wrote to his brother, Robert, about Berolzheimer's latest heart attack: "OM [Onkel (Uncle) Michael] is much better, knock on wood. But one cannot predict when such an attack will occur again—and there is no possibility or method of treatment to prevent such a reoccurrence. Up to now, I was always optimistic in my judgement about his condition because, in general, his heart works well. But this attack was nearly beyond the strength of his heart and I am forced to be less optimistic now."

Melitta had to fight her own battles as well. Waldemar Schweisheimer wrote to Robert:

> "She also suffers, as you know, from quite severe diabetes, which actually can be kept in check quite well, and a chronic heart muscle ailment that makes her suffer at times very much, so that I am frequently very worried about her. However, because she has had this ailment since 1914 (diphtheria), there is certainly hope that she will pull through this time, too. [...] She actually is

frequently sick, apart from her diabetes and chronic heart ailment—but she has been spoiled by OM at nights, she could wake him up at any hour and have him listen to her complaints which he would do patiently since in exchange he was able to sleep in every day till 1 pm. [...] Mama has lost a lot of weight during the last year, but in the last few months she has kept steady and generally feels okay. Both are mentally fully competent, but in many ways behave oddly, and especially Else has to be very patient, like yesterday when she took Mama shopping, which for women even of Mama's age holds a great deal of attraction."

WRITING THE FAMILY HISTORY

Apart from his own early archival research, two of the most important sources of genealogical information for Berolzheimer in Untergrainau were the renowned Dr. Max Freudenthal and Dr. Theodor Harburger (*see also p. 137 f.*). He corresponded frequently with both of them, as well as contributing to journals dedicated to Jewish heritage and genealogy. How intensely Berolzheimer was involved in Jewish history can be gleaned from a letter he wrote to Harburger on August 19, 1930, in which he talks of a "golden wedding band" and his genealogical research, and his interest in helping to establish a Jewish Museum in Munich (*see p. 123*).

Harburger emigrated to Palestine in 1933; Freudenthal, however, lived in Munich until his death on July 11, 1937. The couples occasionally socialized, and the frequent correspondence was eagerly awaited on both sides. The letters written by Freudenthal's widow, Else, to Berolzheimer reveal her desperation over the volume of correspondence and sources left by her husband, and she asked Berolzheimer to sort through them.[8] She emigrated after the pogrom in 1938 to her children in Sweden, but the death of a favourite uncle and her mother's death finally became too much to bear. She committed suicide on April 30, 1940.

By late 1937, with the loss of such a formidable friend as Freudenthal, Berolzheimer must have felt a sense of urgency to finish his own family history and publish his planned book—"The ancestors of Heinrich Berolzheimer and their families." The original version of the manuscript contained nineteen chapters with 197 pages of text and numerous additions, including eighteen lengthy family trees, most of them going back several hundred years. The final manuscript stops at Chapter 9 after a few pages. He was probably anxious to document his German ancestry before the overwhelming impressions of the New World dimmed his memories and knowledge.

While the first part of his family's genealogy was typewritten in Untergrainau, he started the second handwritten part upon his arrival at Hotel Schweizerhof in Zurich on July 26, 1938, remarkably on the very same day he had left Germany for ever. In his very small though perfectly legible handwriting, he used every square inch on the pages of his writing block, often running out of space in the process. He continued writing on board the SS Washington to America; he wrote in his temporary quarters at Waldemar Schweisheimer's in New Rochelle; and he finished it in Mt. Vernon on November 29, 1938.

Begonnen Zürich, July 26th, 1938.

Fortgesetzt Ship "Washington" September 8th, 1938.

Fortgesetzt 228 Eastchester Road, New Rochelle, N.Y. September 15th 1938.

Beendet 300 Hayward Avenue, Fleetwood, Mount Vernon, N.Y. November 29th, 1938.

The translation of his handwritten note in his family history (*fig. 5*) reads:

> *"Started in Zurich, July 26th, 1938*
> *Continued Ship "Washington" September 8th, 1938*
> *Continued 228 Eastchester Road, New Rochelle, N.Y. September 15th, 1938*
> *Finished 300 Hayward Avenue, Fleetwood, Mount Vernon, N.Y. November 29th, 1938."*

Berolzheimer summed up the reason behind his research efforts in a letter to Charles:

> *"... I not only liked to give a remembrance to the boy [Michael G. Berolzheimer], but something he can't get from anybody else. It is true, I asked myself whether the boy even later will be interested in such matters. But it's good to know where we come from—as far as we can know it. And in this special case you and your family certainly are interested in knowing, where your father's name and your eldest son's name came from. You presumably cannot learn that at any time with certainty, except by these sheets. Thus perhaps someday they may be very useful for your descendants, (the more as our family is separated completely and definitely from the land we came from, and only by my book you can find out the old documents, proofing [sic] the relationship and—perhaps—some rights in favor of your boys, in near or farther future) and they may even be inclined to print the manuscripts, in German or in English."*[9]

At least eight people in the extended family were named "Michael" in his honor. Charles, who since his youth had been very fond of his uncle, named his second son after him—Michael George. This prompted a delighted letter from "Dr. Michael," which included an extensive essay on the history and provenance of the name (*see Appendix*).[10] He intended to write up his further research for his great-nephew's third birthday, but in a letter of February 18, 1942, most probably his last letter to Charles, he had to admit that he was so weak and felt unable to fulfill his intention.[11]

A surprise discovery in 2012 also revealed an affectionate bond between Berolzheimer and his step-granddaughter. Ingeborg Heimsoeth Amos, nicknamed "Butzeli" (little child) was the daughter of Robert's wife, Lilly, from her first marriage. Ingeborg frequently visited Untergrainau with her brother Hans-Jürgen, her mother, and Robert. Ingeborg married the attorney Hans Egon Amos and moved to England with him in 1938, when he was called to the bar in London. They named their first child Michael (*fig. 6*), born on March 8, 1939, in Munich, to honor Berolzheimer who had emigrated at the beginning of Ingeborg's pregnancy. The young mother, preparing for the arrival of her newborn son from Germany, was caught up in the outbreak of World War II. With the internment

fig. 5 Michael Berolzheimer's handwritten note in the family history he had compiled

of his parents on the Isle of Man, little Michael Amos spent the first six years of his life in the care of his doting grandmother, Lilly Schweisheimer, and his great-grandmother Lilly Müller. Fleeing heavy air raids on Munich by the Allied Forces, Lilly moved to Ambach on Lake Starnberg and later to Untergrainau where she rented a room at Haus Hirth, next door to Hügel am Weg. Michael Amos was finally reunited with his parents in England in fall 1945.

THE FINAL DAYS AND LAST WILLS

By fall 1938, with their lives so dramatically changed, it became a priority for both Michael and Melitta to write their last will and testament. Berolzheimer obviously lacked knowledge of American law and legal terms, but Philip had made his own will shortly before, in May 1938, with the assistance of his New York lawyer, Herman Goldman. Philip and his lawyer were therefore able to offer advice and legal expertise. Both Michael's and Melitta's rather lengthy and complicated wills were drawn up by Philip's lawyer and signed by them on December 21, 1938. The pogrom on November 9, 1938, led to a time of extreme fear and worry among Jews as Germany had become a dangerous and unpredictable country for Jewish citizens. In their testaments, both Michael and Melitta explicitly excluded anyone from inheriting unless they lived in the "western hemisphere." Although World War II did not break out until September 1, 1939, Berolzheimer took Hitler's threat of European domination seriously, and he did not want to let any of his possessions fall into the hands of the Nazis. In a letter to Charles, Waldemar Schweisheimer stated:

> "It was Uncle Michael's express aim to leave a small security for his three [step-]children. To achieve this, he lived in a very modest way. He even declined things important for his health such as an air-conditioning unit, for financial reasons. Uncle Michael as well as Mama have shown me their confidence by making me executor of their last will. There is probably no one who is better acquainted with Uncle Michael's intentions than I, since my professional care for him has given me an opportunity to come into intimate contact with this extraordinarily lovable and unforgettable man."

Schweisheimer's professional health care was needed more and more. Between March 14 and 21, 1942, Berolzheimer suffered such severe attacks of heart failure that, several times, Schweisheimer believed his patient had died.[12] Berolzheimer pulled through these attacks of extreme slow heart beat, again and again. In earlier years, he had always recovered remarkably quickly, but with advancing old age, his body had become less resilient to health problems and the stress of financial and family worries.

Dr. Michael Berolzheimer died after another lengthy attack on June 5, 1942. He was buried two days later next to his brother, Philip, on the family plot at the Beth-El Cemetery in Queens. Waldemar Schweisheimer wrote to Robert:

> "Yesterday was OM's funeral and we drove to the cemetery in Queens with Charles and Lois whom we picked up. [...] Charles [...] placed the greatest

fig. 6   Michael Amos in front of the gate at Haus Hirth, Untergrainau, c. 1945

emphasis on OM's funeral being conducted in the same manner as Philip's.
Luckily the American funerals are a lot less sentimental than the German ones.
We had asked the cantor not to make any speeches but only say a few prayers
in English. At the cemetery were also Alfred and wife, Edwin and wife,
Edwin's daughter Margot with husband Krakenberger-Craig, both Else's
brothers, Mr. Dinkel, Marie Hopf and daughter, Josefstal and brother, and of
course the four of us. Alfred visited Mama in the afternoon."

Melitta was too sick to attend the funeral. After her husband's death, Melitta gave her granddaughter, Elsieliese, the sad advice "never to marry because of the pain of losing a husband." Melitta died of heart failure fifteen days later, on June 20, 1942, and was buried next to Michael (*fig. 7*). Elsieliese mused: "She died of a broken heart."[13] Schweisheimer also described Melitta's funeral in a letter to Robert:

> *"It was nice weather, the service was short, just a few prayers in English by the Rabbi—a very nice, educated, younger man from Berlin who had also said the prayers for OM and Philip. Mama would have taken great pleasure in the wonderful carpet of flowers; I have no taste for it. I did like, however, that during the prayers bees were humming in the flowers around the casket, and Else drew my attention to the fact when Mama's coffin was in the ground, it wasn't lying level but rather tilted towards the side where OM was resting. I am very sad about her loss, much more than I expected—but I think, married people that have been happy together for such a long time should also die together, and perhaps that makes her content."*

SUPPORT

Emigration proceedings for Jewish citizens were a bureaucratic nightmare. German Jews were stripped of their citizenship when they left, and became formally "stateless." The receiving country, however, needed some sort of citizenship documentation. In order to satisfy the American immigration office, American relatives, who were willing to sign affidavits, vouch for the new immigrants, and declare their willingness to look after them, were essential for hapless immigrants. Although America had still tolerated Hitler's expansion politics in 1938, Jewish families and organizations worldwide knew about the urgent need to facilitate emigration from Germany. The American branch of the Berolzheimer family, too, was asked for help by many German friends and extended family members. Charles Berolzheimer in particular is on record as generously providing help and support, taking over this role from his ailing father around 1940.

Charles knew that help for the European members of his extended family was desperately needed. He often gave without being asked, to avoid situations in which people could lose their dignity by having to beg. By 1940, food had become scarce in certain regions of England because of German air raids and food parcels were a very welcome relief. While Charles ordered food parcels to be sent to Berolzheimer's step-granddaughter, the Amos family in London, as well as other friends there, Waldemar Schweisheimer's wife, Else, sent bi-weekly food parcels to her sister-in-law, Nelly, in England.[14]

fig. 7   Michael and Melitta's graves

Charles supported Uncle Michael's quest for information from Europe with a paid subscription to the London Economist. As a practical and frugal man, Berolzheimer had asked Charles to send him past copies which would otherwise have been thrown away. But Charles, living in California, ordered a separate subscription for Berolzheimer living on the East Coast. It may seem of little significance today, but at a time before television, such a subscription provided important and valuable access to world affairs for Berolzheimer, especially since his bad hearing may have prevented him from following the broadcasts on the wireless spoken rapidly in English. News on the radio was eagerly followed by many people, including Schweisheimer, who expressed his relief at the end of the war that he would no longer have to listen to the radio every hour on the hour.

After Michael Berolzheimer's death, Charles generously transferred the London Economist subscription to Berolzheimer's stepson, Robert Schweisheimer, who had changed his name to Sheridan upon his immigration in 1940 and lived in San Francisco. Charles and Robert had always gotten along well, to the point that Charles had asked his mother after the war to search in the attic for their "antique" Electrolux vacuum cleaner to give to Robert as a joke (Robert having worked as a salesman for that company).

Charles also paid the storage fees incurred by both Robert and Waldemar Schweisheimer for the belongings they had inherited from Berolzheimer and Melitta. Schweisheimer's fees were mostly for Nelly's property, as Melitta had left all the furniture to Nelly. Since Nelly and Leopold still lived precariously in England and Schweisheimer supposedly had at that time no room for Nelly's furniture, it had to be stored elsewhere. The bigger pieces, valuable Biedermeier furniture which the Berolzheimers' had brought from Germany, were later regarded as too cumbersome for Schweisheimer to ship to New Zealand and Schweisheimer told Charles he would sell them. However, according to the list of Waldemar's estate for inheritance tax purposes, these items may in fact have ended up in his own household.

In 1942, Charles helped Robert with a loan to buy a much-needed new car in San Francisco. Charles also facilitated Robert's support payments to the latter's step-daughter, Ingeborg Amos, in London, via Charles' blocked account in London. He also gave him access to his bank funds in London in 1947 to buy a second-hand car when Robert went to London to remarry Lilly. Lilly had been forced to divorce Robert *in absentia* in February 1939 because of Hitler's decree forbidding Jewish-Aryan marriages. She had been trapped from 1938 through 1947 in Germany, unable to travel abroad without her passport, which had been confiscated by the Nazis.

There were others as well who needed or asked for Charles' help, such as his distant cousin, Herman Fels, who drew on the friendship they had enjoyed in their youth. Charles supported him with a monthly payment after the Fels family managed to emigrate to the US. The correspondence between Charles and Herman sheds light on the financial and emotional difficulties that Herman—like many new emigrants—experienced at the time.

In his quiet and generous manner, Charles also supported his much loved "second mother," Frances Greenhood (1866–1955). She was a childhood friend and second cousin of Michael Berolzheimer through their common great-grand-father. She was born in San Francisco the same year as Michael, brought up in Germany, but had returned to America. She was an intelligent, lively, eccentric spinster who loved Charles dearly. He subsidized her family visits to Europe providing her with money for her trip, paid for her board and lodging in a San Francisco hotel after her retirement as a school teacher, and—toward the end of her life—paid for her nursing.

EXECUTORSHIP

In 1938, in their wills, both Michael and Melitta had named Philip Berolzheimer and the Public National Bank and Trust Company of New York to act as executors and trustees of the trusts to be established. Waldemar Schweisheimer was named in second place, should Philip be unable carry out these duties. Since Philip died before Michael and Melitta, Schweisheimer became executor, together with the bank. The bank, however, was unwilling to act since the estate was too small for their expected expenses. Schweisheimer was explicitly authorized to decide about the distribution of Michael and Melitta's residuary estate without any restrictions.

Waldemar Schweisheimer was very concerned about saving legal costs and inheritance taxes. Since Michael and Melitta's deaths occurred so close together, Schweisheimer pressured the lawyer to settle the simpler, final accounting of Melitta's testament first. Melitta had inherited all of her husband's artworks, so Schweisheimer had all those works which were in Berolzheimer's possession at the time of his death appraised by the Philip P. Masterson Company. Brother Robert arrived from California after Melitta's death and the two of them divided up the artworks then owned by Melitta into three parts. Robert took his share of the artworks to California while Waldemar kept his own and his sister Nelly's share. A complete art inventory list written by Berolzheimer is unaccounted for. It is not clear therefore whether all artworks were presented for appraisal, but Schweisheimer used these appraisals, as well as the value of the existing financial bank records, for both Berolzheimers' New York estate tax returns. The value of the Rodin statue was estimated at $3,000, the rest of the art collection at $570.

The estate tax return for Michael Berolzheimer was filed on February 10, 1944, during World War II, when nobody could know what the outcome would be. Schweisheimer did not declare any Berolzheimer assets still in Germany as their status was obviously uncertain. In addition, they had been confiscated by the time of Berolzheimer's death, and it would have taken a lot of time and legal work to decide what action to take. To make things easier for himself, and to save extensive research and legal costs, Schweisheimer therefore remained silent about such assets. Berolzheimer's will was confirmed as executed on February 28, 1944, by Westchester County Surrogate Court.

Attorney Herman Goldman, however, entered a cautionary letter to the surrogate court, explaining in detail how complicated the will was, requiring the establishment of six separate trusts, and how difficult the final administration of the Federal and New York State taxes had become. He had agreed with Schweisheimer to the payment of a very reasonable fee, but "if presently unanticipated difficulties should arise … I will be at liberty to request the reconsideration of the fees thus agreed upon with a view to an increase in the amount thereof." Goldman did not have to deal with the "unanticipated difficulties" of restitution proceed-

fig. 8   Hügel am Weg in 1945

ings, since Schweisheimer had hired New York attorney Robert Held, formerly of Munich, by that time.

Paragraph 3 of Michael Berolzheimer's will states: "All the rest, residue, and remainder of my estate of whatsoever kind, nature, and description, real, personal, and mixed, and wheresoever situated, including all property of which I may have the power of disposition by my will, all of which rest, residue, and remainder is hereafter referred to as my residuary estate, I give, devise, and bequeath as follows: …"

This "residuary estate" turned out to be very valuable when post-war Germany legally stipulated the restitution of stolen or unlawfully acquired property. Not only were Berolzheimer's real estate holdings, including Hügel am Weg (*fig. 8*), eventually restituted to the heirs, but Schweisheimer embarked on an intensive search for the art collection Berolzheimer was forced to leave behind and which was sent on government order to the German auction house, Weinmüller. Although much has been found and restituted, that search is continuing, and—with the authorization of the heirs—has now been taken over by Berolzheimer's great-nephew, Michael G. Berolzheimer (*see Section III in this publication*).

THE SALE AND RESTITUTION OF HÜGEL AM WEG IN UNTERGRAINAU

In January 1940, Lilly asked Berolzheimer for—and was refused—power of attorney to sell the house, as there was no guarantee that Berolzheimer would

ever receive the proceeds. In spring 1940, Count Hermann von Arnim-Muskau heard that negotiations had been going on between a Mr. Neuburger and Georg Keller, the trustee for the Berolzheimers' assets appointed by the German government, as Neuburger was interested in acquiring the house Hügel am Weg.

Count Arnim had owned a small house close to Hügel am Weg in Untergrainau since March 1938, where he spent his vacations in the Bavarian countryside he loved so much. His mother, Countess Sophie von Arnim, born in 1876, suffered from heart problems and used to stay at Haus Hirth for part of the winter. The climate proved to be so favorable for her health that von Arnim wanted her to be able to settle permanently in Grainau. She eventually died in Grainau on August 17, 1949.

Von Arnim approached Lilly Klöckner through his friend and attorney, a Mr. Ritter, since he had heard that Lilly might be able to exert some influence on Keller in von Arnim's favor. Private negotiations were held between Lilly (although she was not authorized by Berolzheimer to do so) and Ritter since influential political pressure had been brought on Keller to sell to Neuburger. Lilly did not want a Nazi to acquire the Berolzheimers' home at any cost, preferring instead to sell to von Arnim whom she considered a decent man.

Von Arnim later wrote to Robert Schweisheimer in his offer of restitution that his mother had taken a fancy to Hügel am Weg, and had insisted that only this house would be satisfactory to her, having lost the magnificent ancestral seat, Muskau Castle, on the German-Polish border, through the events of the war. A woman of many interests, Countess Arnim had become friends with the owners of Haus Hirth, Walther and Johanna Hirth. She had raised four children, was chatelaine at Muskau, suffered the death of her husband Count Adolf von Arnim in 1931, and had written several books about the previous owners of Muskau Castle, as well as a biography of the Romantic painter Carl Gustav Carus. On October 10, 1940, a sales contract was drawn up and signed by Keller for

fig. 9 Robert Schweisheimer's house, Am Priel 25

Michael Berolzheimer, and by the neighbor, Walther Hirth, on behalf of von Arnim. On November 30, 1940, the contract was amended to include von Arnim's mother as joint owner.

With fiscal hearings and permissions frequently delayed and interrupted by Nazi interference in favor of Neuburger, completion of the contract and registration dragged on until November 25, 1941. On that day, a law came into effect confiscating all Jewish property, including of course Berolzheimer's. The state, however, took over the contract and sold Hügel am Weg in February 1942 to von Arnim for 170,000 Reichsmarks.[15] The price was established by an architect, a Mr. Albinger, deemed to be fair and confirmed through taxation.

On December 28, 1945, almost four months after the end of the war, von Arnim wrote a letter to Robert that he would be willing to return Hügel am Weg, admitting that "the house would not have been sold without the immoral pressure of the Nazi government." He emphasized, however, that he has a clean conscience since he entered the negotiations only after he heard that others had already started them, and that he conducted the negotiations in full consent with the only available member of the Berolzheimer family, Lilly Klöckner.

Count Arnim was willing either to give the house back (the government would repay him the purchase price and the house would be returned to Berolzheimer's heirs) or—if the sale were to be considered *a posteriori*, he offered his help to have the purchase price restituted by the government to the rightful heirs directly, writing "... I would ask you to find, together with me, a way to obtain the money you are owed ...."

Waldemar Schweisheimer, as the executor of Berolzheimer's estate, had unlimited authority to deal with his step-father's residual property. He determined that he wanted the house returned, although he then had to deal with the financial accounting for the restitution and the rental income.

During the war and up until October 1945, the house had been rented out by von Arnim to a Mr. Nestler. With the question of post-war ownership in limbo, the military government took over the administration of this rental contract. On September 21, 1946, Dr. Grete Lenz, the property administrator, wrote to Schweisheimer that Nestler had moved out in the meanwhile and a new rental contract was being prepared between the military government and Lilly Klöckner.

Lenz had the authority to act on behalf of the military government and— as a friend of Lilly's—she was eager to help her. Robert and Lilly's house in Munich, Am Priel 25 (*fig. 9*), had been bombed and Lilly had been living in a rented room at Haus Hirth in Untergrainau, together with her young grandson, Michael Amos. Living alone by that time, Lilly rented the whole of Hügel am Weg, paying 418 Reichsmarks a month, plus all taxes and extras, but she was also free to enter into rental agreements with other people. There was a lot of repair and maintenance to be done before the house was in reasonable shape again. Drainage, heating, the bathrooms, and the electrical wiring had to be repaired, sinks replaced, and Melitta's pride—the garden—was in pitiful shape.

Lilly set to work, together with Lenz and a Mrs. Fehn, organizing labor and material. The former gardener, a local man who had originally laid out the garden under Melitta's guidance, came back in fall 1946 to do the necessary garden work. All expenses incurred were met with scorn by Waldemar Schweisheimer in America. Apart from his personal dislike of Lilly, he could not appreciate the need for housing repairs in post-war Germany.

Due to massive destruction caused by allied bombing, many people had become homeless and had to be accommodated in other buildings still intact. The huge influx of German war refugees from the east also had to be dealt with. All housing was therefore controlled by a refugee commissariat that decided who and how many additional people would have to be accommodated by a house owner. Hügel am Weg was a large house and it became a post-war concern for Lilly to balance the available space with the number of required residents so as not to render the house worthless through abuse.

The fields and woodland in Grainau belonging to Berolzheimer were still administered in 1946 by the tax office which received the leasehold payments. Although the handling of property had actually been transferred to German civil servants, the military government continued to supervise it. The hope was expressed, however, that Jewish owners would soon have their property restituted.

By October 1946, after some bitter arguments, Robert and Waldemar Schweisheimer agreed not to touch the Berolzheimer inheritance until the restitution problem had been resolved. News of their father Eugen's death in Theresienstadt concentration camp in 1942 had finally reached them in June 1945, and presented them with another problematic inheritance.

Their father had named Waldemar Schweisheimer in his last will as executor and sole heir; Robert and Nelly had been disinherited with the—later clearly disputed—argument that Eugen did not know their whereabouts. Schweisheimer believed, therefore, he could claim the restitution of all his father's estate, including a Munich property, Brabanter Strasse 2, which was part of his father's banking assets.

Robert, however, presented a written agreement between himself and his father, which made him a partner in the banking business with a fifty percent share, and full ownership in the case of his father's death; it also did not hold him responsible for any debts up to the end of 1939. He therefore fought what he considered an invalid testament, made under pressure. The post-war courts had to determine who was right; they sided with Robert.

By the end of 1948, restitution claims had been submitted for the Berolz-heimer estate, Eugen Schweisheimer's personal estate, Eugen's banking business, Robert Schweisheimer's personal estate, as well as Lilly Klöckner's confiscated shares in the Klöckner family's vast steel company. It had become a complicated legal business.

Hügel am Weg was returned to the heirs in 1949 and, after stalling for a long time, was ultimately sold on October 31, 1957, by Waldemar Schweisheimer to the United Engineering Trust of Vaduz, Liechtenstein, for 150,000 Deutsch-marks, then approximately $37,000.

EPILOGUE

The unraveling of the previously unknown and undocumented history of Michael Berolzheimer's life, seventy years after his death, has proven his pivotal position within the Berolzheimer family. His life's vocation of researching and writing an extensive family genealogy, and the collecting of art as his life's pleasure, deeply—although sometimes unknowingly—impacted the generations that followed him.

The execution of Berolzheimer's last will sadly divided some family members over half a century ago. Efforts for the restitution of his dispersed art collection are on-going, and members of the extended family living all around the globe, in Europe, Australia, New Zealand, Asia, and the Americas have been traced and are reconnecting.

Michael Berolzheimer, in his gentle ways, had a surprising influence on many members of later generations. He may have lacked the business acumen of his older brother, Emil, or the relaxed, social competence of his younger brother, Philip, but his kind, quiet, unassuming manner, his deep affection for those he loved, the diligence he demonstrated in his research work, and not least his passion for the arts, history, Judaism, and culture, made him a remarkable man, and earned him a place in the Berolzheimer family as one of the most cherished ancestors.

1 Heinz and Thea Ruth Skyte (née Ephraim), *Our Family*, T-Online publication, last updated 02/13/2009, http://rijo-research.de

2 For the full story, see http://members.gaponline.de/alois.schwarzmueller/juden_in_gap_index/index_juedische_buerger.htm; Alois Schwarzmüller, "'Juden sind hier nicht erwünscht!' Zur Geschichte der jüdischen Bürger in Garmisch-Partenkirchen von 1933 bis 1945" in: Verein für Geschichte, Kunst und Kulturgeschichte im Landkreis Garmisch-Partenkirchen (ed.), *Mohr-Löwe-Raute. Beiträge zur Geschichte des Landkreises Garmisch-Partenkirchen*, vol. 3, 1995, pp. 184–232.

3 It is not known how and which artworks were brought at what time to America. Unsubstantiated family lore talks of secret help by the American diplomat Sumner Welles, and the musician Olga Samaroff, who may have already smuggled some of Berolzheimer's artworks out of Germany before his emigration. Whatever the case, it was his art collection that was intended to provide for his livelihood in America. What he did not count on was the lack of interest in the American art market for his print collection, which he had valued at German market prices.

When he tried to sell Rodin's *Saint Jean-Baptiste* in 1940, in order to raise money to support his stepchildren, he did not find a buyer. Only after his death did Waldemar Schweisheimer succeed in finally selling it to the Saint Louis Art Museum.

4 Roszika Edle von Wertheimstein (1870–1940) was married to the English banker Nathaniel Charles Rothschild (1877–1923.) She was well known for her generous engagement in the rescue and care of German Jewish children.

5 Michael G. Berolzheimer, in an interview with Noeline Friedberg, 2013.

6 Leopold's oldest sister, Johanna Simon-Friedberg had died in 1920, leaving her three children and her American husband living safely in the US. Leopold's two other living sisters, Frieda and Elisabeth, however, as well as his brother, Hans, became victims of the Holocaust. Gedenkbuch Karlsruhe. www.karlsruhe.de/b1/stadtgeschichte/gedenkbuch.de

7 For German victims of the holocaust see http://www.bundesarchiv.de/gedenkbuch/directory.html.de

8 Leo Baeck-Institut, Center for Jewish History, New York, Michael Berolzheimer Collection.

9 Michael Berolzheimer's unpublished family history.

10 Ibid.

11 Ibid.

12 Letter from Waldemar Schweisheimer to Robert, March 21, 1942. Schweisheimer later charged Berolzheimer's estate $1000 for his medical services.

13 Interview with Elsieliese Thrope, 2000.

14 Letter from Waldemar to Robert, April 3, 1943: "We had quite a cheerful letter from Nelly today in which she wrote gratefully about Mama's fur coat which Else had sent her (Else sent her since last June every 2 weeks a parcel) as well as about a radio which she had bought upon my urgent suggestion; for some strange reason she did not own one before."

15 To provide some idea of the value in real terms of the amounts given here and elsewhere in this volume in Reichsmarks, Marks, etc., and some approximate equivalent of these sums in US dollars today, please see Appendix.

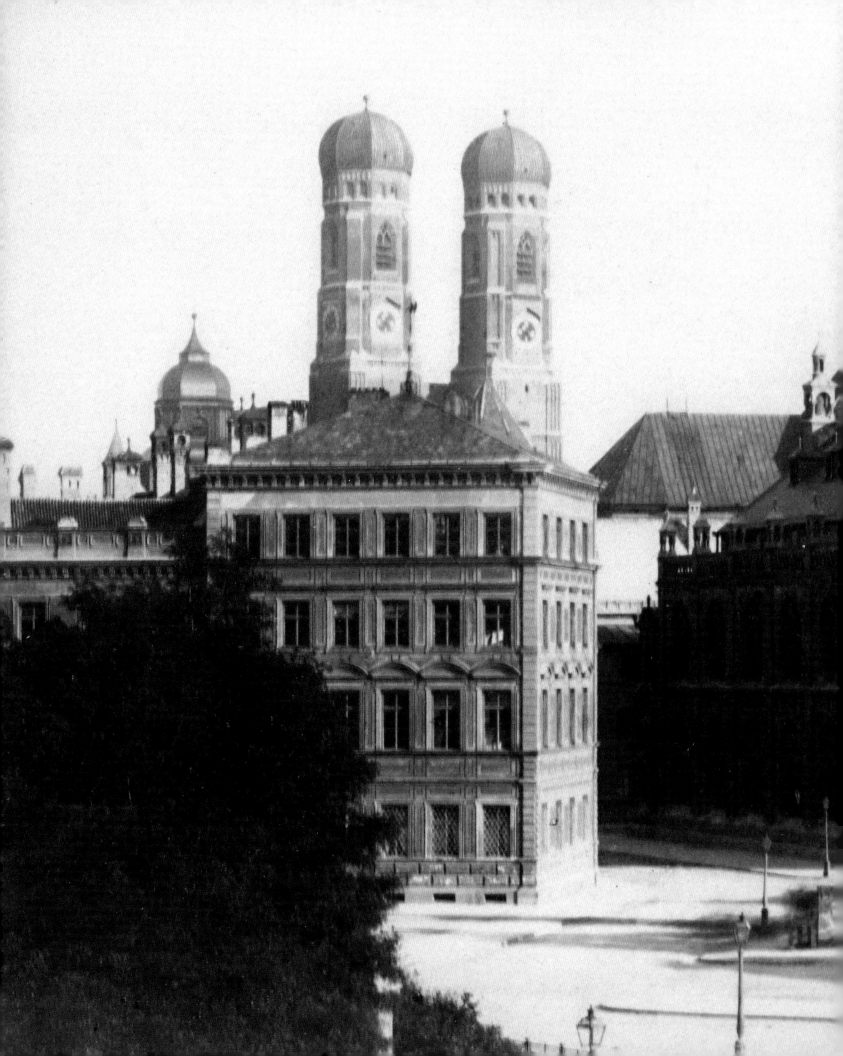

JUDAISM AND GENEALOGY

MICHAEL BEROLZHEIMER AS
A PATRON OF THE ARTS

Apart from his interest in old drawings and prints, as well as in genealogy, Michael Berolzheimer focussed more and more on Jewish art from the 1920s onward, and was committed to the idea of a Jewish Museum being established in Munich. Through his family's patronage of the Berolzheimerianum in Fürth and later his own involvement with the Künstlerhaus and Luitpoldhaus in Nuremberg, Berolzheimer was familiar with the needs of public art and educational institutions.

A JEWISH MUSEUM FOR MUNICH

The history of Jewish museums goes back to the end of the nineteenth century. The first museum of its kind in the world opened in 1895 in Vienna. This was followed by other institutions, for example in Prague (1906), Budapest (1912), Frankfurt am Main (1922), and London (1932).[1]

The idea of setting up a Jewish Museum in Munich (*fig. 1*) was first mooted in the 1920s. In 1926, the Munich art historian Theodor Harburger (1887–1949) was commissioned by the Association of Jewish Communities in Bavaria to draw up an inventory of all the ritual objects that existed in Bavarian synagogues. Such an inventory was of considerable importance, as many rural Jewish communities were on the brink of being dissolved, due to the increase in the number of people migrating to larger cities. The continued existence of many synagogues, with the ritual objects they housed, was in jeopardy. Between 1927 and 1932 Harburger visited more than 200 communities which had synagogues, took over 800 photographs, and made countless notes about ritual objects, the interiors of synagogues, and gravestones in Jewish cemeteries.[2] As a result, the multifaceted religious and cultural life in rural Jewish communities since the sixteenth century was documented and preserved for posterity.

On January 26, 1928, Harburger wrote to Berolzheimer in Untergrainau for the first time: "I am grateful to His Eminence, the rabbi Dr. Freudenthal,[3] who kindly informed me that you wish to be given details of the inscriptions on gravestones in Kriegshaber cemetery to trace your family's history.[4] Last year

I noted down all the inscriptions, where found, and took photographs of individual gravestones of art historical interest. I gladly remain at your disposal of course for your research. Perhaps you could kindly let me know exactly what you are looking for."[5] This offer of Harburger's to Berolzheimer led to an extensive correspondence over more than ten years, largely on the subject of Jewish genealogy. After he had returned from carrying out research, or sometimes even during such trips, Harburger regularly sent gravestone inscriptions to Berolzheimer. He also channeled Berolzheimer's interest away from only researching his own family toward Jewish art in general, and was able to win Berolzheimer's commitment to founding a Jewish museum in Munich.

Harburger curated the successful "Ausstellung jüdischer Kult-Geräte und Einrichtungen für Synagoge und Haus" (Exhibition of Jewish ritual objects and furnishings for synagogues and the home) in 1930 in Munich, further helping the idea of establishing such a museum in the Bavarian capital. On June 30, 1930, while the exhibition was still running, the "Verein für jüdische Museen in Bayern" (Association for Jewish Museums in Bavaria) was established, and Harburger wrote the very next day to Berolzheimer about the association's aims.[6] In August 1930, Berolzheimer wrote of his attempts to convince relatives to donate to the projected museum. "Mr. Ernst Sahlmann of Fürth has a golden wedding band, probably from the sixteenth century. He inherited it from his mother, Mrs. Bertha Sahlmann, née Berolzheimer, she in turn from her uncle, Gustav Berolzheimer […]. I have tried in vain to gain the band as a donation for the projected Jewish musuem."[7] In fall 1930, the "Jüdisches Echo" (Jewish Echo), a magazine published in Munich, reported that "men and women from all circles of Jewish society in Bavaria," who were impressed by the exhibition, "have joined forces to protect and care for historic Jewish artifacts wherever these are endangered. These efforts have now led to the founding of the Association for Jewish Museums in Bavaria."[8]

The article went on to outline the main goals of the new association—collecting exhibits, raising funds, and ensuring public access to the collection—and invited interested members of the public to participate. The names of the president, the rabbi Dr. Leo Baerwald,[9] and the secretary of the association, Theodor Harburger, were given as contacts. On April 22, 1931, the first members' meeting was held in Munich, at which Rabbi Baerwald was re-appointed president. Berolzheimer was elected to the four-member board of management.[10] From that time onward, in addition to the clarification of genealogical questions, which remained the central topic of the correspondence between Berolzheimer and Harburger, the association and the creation of a collection were recurrent topics in their letters. When the auction house Hugo Helbing held the sale of the Sally Kirschstein Judaica Collection[11]—one of the most important private collections of its kind up until World War II—Berolzheimer and Harburger discussed possible acquisitions for the museum association. Berolzheimer thanked Harburger on this occasion for agreeing to bid in his name for lot number 387 in the "cat[alog] Kerschstein" [sic]—a "copperplate engraving of 1704, a portrait of my ancestor Samuel Oppenheimer,"[12] specifying an upper limit of sixty to seventy Marks.[13] Harburger later reported to Berolzheimer that he had been outbid and that the print had gone into other hands.[14]

The goals set by the museum association were hard to reach, not least of all due to the turbulent economic and political circumstances of the times. Progress

fig. 3   Portrait of Samson Wertheimer (1658–1724) by Eduard Kräutler (1835–1901), oil on canvas. This is a copy of an older painting, now lost, from the second half of the nineteenth century, held in the Wien Museum, Vienna

in assembling a collection was slow, although Harburger was able to acquire several interesting objects. Shortly before the National Socialists seized power in 1933, a meeting for members of the association was held in the apartment of the Munich dentist and Judaica collector Dr. Heinrich Feuchtwanger.[15]

The association's activities over a period of several years after 1933 are also documented in correspondence between Berolzheimer and Harburger. In 1934, Berolzheimer offered a lithographic portrait of Simon Gleisdörfer of Regensburg to the museum association.[16] However, this offer no longer reached Harburger in Munich, as he had emigrated with his wife to Palestine shortly before, where they later established a bed-and-breakfast business, first in Tiberias, later in Nahariya. With the departure of the association's president, its activities came to a standstill. The small collection was probably housed in the offices of the Israelite Cultural Community Munich in Herzog-Max-Strasse. What happened to the objects after the demolition of the synagogue (*fig. 2*) and the adjoining buildings in June 1938 is not known.

More than eighty years after the event, a case of looted art was solved on the strength of the detailed exchange of letters between Berolzheimer and Harburger. In a letter to Harburger in 1929, Berolzheimer pointed out a Hanukkah lamp, traditionally used during the Jewish celebration of the same name in December, which had been the property of the famous Austrian Court Jew Samson Wertheimer (1658–1724; *fig. 3*) in the early eighteenth century. It was now owned by the Oppler family of Hanover, having been passed down the Wertheimer line.[17] Berolzheimer wrote that he had been given a photograph of the lamp by the family and permission to print it, and asked Harburger if he would be interested in publishing an essay about it.[18]

The Wertheimer-Oppler Hanukkah (*fig. 4*) is one of a group of four lamps known to have been made around 1713 in the workshop of Thomas Tübner in Halberstadt (Prussia), either bearing his hallmark or attributed to him (*fig. 5*).[19] Wertheimer was Chief Rabbi of Hungary and Moravia and Rabbi of Eisenstadt. He was also an Austrian financier, Court Jew, and *shtadlan* (intercessor) to the Austrian emperors Leopold I and Charles VI. A portable Torah ark owned by Wertheimer can be found in the collection of the Jewish Museum in Paris.[20]

In their extensive correspondence, Berolzheimer and Harburger discussed the lamp and contacted Sigmund Oppler in Hanover to request a photograph of better quality than the one they already had.[21] In his letter of February 19, 1929, to Harburger, Berolzheimer traced the provenance of the lamp in meticulous detail as follows:[22]

1. Samson Wertheimer (1658–1724)
2. To his eldest son, Wolf Simon Wertheimer (1681–1763/65), Vienna and Munich
3. To his grandson, Josef Wertheimer, Bayreuth[23]
4. To his son, Philipp Wertheimer (c. 1747–1810), Bayreuth
5. To his daughter, Recha (d. 1834), married to Samuel Löb Gleisdorfer (1770–1835), Regensburg
6. To their daughter, Sophie (1810–62), married to Dr. Hermann Cohen (d. 1869), Hanover
7. To their daughter, Ella (1843–1912), married to the architect Edwin Oppler (1831–80), Hanover[24]
8. To their son, Dr. Sigmund Oppler (1873–1942), Hanover and Amsterdam[25]
9. Dissappearance of the lamp after 1938
10. Gift of Morris Troper (1892–1963) to the Central Synagogue, New York, c. 1950
11. Submitted by the Central Synagogue for auction at Sotheby's New York, "Important Judaica," December 13, 2006, lot 53 (withdrawn prior to auction)
12. Restituted by the Central Synagogue to the Oppler family in Washington, D.C., 2007
13. Submitted by the Oppler Family for auction at Sotheby's New York, "Important Judaica," December 15, 2010, lot 26
14. Acquired for the collection of Dr. David and Jemima Jeselsohn, Switzerland

In 1931, art historian Elisabeth Moses published a photograph of the lamp, with no further details, in her book on the history of Jews in the Rhineland.[26] Another illustration with a description of the lamp—which belonged to the Central Synagogue in New York by that time—was published in 1989 (*fig. 5*).[27]

Information on the provenance and history of the Hanukkah lamp had previously been lost. Together with thirty-seven other Judaica objects, the lamp was donated by Morris Troper, a New York attorney, to the New York Central Synagogue, probably in the 1950s.[28] Troper had been working for the American Jewish Joint Distribution Committee (JOINT) since the 1920s, and had become chairman of its European Executive Council. In this capacity, he had worked, for instance, to save Jewish passengers on the SS St. Louis.[29] He also worked for JOINT in Europe after 1945.[30] How the Wertheimer-Oppler Hanukkah lamp came into his possession, however, is not known.

When the lamp was submitted to an auction of Judaica in New York[31] in 2006 by the Central Synagogue, the present author was able to identify it as the one that had once belonged to the Oppler family, thanks to documents in the Michael Berolzheimer Collection, given by his nephew, Charles Berolzheimer, to the Leo Baeck Institute in New York. The lamp was withdrawn from the sale and restituted to the heirs of the Oppler family in 2007, who put it up for sale at a later Judaica auction held at Sotheby's in 2010.[32] The lamp—now with its complete history—fetched eight times the estimate it had been given three years earlier, and is now in a private collection in Switzerland.[33]

It would not have been possible to find the rightful owners of the lamp without Berolzheimer and Harburger's work, nor would its impressive provenance that reaches back to the early eighteenth century have come to light. It may be

fig. 4   The Wertheimer-Oppler Hanukkah made in Halberstadt in 1713, now in a private collection in Switzerland

fig. 5   One of four Hanukkah lamps made by the master craftsman Thomas Tübner of Halberstadt, in c. 1710/1715, now in the Jewish Museum, New York

one of history's peculiar ironies that Berolzheimer, who himself lost part of his art collection during the Shoah,[34] was instrumental in solving another art robbery almost seventy years after his death and eighty years after his research work.

EPILOGUE

Shortly after his forced emigration to the USA, Michael Berolzheimer once again demonstrated his expertise in Jewish history and tradition. A few days after the birth of his great-nephew Michael George, he thanked the child's parents—his nephew Charles P. Berolzheimer and his wife, Lois Elizabeth—for naming the child after him, and took the opportunity to explain the meaning of the boy's two names on seven closely handwritten pages.[35] He pointed out the Hebrew roots of the first name and the link to his native city, Fürth, where "St Michael's country fair"—a popular festival—was held in honor of the patron saint of the Protestant church. In the second part of his explanation, he threw light on the name George, closing with a wish, in rather awkward English, for the newborn child: "So we hope your boy will become—in peace—a fighter for good and right and true, in harmony with his elder brother, like this older generation['s] friendly and affectionate brothers, your father and myself …."[36]

Once again, this letter underlines the traditions to which Berolzheimer was born, and how dealing with these traditions changed. This was especially true in the nineteenth century. In Fürth, Berolzheimer probably received a modern, humanistic education, coupled with fundamental teaching in traditional Jewish religious rites, which would still have been practiced in the old Jewish congregation during his childhood. As for so many of his generation, religious life had become less important, although the ties to Judaism, in the form of a community with a shared fate and tradition, remained. Synagogues were no longer places with which people identified themselves closely, but rather places to reflect on where they came from (*fig. 6*). In Berolzheimer's case, family research became pivotal to discovering his own personal identity. Other involvements, like his commitment to a Jewish Museum in Munich, also underline this interest. Berolzheimer could always build on his solid, fundamental knowledge and his familiarity with the Jewish tradition. Like so many German Jews of his generation, he no longer lived out this Jewish tradition, but he did not deny it either.

fig. 6   The main entrance to the new synagogue on St. Jakobs Platz, Munich

1 Grace Cohen Grossman, *Jewish Museums of the World,* Southport 2003.

2 "Theodor Harburger, Die Inventarisation jüdischer Kunst- und Kulturdenkmäler in Bayern," edited by the Central Archives for the History of the Jewish People and the Jüdisches Museum Franken – Fürth & Schnaittach, 3 vols, Fürth 1998.

3 Dr. Max Freudenthal (1868–1937) was rabbi in Nuremberg from 1907–34 and later lived in Munich.

4 There was an important rural Jewish congregation in Kriegshaber, now a district of Augsburg.

5 Letter from Harburger to Berolzheimer, 01/26/1928, Leo Baeck Institute New York, Michael Berolzheimer Collection (AR 4136), Series F sub dato.

6 Ibid., 07/01/1930.

7 Ibid., 08/19/1930.

8 On the founding of the "Verein für jüdische Museen in Bayern e.V," see the *Jüdisches Echo*, year 17, no. 48 (1930), p. 688.

9 Dr. Leo Baerwald (1883–1970) was rabbi in Munich from 1918–40, and from 1941–55 in the Beth Hillel Congregation in Washington Heights, New York.

10 *Jüdisches Echo*, year 18, no. 18 (1931), pp. 276–77.

11 "Die Judaica-Sammlung S. Kirschstein Berlin. Kultgeräte für Haus und Synagoge / Manuskripte / Gemälde / Miniaturen / Graphik / Urkunden / Bücher. Versteigerung in der Gallerie Hugo Helbing München," Munich 1932.

12 Letter from Berolzheimer to Harburger, 07/10/1932, Leo Baeck Institute New York, Michael Berolzheimer Collection (AR 4136), Series F sub dato. On the copperplate engraving of Samuel Oppenheimer (c. 1635–1703) see Alfred Rubens, *A Jewish Iconography,* London 1981, no. 1960.

13 Letter from Harburger to Berolzheimer, 15/07/1932, Leo Baeck Institute New York, Michael Berolzheimer Collection (AR 4136), Series F sub dato.

14 To provide some idea of the value in real terms of the amounts given here and elsewhere in this volume in Reichsmarks and Marks, and some approximate equivalent of these sums in US dollars today, please see Appendix.

15 On Feuchtwanger see: Barbara Staudinger (ed.), *From Bavaria to Eretz Israel. Tracing Jewish Folk Art,* exh. cat, Jewish Museum Munich, Munich 2007.

16 Letter from Berolzheimer to Harburger, 07/27/1934, Leo Baeck Institute New York, Michael Berolzheimer Collection (AR 4136), Series F sub dato.

17 Berolzheimer was related, albeit distantly, to the Wertheimers through his great-grandmother and there are a number of Wertheimers in another branch of the family. It may well have been a topic close to his heart to find an object as important as a Hanukkah lamp for the new Jewish Museum in Munich, and would have explored possibilities within his own family. Since Berolzheimer corresponded so extensively and the Wertheimer family was so well connected, he may well have known the person who owned the lamp.

18 Ibid., 01/23/1929.

19 Susan L. Braunstein, *Five Centuries of Hanukkah Lamps from the Jewish Museum: A Catalogue Raisonné,* New Haven/London 2005, pp. 68, 237. On p. 68. Braunstein mentions the Wertheimer-Oppler lamp twice, once as pre-war Oppler property and once as property of the Central Synagogue, New York.

20 Vivian B. Mann, Richard I. Cohen, *From the Court Jews to the Rothschilds,* The Jewish Museum New York, New York 1997, cat. no. 129.

21 Leo Baeck Institute, New York, Michael Berolzheimer Collection, AR 4136, Series F, correspondence between Berolzheimer, Harburger, and Sigmund Oppler, letters of Jan. 23, 1929; Jan. 25, 1929; Jan. 27, 1929; Jan. 30, 1929; Feb. 13, 1929; Feb. 17, 1929; Feb. 19, 1929; March 15, 1929; March 17, 1929; March 20, 1929; March 25, 1929; and March 27, 1929.

22 The dates of birth and death have been taken from www.loebtree.com.

23 This generation is missing in Berolzheimer's listing.

24 Peter Eilitz, "Leben und Werk des königl. hannoverschen Baurats Edwin Oppler" in: *Hannoversche Geschichtsblätter,* N.F. 25, 1971, pp. 127–310.

25 Dr. Sigmund Oppler and his wife committed suicide in Amsterdam in September 1942 to escape deportation. See http://www.joodsmonument.nl/page/559930

26 Elisabeth Moses, *Jüdische Kunst- und Kulturdenkmäler in den Rheinlanden,* Düsseldorf 1931, p. 161.

27 Cissy Grossman, *The Jewish Family's Book of Days,* New York 1989, pp. for November 7–11.

28 "War and Remembrance" in *New York Times,* February 7, 1997.

29 Sarah Ogilvie, Scott Miller, *Refuge Denied: The St. Louis Passengers and the Holocaust,* Madison 2006.

30 *American Jewish Year Book,* vol. 65, 1964, p. 438.

31 Sotheby's New York, "Important Judaica," December 13, 2006, lot 53.

32 Sotheby's New York, "Important Judaica," December 15, 2010, lot 26. See also: Bernhard Purin, "Im Zeichen des Schützen. Ein Chanukka-Leuchter aus Halberstadt bei Sotheby's, New York" in: *Kunst und Auktionen,* year 38, no. 23, December 3, 2010, pp. 5–6.

33 The lamp, used by one generation of the family in Munich during the eighteenth century, was exhibited in winter 2013/spring 2014 at the Jewish Museum Munich. See: Bernhard Purin, *Samson's Lamp. A Hanukkah Lamp once owned by the Wertheimer Family,* Munich 2013.

34 Shoah is the Hebrew word for the programmatic mass murder of Jews, among others, during World War II by the Nazis throughout German-occupied territories, generally referred to as the Holocaust in the non-Jewish, English-speaking world.

35 The original letter is in the ownership of the family. A copy is in the Leo Baeck Institute, New York, Michael Berolzheimer Collection, AR 4136, Series H.

36 Ibid.

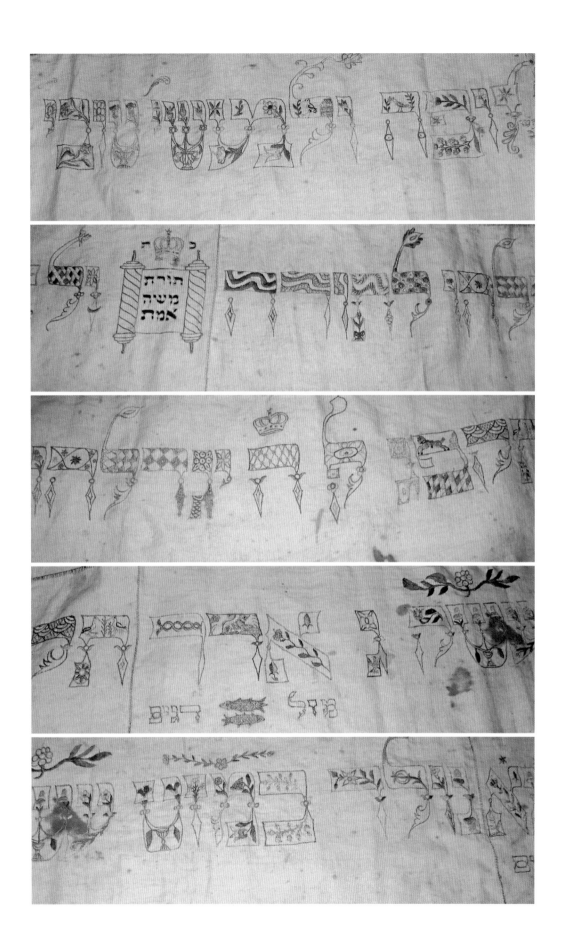

THE STORY BEHIND THE WIMPEL

It must have seemed an odd Christmas gift to Emile Albert Berol (1911–93) when he received a long, strange-looking, embroidered cloth from his great-uncle, Michael Berolzheimer, in December 1939 (*fig. 1*). By that time, Berolzheimer had settled into his new home in America, had unpacked his belongings shipped from Germany, and had already written his last will and testament. Berolzheimer had made some very deliberate decisions as to who eventually should receive his possessions, with family heirlooms requiring special consideration since he had no direct descendents. He had already dedicated his most important item, the carefully researched, handwritten family history to his brother, Philip. And he wanted to pass an old Berolzheimer heirloom, the wimpel or Torah binder— known in Hebrew as a *mappah*—into what he considered the "proper" hands.

This Torah binder came from Isidor Berolzheimer (1823–87), Michael Berolzheimer's great uncle—a brother of Michael's grandfather, Daniel (1810–59). In keeping with an ancient Jewish tradition, a newborn baby boy's cradle was draped with a wimpel, a long, narrow piece of linen used as a swaddling cloth at the boy's circumcision ceremony (*brit milah*). After this initiation, the cloth would be richly embroidered with the birth date and name of the child as well as traditional blessings and personal wishes.

The inscription in Hebrew on Isidor's cloth was translated by Berolzheimer himself and reads:

> "Israel, called Iserl, little son of Menachem, called Mendel Berolzheim, was born Friday, the 3. Adar of the year 5583 Jewish era, usual 1823. May to the parents the good luck be given to bring up the boy in the Thora and in the prayers and to guide him happily to the marriage-altar."

Wimpels were generally made of linen or cotton, but well-to-do families sometimes used silk or worked the cloth with silk thread (*fig. 3*). According to popular tradition, if a wimpel "rustled" (i.e. was made of silk), the boy must have enjoyed a privileged upbringing. When a child is first introduced to the teachings of the Torah, normally around the age of three, the wimpel is taken to the synagogue for the Shabbat morning service. After the Torah reading, it is wrapped

fig. 1 The Berolzheimer Torah binder with its decorative embroidery and inscription

now Mt. Vernon, N.Y.
300 Hayward Ave., Fleetwood

Christmas 1939

Dear Brother,

wishing you a merry christmas and a happy new year I beg your permission for sending you this family relic and, since embroidery of Hebrew letters may perhaps be strange and unintelligible to you, also for adding some comment. First of all: What was the meaning and aim of such kind of strip of embroidered stuff? After the birth of a jewish boy his mother wrote in embroidered Hebrew letters a sentence on such a strip, which was then used as a pennon, hanging above the child's cradle. If the boy came from a good family, the people used to say: „Bei ihm hat die Wimpel gerauscht" – the pennon has rustled with him, id est: his pennon was done of or embroidered with silk (because silk is rustling), id est: he has good manners, because his nursery was a good one. And if a man had no good manners, the people said: „Bei ihm hat die Wimpel nicht gerauscht." After used as pennons this strips got to the synagoge, where they were used for wraping round the Thora-roll (because the Jewish code is handwritten on pergament-rolls still to-day like in oldest ages).

This pennon anyhow either got not to the synagoge but remained with the family Berolzheimer, or perhaps was sent back to the family from the synagoge, because this child was baptized when he was a young man.

Now the translation of the Hebrew text of the pennon into English:

Israel, called Iserl, little son of Menachem, called Mendel Berolzheim, was born Friday, the 3. Adar of the year 5583 Jewish era, usual 1823. May to the parents the good luck be given to bring up the boy in the Thora and in the prayers and to guide him happily to the marriage - altar.

The father of this boy was „Menachem, called Mendel Berolzheim". „Menachem" is a Hebrew name, translated „consoler". It was the name of one of the last kings of the State of Israel in Palestine, who was vassal to the king Tiglat- Pileser III. of Assyria (754-727 B.C.). „Menachem" also was one of the various names of Messiah (Hebrew:

Maschiach, English: Anointed; Greek: Christos, Meaning: Saviour).

This abbreviation of "Menachem" is the name "Mendel". With this name your great-great-great-grandfather used to be called. But his official name, in documents, especially in the register and also with the signature of his last will is "Emanuel". And this is also the name he is known with my father and myself. And according to this name your grandfather got the name "Emil", and yourself the name "Emil", which is in reality a latin name of course, while "Emanuel" is the Greek form of the Hebrew "Immanuel" (God with us), symbolic name of the Messiah-Boy, whose birth the prophet Isaja (7-8) announced.

Emanuel Berolzheimer, born 1787 in Berolzheim on the Altmühl-River, in the house No. 13, died in Fürth, Sterngasse No. 19, October 18th, 1827. He was married to Babeta, daughter of Daniel Offenbacher, and, according to the name of the father of Daniel Offenbacher, this son of Emanuel and Babeta was called "Israel" (it self "fighter for God", the name given to Jacob in honour of his combat against the angel. The name "Israel" is mentioned first time in document at the inscription of the stele of Pharao Merneptah, 1220 B.C., son of Ramses II of the 19th dynasty; this stele is in custody of the museum of Cairo, Egypt.

The name "Isri" is the pet name of "Israel".

In reality nobody of the family Berolzheimer, not even his descendants (except myself) knew his name "Israel"; he himself didn't know it, since he was called "Isidor". That's a funny thing: "Habent sua fata libelli" - books have their fate. But not only books. Also names: Before the beginning of the 19th century no jew in the whole world had this name "Isidor". On the contrary: "Isidor" is a Greek name, coming originally from Egypt, present by the goddess Isis. And later a man, named "Isidor", was the head of the antisemitish delegation from the city of Alexandria, Egypt, to the Emperor Caligula. Even because "Isidor" was not a Jewish name, the jews in the beginning emancipation, in consequence of the French revolution and Napoleon I, liked it instead of the Jewish "Israel". Such a great numb-

of Jewish boys got the antisemitish names Isidor, that it developed into a specific Jewish name, so that the Jews it again abolished on the end of the 19th century.

Our uncle "Isidor" anyhow kept this name, from birth - February 24th, 1823 - until death - Bolzano 1887 -, though he got quite another name with his christening - April 26th, 1848: "Ludwig Carl August".

He lost his fortune twice in game of hazard in Monte Carlo, Riviera, and my father gave him a job in his office with Berolzheimer v. Leibler in Fürth. I remember him very well, limping a bit.

My story is grown longwinded. And I don't know even, whether or not my badly writing English is intelligible at all. At all events the pennon perhaps may give you a little joy and may be a remembrance to your ancestors Emanuel and his wife Babeta.

Fondly, yours

Uncle Michael.

Mr Emile Albert Berolzheimer
34 West 74th Street
New York, N.Y.

fig. 2 Michael Berolzheimer's handwritten letter dated Christmas 1939, erroneously beginning with "Dear Brother" but addressed and sent to Emile Albert Berolzheimer

around the Torah scroll—giving rise to its other name, the Torah binder. The wimpel would be also be wrapped around the scroll during a boy's *bar mitzvah*, the Jewish coming-of-age ritual at the age of thirteen, and later during his wedding ceremony, considered the two most important personal events in a male's life when the Torah binder would be used.

Nobody in the Berolzheimer family or even Isidor's own descendants (except Berolzheimer) knew his proper name was "Israel"; even Isidor himself did not know. In his letter (*fig. 2*), Berolzheimer explains the derivation of Isidor from the Greek, in turn originating from the Egyptian, meaning a "present by the goddess Isis." With the beginning of the emancipation of Jews, and as a consequence of the French Revolution and the rule of Napoleon I, parents in Europe began using the non-Semitic name "Isidor" instead of the Jewish "Israel," although the former was in fact considered a specifically Jewish name. It fell out of fashion in Germany at the end of the nineteenth century when the law on equality came into force in 1871, and hopes were raised that Jews would finally achieve recognition as citizens with equal rights, rendering any need to assimilate names superfluous.

Isidor was born in Fürth on February 24, 1823, into the Jewish tradition and named after his great-grandfather Israel Offenbach. Twenty-five years later, in 1848, he converted to Catholicism and took on the name of his godfather, Ludwig Carl August, although everybody continued to call him Isidor. Isidor married Dorothea Mahl, a Protestant, in the Catholic church of a small village, Bartenstein, in Franconia. Amalie, their only child to survive infancy, was brought up in the Protestant faith and inherited her parents' musical talent. Amalie's oldest son, Herman Carl Hiller, might have been the logical recipient of this family heirloom once made for his grandfather.

When he was twenty years old, Herman Carl Hiller, a professional musician, went to America, shortly after the death of his father in August 1892. Ship records list him as arriving in New York on January 13, 1893. He returned to Europe several times but eventually settled in Oakland, California. Judging by a local newspaper advertisement of 1926, he earned his living as a music teacher. Although Berolzheimer knew of Amalie's son and mentioned him in the family history, he did not know Hiller's first name and was therefore unable to ask his nephew, Charles, who actually lived nearby in Stockton, California, to pass the heirloom on to Isidor's grandson.

Berolzheimer may possibly have been given the wimpel, bereft of its ceremonial purpose, by his father, Heinrich, a prominent member of the Jewish cultural community in Fürth. Heinrich had taken pity on his gambling-addicted Uncle Isidor, who had twice lost his fortune in Monte Carlo, giving Isidor a job at the Fürth pencil factory. His great-nephew therefore would have had memories of his "Uncle Isidor," who walked with a limp, from when he was a young man.

Berolzheimer's intention may well have been to donate the Torah binder to the Jewish Museum once planned in Munich (*see also p. 123*). However, the museum did not materialize after its initiator, Theodor Harburger, emigrated to Palestine in 1933, leaving Berolzheimer with this curious family heirloom. In the end, he decided to give it to his eldest brother Emil's grandson, Emile Albert, both their names being derived from their forefather Mendel/Emanuel Berolzheimer, mentioned on the wimpel itself.

Although this artifact provides just a brief glimpse into the Berolzheimer family's long history, the story of this cloth bears witness to the rich traditions and ceremonies of the Jewish people. At the same time, it further highlights Michael Berolzheimer's profound knowledge and respect for family history and tradition.

fig. 3   A late eighteenth-century Torah binder showing similarly precise embroidery work, linen, Jewish Museum Munich (Gift of Eric Bloch, Philadelphia)

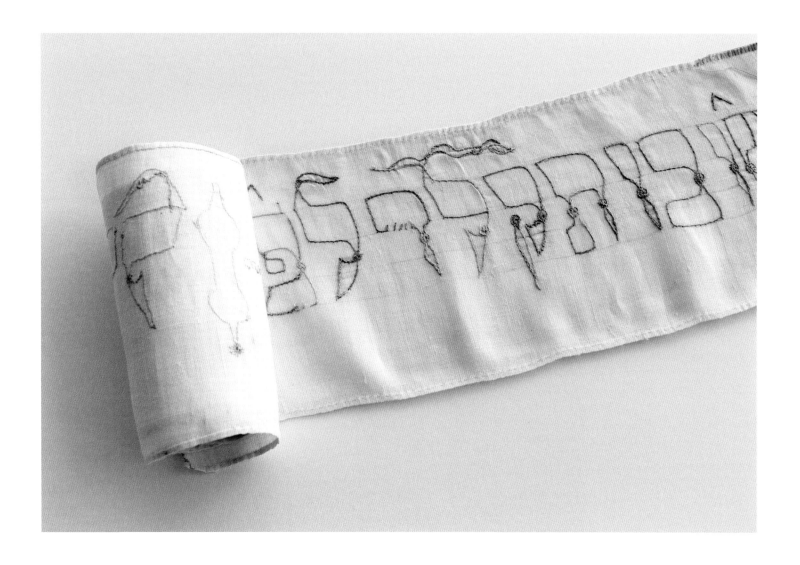

der Eremit in seiner Klause.

MICHAEL BEROLZHEIMER
AS A GENEALOGIST

Dr. Michael Berolzheimer (*fig. 1*) devoted much of his time and attention to the genealogical research of Jewish families in Bavaria. He began his research in the 1920s, after having moved permanently to the quiet locality of Untergrainau, and genealogical research continued to preoccupy him up to his death in 1942. His meticulously detailed research notes always cited the sources which supported his conclusions about individuals and their vitae. These findings constitute some of the most complete data on Jewish families in Franconia. As a result, many Jewish families from the communities in which Berolzheimer carried out his detailed research, have since been able to expand their family trees to include previously unknown relatives.

Natural decay as well as the willful destruction of Jewish gravestones and cemeteries, the desecration of synagogues and Israelite cultural centers in the Third Reich, and the loss of administrative records, libraries, and archives through allied bombings in World War II, all contributed to Berolzheimer's work becoming an irreplaceable resource and reference for genealogical research in Germany and elsewhere.

Berolzheimer was fascinated by the origins and derivation of Jewish family names. Much of his research covered Bavarian Jewish families who had to give up their patronymic naming[1] following a law in 1813, which required each family to adopt a surname that would continue from one generation to the next. His goal was to write a history of the extended Berolzheimer family, to include the families of those who had become related to the Berolzheimer name through marriage. He would often comment on the derivation of names in his correspondence with family members, and later in life wrote to the younger children in the family in particular to describe their forebears and the history of their names.

Berolzheimer developed a network of people with a similar interest who shared details of specific families to enhance his own research, and conscientiously cited the sources of this information in his notes and manuscripts. He organized his research into family lines and began writing separate chapters for each family name. By the summer of 1934 he had written 197 pages, roughly divided into nineteen chapters.[2]

The research required detailed knowledge of the events in the lives of Jewish residents across Bavaria, particularly in Fürth and Nuremberg. Since most

fig. 1 "The Hermit in his cell" – Michael Berolzheimer in his study at Hügel am Weg, c. 1935 documents were written in Hebrew, he made transcriptions and translations of the data found and related them to other family facts he had accumulated. In many cases, he found additional names and dates to supplement government records.

Corresponding with distant relatives and friends who learned of his interest, he was able to gain useful information from other towns and villages in Germany as well, and—as elsewhere—carefully acknowledged this assistance. On page 180 of his preliminary text, for example, he expresses thanks to Adolph Eppstein of Feuchtwangen for information on the descendants of Fanny (Sulzbürg) Oettinger (1838–98). The next footnote on that page thanks Martha Oettinger of Munich for details about her late husband and Fanny's younger brother, Isak Oettinger (1840–99). The following note relates to Rosalie Oettinger and acknowledges information given to Berolzheimer by Else Bensinger of Munich. Else was Fanny and Isak's sister; she died in November 1931. Although Berolzheimer's compiled this text long after his first contact with these informants, he took care, as always, to acknowledge them as the source of his facts. Such care and attention to providing the necessary evidence is essential to sound genealogical scholarship.[3]

One example of a typical, handwritten draft of a person's life, authenticated with source notes, reads: "Antonie (Toni, Telzele) Berolzheimer, was born in Fürth on April 4, 1813 [Birth register II, page 18, no. 89] and died in Baden-Baden on January 27, 1885. She was married in Fürth on August 22, 1831 [Marriage Register 14/72] to the jeweler David Mannheimer."[4]

Between 1927 and 1939, Berolzheimer corresponded with several other people interested in the genealogical research of Jewish families in Germany. Perhaps the most prolific collaboration was with rabbi Dr. Max Freudenthal, who greatly stimulated Berolzheimer's thinking. They exchanged frequent letters full of ideas and information until the rabbi's death in 1937. Freudenthal translated the Testamenten Books of the Jewish community in Fürth. Berolzheimer then copied them and created an index for the resulting list. He also created a series of smaller family trees for about fifty families in the register. Freudenthal engaged Berolzheimer in his research on some of the families too, occasionally finding other families with the same family name in communities where Berolzheimer had been working. Their correspondence created a strong bond of friendship and mutual esteem, and Berolzheimer remained in touch with Dr. Freudenthal's widow until 1939.[5]

Theodor Harburger (1887–1949), who emigrated from Munich in 1933 to Tiberias in Palestine (*see p. 65*), also enjoyed an extensive period of correspondence with Berolzheimer, about both art and family history. Harburger, who had lost his father in 1919, was a generation younger than Berolzheimer, and much more mobile to seek out archives and cemeteries for information. Harburger's interests resonated with Berolzheimer and he made extensive use of Harburger's sources.[6]

Berthold Rosenthal (1875–1957), a schoolteacher and genealogist mostly interested in Jewish families from southwestern Germany, first contacted Berolzheimer in September 1930. His question led to a series of exchanges of research results over the next twenty months. In summer 1937 a brief exchange of letters renewed their collaboration.[7] Rosenthal emigrated to the USA in 1939. Berolzheimer's own library of research resources eventually included lists of

fig. 2   Philip, Heinrich, and Emil Berolzheimer

Jewish registries from many communities in Bavaria and beyond. To trace his ancestors, he became particularly interested in the records of the Franconian villages of Markt Berolzheim and Redwitz an der Rodach, the larger centers of Fürth and Heidenheim, as well as the more distant cities of Leipzig, Prague, and Vienna.

In 1938, even as he was preparing to leave Germany for America, Berolzheimer reorganized his manuscript into a new format that he called "The Ancestry of Heinrich Berolzheimer and his Family."[8] He rearranged the order of the chapters which he had used in his first compilation, and moved the Berolzheimer section from the end to the front of the manuscript. The first two chapters of the revised version were entitled the "The Family Berolzheimer" and "Dedicated to my brother Philip Berolzheimer." After arriving in New York, Berolzheimer gave Philip this section of his rewritten work.

On May 22, 1942, Philip Berolzheimer died. His affairs, including his manuscript, passed to his son, Charles P. Berolzheimer (*fig. 3*). On June 5, 1942, Michael Berolzheimer's stepson and executor, Waldemar Schweisheimer, found the original manuscript of the projected genealogical publication among Berolzheimer's papers. On December 26, 1945, Schweisheimer sent this manuscript—without the Dispeker information about his mother's side of the family, which he considered irrelevant to the Berolzheimer family history and therefore kept to himself—to Charles Berolzheimer as a Christmas gift, thus complementing the revised chapters that Charles had inherited from his father, Philip. By the time of his death, Michael Berolzheimer had completed eight chapters and begun a ninth. This revised manuscript amounted to 459 pages of text, plus eight pages of Berolzheimer names. It had, at that time, still to be proven if these people were related to the family or not.

In 1968, Charles began talks with the Leo Baeck Institute in New York City. The institute focuses on preserving the stories of German-Jewish families

fig. 3 Charles Berolzheimer at the Berolzheimerianum next to the bust of its founder, Heinrich Berolzheimer, photographed in the early 1990s

who had fled Europe and settled in America. Part of the conversation involved Eric Midas, who had worked with Berolzheimer on some Jewish records in Fürth. Midas had begun working with the Leo Baeck Institute to organize record collections deposited there. He was familiar with Berolzheimer's work, and ultimately all of Berolzheimer's papers were transferred to the institute. Midas began to index the material and sort it into a usable format for research purposes.[9]

The Leo Baeck Institute separated the photographs from the other documents. A microfilm copy of the entire archival collection was prepared in 2002 and made accessible to interested parties. In 2009, the three rolls of microfilm were placed in the Internet Archive and have since been published on the Internet under www.archive.org, "Michael Berolzheimer Collection, 1325–1942." Its appearance on the Internet has made the collection widely available to other genealogists with an interest in Jewish communities in Bavaria. By early 2014, the collection had been downloaded more than 1050 times and used on-line innumerable occasions.

Other collections donated to the Leo Baeck Institute have drawn heavily on Michael Berolzheimer's work and even expanded on it with facts which were not previously available to Berolzheimer himself. Charles P. Stanton of Brooklyn, for example, became aware of the Berolzheimer work through correspondence with E. Albert Berol in 1981 — the latter's family having abbreviated the name Berolzheimer to Berol. Stanton was working with a much broader base of Jewish families in the Franconia area of Bavaria. He created very clear family charts and contacted many families seeking additional information where there were blanks in the trees. He also had access to all the Berolzheimer material. When Stanton's collection of 2000 family charts and correspondence was gifted to the Leo Baeck Institute and prepared for Internet circulation, it provided an excellent companion to the material in the Berolzheimer archive. The material in both collections is now being used to support current research into the Berol and Berolzheimer families.[10]

fig. 4 Lina and Heinrich Berolzheimer's graves

Additional factual information obtained by Stanton was able to enhance some of the original charts in the Berolzheimer collection from forty years earlier. For example, Berolzheimer showed that Hermann Wolf (Branch 3 IV 8/25) died on 22 April, 1845. Because there was no year stated for his birth in the Berolzheimer tree, Hermann Wolf appeared at the first spot on his generation's chart. In the Stanton tree, with new information that he was born on May 10, 1842, in Sulzbürg (Upper Palatinate/Bavaria), Hermann now follows several older siblings in the documentation of the family.[11]

After Berolzheimer's death, his nephew, Edwin, asked Waldemar Schweisheimer for a copy of the family history, which later passed into the hands of Edwin's son, E. Albert Berol. Albert intended having this family history translated into English by Dr. Lino Lipinski de Orlov (1908–88), curator of the John Jay Museum in Katonah, New York, but Lipinski died before the translation could be completed. Lipinski is nevertheless credited by Charles P. Stanton as the source of the Berolzheimer material which formed the basis of many of the charts in the Stanton Collection at the Leo Baeck Institute.[12]

It took two more years for Rita K. Coughlin and Avery L. Ross to complete the lineage tables. This led to a simple format of the Berolzheimer family history with the basic information taken from Berolzheimer's research, expressed in a systematic way for easy reference. This family information was finally circulated by Albert Berol in 1990 to family members as "The Berol and Berolzheimer Genealogy."[13]

Extending Albert's work with modern software, the task began to transfer all Berolzheimer's genealogical data available into *ancestry.com* files. At the request of Michael G. Berolzheimer, the present author is continuing this task, adding updates to family information learned since 1990, making genealogical information more accessible to the family, allowing for future updates, and seeking previously unrecognized branches of the extended Berolzheimer family. The current genealogy contains over 2080 names.

1 Traditionally, the Jewish patronymic system comprises the first name followed by *ben* (meaning "son of" or *bat* ("daughter of") and the father's name. Variations include *bar* in Aramaic (for a son) or *ibn* in Arabic. While family surnames were already being used by Sephardic Jews in Iberia, among other regions, back in the tenth or eleventh centuries, Ashkenazi Jews in Germany and Eastern Europe did not adopt surnames until the early nineteenth century.

2 The genealogical records and original manuscripts are at the Leo Baeck Institute in New York City. They are available on the Internet under www.archive.org as the "Michael Berolzheimer Collection, 1325–1942," in the form of images from three rolls of microfilm. All references to these films are presented by reel number and respective page number.

3 In Berolzheimer's manuscripts the text is a mix of typed and handwritten paragraphs. The text for the Oettingers is found on Reel 01, p. 1093, for example. The author inserted a small, numbered footnote marker on that page and wrote the notes (*Anmerkungen*) on a separate page. In this case, these notes are to be found on Reel 01, p. 1119.

4 Found in Berolzheimer's handwritten text at the bottom of page 120/top of page 121. Reel 01, pp. 179–80. The notes are at the bottom of each page.

5 The extensive correspondence between Berolzheimer and Freudenthal can be found on Reel 03, pp. 502–624, in reverse chronological order from 1926 to June 1937. Subsequent correspondence with his widow, Else Freudenthal, appears on Reel 03, pp. 472–89.

6 The Harburger correspondence can be found on Reel 03, pp. 625–738.

7 The Rosenthal papers in the Internet archive comprise the originals of most of the letters from Berolzheimer and are easier to read. The handwritten notes from Rosenthal to Berolzheimer are in the Berolzheimer collection at the Leo Baeck Institute.

8 The title of the revised version is in English only. The inventory at the Leo Baeck Institute however lists the document under "Die Ahnen des Heinrich Berolzheimer und ihre Familien, von Dr. Michael Berolzheimer."

9 A succinct summary of the contents of the Berolzheimer Collection at the Leo Baeck Institute is found on twelve typewritten pages, in German, on Reel 01, pp. 27–38.

10 The "Charles P. Stanton Family Collection 1802–2001" at the Leo Baeck Institute can be accessed under www.archive.org/details/charlesstanton

11 Stanton Family Collection, Berolzheimer Family Chart IV, under www.archive.org/stream/charlesperrystanton_05 _reel05#page/n473/mode/1up

12 Ibid., p. 469ff.

13 Berolzheimer Collection, Reel 03, p. 1038ff., with the actual family charts found on pp. 1078–155.

FAMLIY TREE

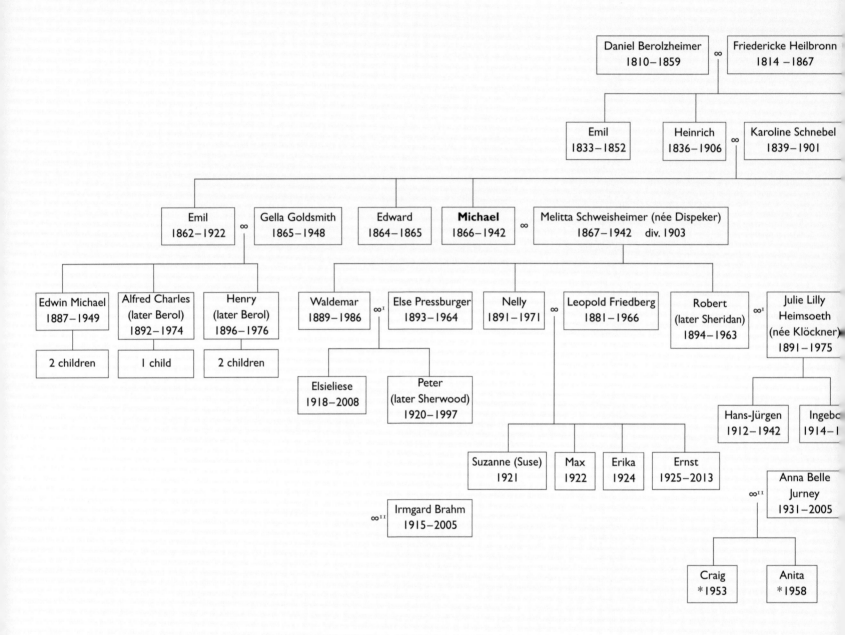

Excerpt from the Berolzheimer family tree. For reasons of clarity,
not all spouses, children, and subsequent generations are shown.

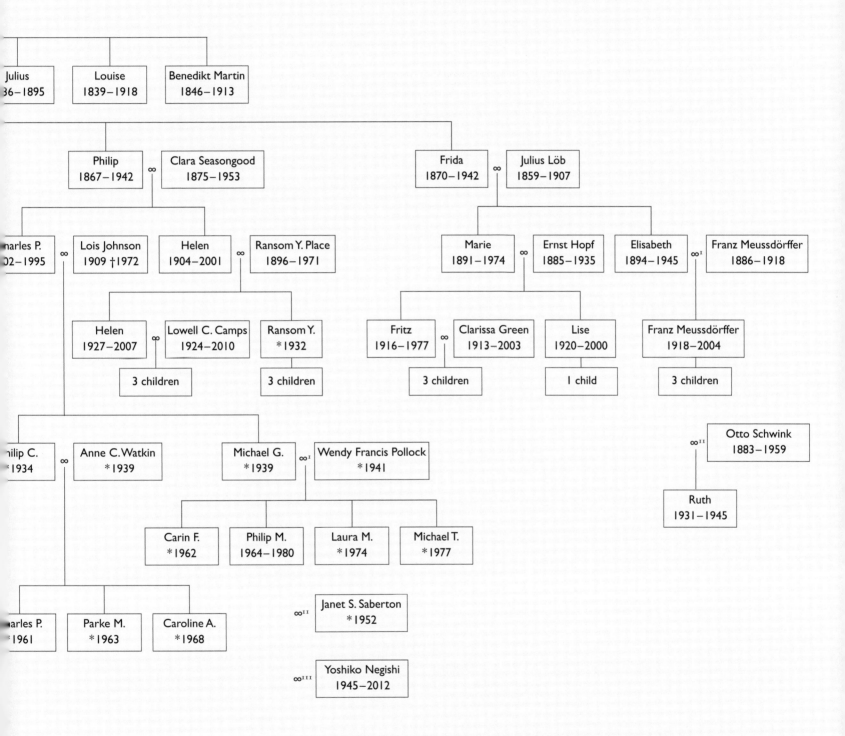

Julius
36–1895

Louise
1839–1918

Benedikt Martin
1846–1913

Philip
1867–1942

∞

Clara Seasongood
1875–1953

Frida
1870–1942

∞

Julius Löb
1859–1907

arles P.
02–1995

∞

Lois Johnson
1909 †1972

Helen
1904–2001

∞

Ransom Y. Place
1896–1971

Marie
1891–1974

∞

Ernst Hopf
1885–1935

Elisabeth
1894–1945

∞I

Franz Meussdörffer
1886–1918

Helen
1927–2007

∞

Lowell C. Camps
1924–2010

Ransom Y.
*1932

Fritz
1916–1977

∞

Clarissa Green
1913–2003

Lise
1920–2000

Franz Meussdörffer
1918–2004

3 children

3 children

3 children

1 child

3 children

Otto Schwink
1883–1959

∞II

hilip C.
*1934

∞

Anne C. Watkin
*1939

Michael G.
*1939

∞I

Wendy Francis Pollock
*1941

Ruth
1931–1945

Carin F.
*1962

Philip M.
1964–1980

Laura M.
*1974

Michael T.
*1977

arles P.
*1961

Parke M.
*1963

Caroline A.
*1968

∞II

Janet S. Saberton
*1952

∞III

Yoshiko Negishi
1945–2012

WHO'S WHO

A brief list of selected figures mentioned in this publication for ease of reference. Compiled by Dietlind Bratengeyer.

AMOS, Hans Egon, 1908–95: Moved with wife, Ingeborg Heimsoeth, to England in 1936; changed his name to Hugh E. Amos; was called to the bar in 1938; Michael, Christopher, and Jeremy's father

AMOS, Ingeborg ("Butzel"): See Heimsoeth, Ingeborg

AMOS, Michael, b. 1939: Michael Berolzheimer's step-great-grandson; Lilly Klöckner's grandson; named after Michael Berolzheimer; born in Munich and stayed behind in Germany during World War II in the care of his grandmother until 1946

BEROL, Alfred Charles, 1892–1974: Michael Berolzheimer's nephew; Emil Berolzheimer's son; changed surname in 1943

BEROL, Emile Albert, 1911–93: Michael Berolzheimer's great-nephew; Edwin M. Berol's son; changed surname in 1942

BEROL, Henry, 1896–1976: Michael Berolzheimer's nephew; Emil Berolzheimer's son; changed surname in 1947

BEROLZHEIMER, Charles Philip, 1902–95: Michael Berolzheimer's nephew; Philip Berolzheimer's son; married Lois Johnson; Philip Charles and Michael George's father

BEROLZHEIMER, Clara, 1874–1953: Michael Berolzheimer's sister–in–law; Philip Berolzheimer's widow; married Edgar Bromberger, Chief Magistrate of New York, in 1947

BEROLZHEIMER, Daniel, 1810–59: Michael Berolzheimer's grandfather; founder of Berolzheimer & Illfelder Pencil Company

BEROLZHEIMER, Edwin Michael, 1887–1949: Michael Berolzheimer's nephew; Emil Berolzheimer's son

BEROLZHEIMER, Emil, 1862–1922: Michael Berolzheimer's brother; succeeded Heinrich Berolzheimer as manager of Eagle Pencil Company; married Gella Goldsmith,1865–1948; Edwin, Alfred, and Henry's father

BEROLZHEIMER, Frida, 1870–1942: Michael Berolzheimer's sister; married Julius Loeb, 1859–1907; Marie and Elisabeth's mother

BEROLZHEIMER, Heinrich, 1836–1906: Michael Berolzheimer's father; partner in Berolzheimer & Illfelder Pencil Factory in Fürth; later owner of Eagle Pencil Company in New York

BEROLZHEIMER, Karoline ("Lina"): See Schnebel, Karoline

BEROLZHEIMER, Melitta: See Dispeker, Melitta

BEROLZHEIMER, (Dr.) Michael, 1866–1942: Court counselor, attorney, art collector, genealogist; principal figure of this publication

BEROLZHEIMER, Michael George, b. 1939: Michael Berolzheimer's great-nephew and namesake; Charles Philip Berolzheimer's son; publisher and editor of this book

BEROLZHEIMER, Philip, 1867–1942: Michael Berolzheimer's brother; President of Eagle Pencil Company 1922–25; City Chamberlain of New York

BEROLZHEIMER, Philip Charles, b. 1934: Michael Berolzheimer's great-nephew; Charles Philip Berolzheimer's son

BRAHM, Irmgard, 1915–2005: Waldemar Schweisheimer's second wife

DISPEKER, Melitta, 1867–1942: Michael Berolzheimer's wife; divorced Eugen Schweisheimer in 1903 with whom she had three children—Waldemar, Nelly, Robert

DRIESEN, Frieda: See Friedberg, Frieda

FREUDENTHAL, Max, 1868–1937: Friend of Michael Berolzheimer's; historian and genealogist; rabbi in Nuremberg 1907–34; retired to Munich

FRIEDBERG, Frieda, 1893–1943: Nelly Schweisheimer's sister-in-law; married a banker; emigrated to Belgium, then moved to St. Cloud, near Paris; helped Melitta's grandchildren to cross Europe from Italy to England; arrested in Marseille and deported to Auschwitz death camp

FRIEDBERG, Leopold, 1881–1966: Attorney from Karlsruhe; married Nelly Schweisheimer; escaped to England in 1939; emigrated in 1947 with Nelly to New Zealand to join their children—Suzanne (Suse Johanna), Max Eugene, Erika Ruth, Ernst Michael

HEIMSOETH, Hans-Jürgen, 1912–42: Michael Berolzheimer's step–grandson

HEIMSOETH, Ingeborg, 1914–69: Michael Berolzheimer's step-granddaughter, nicknamed "Butzel"; married Hans Egon Amos in 1936; moved to England; Michael, Christopher, and Jeremy's mother

HEIMSOETH, Rudolf, d. 1968: Lilly Klöckner's first husband; owner of company producing the "Enigma" cipher machine; Hans-Jürgen and Ingeborg's father

JOLLES, Boguslav, c. 1845–d. 1912: Member of a Jewish family of bankers from Berlin and Dresden; owner of an art collection auctioned in Munich by Hugo Helbing in 1895 and acquired by Michael Berolzheimer

JURNEY, Anna Belle, 1931–2005: Robert Schweisheimer (Sheridan)'s second wife; Craig and Anita's mother

KLÖCKNER, Lilly, 1891–1975: Michael Berolzheimer's step-daughter-in-law; divorced Rudolf Heimsoeth (two children—Ingeborg and Hans-Jürgen); married Robert Schweisheimer (later Sheridan) in 1921, anti-semitic law in Germany forced her to divorce him in 1939; remarried Robert in 1947 in London and emigrated with him to the USA; original divorce annulled in 1948; divorced again legally in 1952

PRAGER, Michael Sigmund, 1866–1943: Michael Berolzheimer's cousin and close friend, son of Jeanette Prager, née Schnebel; studied at Munich University with Michael Berolzheimer; emigrated to join his son, Kurt Adolf, in the Netherlands; deported from Westerbork to Sobibór extermination camp

PRAGER, Paula: See Sahlmann, Pauline (Paula)

PRESSBURGER, Else, 1893–1964: Waldemar Schweisheimer's wife

SAHLMANN, Pauline (Paula), 1869–1943: Wife of Michael Berolzheimer's cousin, Michael Prager; close friend of Michael and Melitta; emigrated with her husband to join their son in the Netherlands; deported from Westerbork to Sobibór extermination camp

SCHNEBEL, Karolina, 1839–1901: Michael Berolzheimer's mother; married Heinrich Berolzheimer; Emil, Edward (died in infancy), Michael, Philip, and Frida's mother

SCHWEISHEIMER, Elsieliese, 1918–2008: Michael Berolzheimer's step–granddaughter; married Nolan Thrope; Michael Thrope's mother

SCHWEISHEIMER, Eugen, 1858–1942: Melitta Dispeker's first husband (Waldemar, Nelly, and Robert's father); owner of the Munich banking business E. & J. Schweisheimer; deported 1942 to Theresienstadt where he was murdered

SCHWEISHEIMER, Irmgard: See Brahm, Irmgard

SCHWEISHEIMER, Julius, 1863–1942: Eugene Schweisheimer's brother; partner in Eugen's banking business; deported 1942 to Theresienstadt where he was murdered

SCHWEISHEIMER, Moritz, 1862–1942: Eugen Schweisheimer's brother; deported to Theresienstadt in 1942 where he was murdered

SCHWEISHEIMER, Nelly, 1891–1971: Michael Berolzheimer's step-daughter; married Leopold Friedberg in 1920; Suzanne (Suse Johanna), Max Eugene, Erika Ruth, and Ernst Michael's mother; sent children to safety in New Zealand; escaped with Leopold to England in 1939; emigrated to New Zealand in 1947

SCHWEISHEIMER, Peter, 1919–97: Michael Berolzheimer's step-grandson; changed name to Sherwood; married Resi Pott; Douglas's father

SCHWEISHEIMER, Robert, 1894–1963: Michael Berolzheimer's stepson; married Lilly Heimsoeth, née Klöckner in 1921; partner in his father's banking business; fled to England in 1938; emigrated to the USA in 1940; changed his name to Sheridan; divorced under Nazi law in 1939; remarried Lilly in 1947; divorced Lilly again in 1952; father of Heide (died in infancy); married Anna Belle Jurney in 1954; Craig and Anita's father

SCHWEISHEIMER, Waldemar, 1889–1986: Michael Berolzheimer's stepson; medical doctor and writer; married Else Pressburger (1893–1964); Elsieliese and Peter's father; emigrated to the US in 1936; executor of Michael and Melitta Berolzheimer's last will; widowed; married Irmgard Brahm in 1966

SHERIDAN, Anita Lily Maria, b. 1958: Michael Berolzheimer's step-granddaughter

SHERIDAN, Craig, b. 1953: Michael Berolzheimer's step-grandson

SHERIDAN, Lilly: See Klöckner, Lilly

SHERIDAN, Robert: See Schweisheimer, Robert

SHERWOOD, Peter: See Schweisheimer, Peter

J. J. Dillis.

THE BEROLZHEIMER COLLECTION

ART ROBBERY: A PERSPECTIVE

fig. *1*   Nicolas Guibal (1725–84)
Pluto's Abduction of Proserpina, n.d.,
pen in brown ink with brown and gray wash
over graphite, restituted by the Albertina, Vienna

"On March 9 and 10, 1939, I shall be auctioning two Munich collections—original artists' drawings and miniatures. [...]. Most of the sheets to be auctioned come from two Jewish collections,"[1] the Munich art auctioneer Adolf Weinmüller announced two weeks earlier on February 24. One of the Jewish collections was Dr. Michael Berolzheimer's.

On December 3 of the previous year, new legislation on the handling of Jewish assets had come into effect.[2] Weinmüller sought to fight the restrictions this imposed on his business, which he felt not only threatened his own existence but also that of all others working in the same field. He was particularly critical of a clause in a related by-law passed shortly afterward on January 16, 1939, which prohibited Jews from acquiring, pledging or selling jewelry and works of art on the open market if the price of an object exceeded 1000 Reichsmarks.[3] Items worth more were not to exchange hands privately or be offered for sale to the general public, but be handed in to a central post in Berlin, established later specifically for this sole purpose.

Weinmüller feared that the enforcement of this legislation would directly effect the success of the auction he was planning for March 9 and 10, as well as "the profitable activity [of his] business as a whole."[4] He felt it to be totally unacceptable for Munich, as a center of German art, if "all cultural assets owned by Jews [were] to be handed in to a post in Berlin not yet even established, [thus] bypassing the local market. This type of centralization," Weinmüller continued, "would be a considerable danger to trade in Germany as a whole, as Berlin is certainly not the only German city which trades in art."[5] In the same text he went on to say that art dealers and auctioneers in Munich could definitely not do without the cultural objects placed on the market by Jewish clients as there were "no more large, complete collections in Munich owned by Aryans to be sold."[6] In fact the auction he was planning "comprised some $^1/_3$ works in Aryan and some $^2/_3$ in Jewish ownership, with the most valuable items being in Jewish ownership."[7]

On February 22, 1939, Weinmüller submitted a number of documents to the police headquarters in Munich. This was the standard procedure when applying for permission to hold an auction. A few days earlier, he had published an advertisement in the journal *Weltkunst* announcing the sale of historical and modern miniatures and original artists' drawings, as well as the two collections mentioned above.[8] Leafing through a copy of the auction catalogue or reading the advertisements, those interested in art and in acquiring the works, however, were not informed as to the names of the collections in question—unlike the appropriate authorities and Party offices. In the "list of owners" in the catalogue itself, those items in "non-Aryan" ownership were simply marked as such.[9] The auction house Weinmüller was in fact complying with strict guidelines stipulated in the so-called "Tarnverordnung" (lit.: camouflage legislation) passed on April 22, 1938, in keeping with a recommendation published in a manual that same year.[10] Drawing attention to individual collections or items, based on the time-honored principle of a "full provenance," was no longer possible and was subject to a number of restrictions.

In the preface to the catalogue, an extremely positive appraisal of Berolzheimer's collection of drawings is given by an expert: "The majority of drawings are by German artists. The surprisingly large number of drawings by Romantic artists, which are also significant due to their exceptional artistic quality, unites the most important names of those masters sought at present with particular interest and notable appreciation."[11] Praise for a collection is also, indirectly, an acknowledgement of the achievements of those who summoned the will and energy to assemble the items in the first place and to look after them.

In the Third Reich, no explanations were allowed to be given for the blatant contradiction in Nazi propaganda with regard to the correlation between "Judaism, degenerate art, subversion regarding traditional 'German' social norms and values" and the collections of German art, amassed over many decades by German Jews that were so familiar to the public. By obliterating the names of Jewish benefactors from the collective memory and anonymizing collectors who had to auction their possessions on a large scale before they were able to leave Germany, it was not only intended that their achievements and work should no longer be recognized, but that the people themselves would also simply be forgotten. The radical, popular saying "Jews always have a hand in decay" also found its way into art historical treatises.[12]

In 2011, twenty-nine drawings originally in the Berolzheimer Collection, which had been restituted by the Albertina in Vienna to the heirs (*figs 1, 2*), were presented for sale at the Art Paris fair. An article printed at that time referred to how no consideration or credit had been given to Berolzheimer and his involvement in the world of art: "For the Nazis, Michael Berolzheimer's cultural commitment and his position over many years as an honorary member of the Acquisitions Committee at the Alte Pinakothek and the Graphische Sammlung München did not play any role whatsoever."[13]

After the end of the Nazi era, the art auctioneer Adolf Weinmüller, like many others, showed little interest in providing information about his role in the dispersal of Berolzheimer's collection or in making amends. As such, he failed to contribute towards honoring the name of the collector and his collection. Despite the restitution of a number of works, the whereabouts of several hundred drawings still remains unknown to this day.

The impact and work of Berolzheimer and other Jewish art collectors have increasingly become the subject of historical research in the past few years, since—as a result of agreements reached at the Washington Conference in 1998 on the return of Holocaust-era assets—museums and other public collections in

fig. 2   Abraham Bloemaert
Ruins of a Farmstead, c. 1585–90, pen in brown ink with brown and gray wash over black chalk, restituted by the Albertina, Vienna

Germany and abroad are obliged to examine acquisitions made after 1933 for any links to the expropriation and persecution policies of the National Socialists.

It has been institutions in Munich such as the Bavarian State Picture Collections, the Städtische Galerie im Lenbachhaus, the Zentralinstitut für Kunstgeschichte, the Jewish Museum Munich, the Bavarian National Museum, the Münchener Stadtmuseum, and the Staatliche Graphische Sammlung, in particular, but also the Institut für Zeitgeschichte, the Bavarian State Library and the Library of Ludwig Maximilians Universität, as well as the City Archives and the Bayerische Wirtschaftsarchiv, which have undertaken or cooperated in research into the whereabouts of artworks and cultural assets primarily from the collections of persecuted and exiled Jews from Munich.

Members of staff at several of the institutions mentioned above have also made important contributions to research on the Berolzheimer Collection and the fate of the artworks. Their findings have helped close gaps in the field of research as well as illustrate the life and work of a collector and the fate of his collection in various temporal, regional, and art-historical contexts.

1   Meike Hopp, *Kunsthandel im Nationalsozialismus: Adolf Weinmüller in München und Wien,* Cologne et al. 2012, pp. 163–69, here p. 164.

2   "Verordnung über den Einsatz Jüdischen Vermögens," passed on December 3, 1938.

3   To provide some idea of the value in real terms of the amounts given here and elsewhere in this volume in Reichsmarks, and some approximate equivalent of these sums in US dollars today, please see Appendix.

4   Hopp, op. cit. (see note 1), pp. 163–64.

5   Ibid.

6   Ibid., p. 164.

7   Ibid.

8   Ibid., p. 165.

9   *Buchminiaturen und Handzeichnungen aus älterer und neuerer Zeit. Zwei Münchener Sammlungen und andere Beiträge,* catalogue no. 19, auction held on March 9 and 10, 1939, at the Kunstversteigerungshaus Adolf Weinmüller, Odeonsplatz 4, Munich 1939.

10   Legislation against supporting the concealment of Jewish businesses from April 22, 1938, *RGBl,* 1938, p. 404; Werner Markmann and Paul Enterlein, *Die Entjudung der deutschen Wirtschaft. Arisierungsverordnungen vom 26. April und 12. November 1938,* Berlin 1938, pp. 64–65.

11   Benno Grimmschitz, "Preface" in: *Buchminiaturen und Handzeichnungen,* op. cit. (see note 9), p. 8. "Benno Grimmschitz" is probably the pseudonym of Dr. Bruno Grimschitz (1892–1964), curator and director of the Österreichische Galerie im Belvedere, Vienna, who was called upon as an expert for the auction house Weinmüller and other institutions, including the Dorotheum in Vienna, in particular.

12   Hans Weigert, *Geschichte der deutschen Kunst. Von der Vorzeit bis zur Gegenwart,* Berlin 1942, p. 498.

13   Annette Lettau, "Deutsche Romantik in Paris. Die Galerie Arnoldi-Livie hat ein spektakuläres Zeichnungskonvolut aus einer lange verschollenen Sammlung im Angebot" in: *Die Zeit,* 03/31/2011, no. 14; www.zeit.de/2011/14/Kunstmarkt; 01/08/2013.

MICHAEL BEROLZHEIMER'S ART COLLECTION

fig. 1 Johann Georg Bergmüller, *The Founding of Steingaden Monastery*, 1739; design for the west ceiling fresco of the monastery church; pen in black and brown ink over graphite, partially with gray and rose wash, heightened with white on blue dyed paper, restituted by the Albertina, Vienna

fig. 2 Michael Ostendorfer, *The Sudarium of St. Veronica*, 1520, oil on panel, now in the Bayerische Staatsgemälde-sammlungen, Munich

Rediscovering private collections is like opening doors which have been closed for a long time. Full of suspense, one comes across unknown, surprising or forgotten works of art. There are many reasons why they are not known to a wider public—a collector's discretion and modesty, or the enjoyment of an exclusive, intimate privilege, for instance. However, the dark chapter in Germany's history between 1933 and 1945 also led to the eradication of collectors and collections from the public mind.

On a local level in Munich, it was not until 2007 that a general awareness of the once thriving art collecting scene in the Bavarian capital in the 1920s and '30s was reawakened by the "Collecting Images" series of exhibitions at the Jewish Museum Munich, in which the treasures and quality of collections owned by wealthy, influential, Jewish families—the Pringsheims, Thannhausers, Wallachs, and Bernheimers—were displayed.[1] Berolzheimer's medium sized collection of paintings and probably very large number of works on paper, comprising prints and original drawings from the seventeenth to the nineteenth centuries, is to be counted among those art treasures to be found in the early 1930s in Bavaria.[2]

Until the night of the pogrom in 1938, more than 250 art collections and art dealers with a Jewish family background existed in the Munich area.[3] Of these collections, seventy were confiscated between November 1938 and January 1939, and the works distributed among museums in Munich.[4]

In order to reconstruct Berolzheimer's collection and detail the works it contained, reference has to be made to a number of different sources including gifts, auction catalogues (such as the 1939 Weinmüller catalogues), and records made at the so-called "collecting points." A further picture of the collection's contents was gained in 2011 through the Arnoldi-Livie publications on restituted drawings (*fig. 1*).[5]

Two paintings in Berolzheimer's ownership by German Old Masters were given to the Bayerische Staatsgemäldesammlungen (The Bavarian State Painting Collections). One is a work by Michael Ostendorfer from 1520 depicting the sudarium of St. Veronica (*fig. 2*); the other is the left wing of an altar with an image of St. Ulrich.[6] According to the list of artworks in the database at the Deutsches Historisches Museum in Berlin related to the "Central Collecting

fig. 3   Anselm Feuerbach, *The Berolzheimer Children*,
1877, oil on canvas; depicting Betty and Martin, the
children of Sigmund Berolzheimer, a great-uncle of
Michael Berolzheimer. Martin died aged 10; Betty's
daughter was the famous violinist Charlotte (Lotte)
Harburger, whose portrait was painted by Franz von
Stuck (opposite)

fig. 4   Franz von Stuck, *Portrait of a Lady*, 1907, oil on canvas

Point" in Munich, Berolzheimer also owned a painting on panel by Lucas Cranach depicting a bearded man.[7]

Another list of works owned by Berolzheimer and sold in the owner's absence at the end of November 1938 by the Munich auction house Weinmüller,[8] included a painting by Anselm Feuerbach of a lady dressed for a ball (*Dame mit rosa Kleid* / Lady in a Pink Dress),[9] a charcoal drawing of a Dutch village street by Max Liebermann, two preliminary sketches and an oil study for *The Poor Poet* by Carl Spitzweg (*see p. 166*),[10] as well as landscapes by Anton (Toni) Hermann von Stadler and Heinrich von Zügel.[11]

Data on Galerie Heinemann provided by the Germanisches National-museum in Nuremberg documents further artworks. Berolzheimer owned some ten other works by Anselm Feuerbach, as well as paintings by Friedrich August von Kaulbach, Alfred Plauzeau, Gabriel Schachinger, Toni Stadler, Franz von Stuck, Hans Thoma, Ludwig von Zumbusch, and Fritz von Uhde.[12] Collecting works by Anselm Feuerbach had tradition. In 1877, Feuerbach painted *The Berolzheimer Children*, showing them looking at a picture book together (*fig. 3*). Henriette Feuerbach's letters reveal that Berolzheimer's uncle, Sigmund, and his wife Clara, belonged to Feuerbach's circle of friends and also advised them in legal matters.[13]

Around the turn of the century, court musical director Hermann Levi (1839–1900) and Mary Fiedler, widow of art historian Konrad Fiedler, already owned a significant collection of Feuerbachs as well, which hung in their house in Munich and in Villa Riedberg in Partenkirchen, built for them by Adolf von Hildebrand.[14] Since the 1890s, the market town of Partenkirchen—just a few miles from the Berolzheimers' house in Untergrainau—had developed into a meeting place for artists, writers, and collectors from Munich's cultural scene, including Franz von Lenbach, Adolf von Hildebrand, and Paul Heyse. Entries in the Berolzheimer's guestbook in fact also record visits by the family of the writer and publisher Georg Hirth (1841–1916), the architect Gerhard Herms, Eugen Kirchner (1865–1938)—the painter and creator of the humorous "Fliegende Blätter" drawings—and others (see also pp. 88–93).

fig. 5 Auguste Rodin, *St. John the Baptist,* 1880, bronze, now in the Saint Louis Art Museum

Berolzheimer's collection did not remain static over the years. Its content varied, with a number of artworks being sold through the Galerie Heinemann. The exquisite *Portrait of a Lady* by Franz von Stuck in Berolzheimer's collection is also to be found in the gallery's records and illustrated in the gallery's 1907/08 catalogue (*fig. 4*).[15] It was bought in 1907 for 2700 Marks by "Justizrat Berolzheimer" of Munich—most likely Lotte Harburger's grandfather, Justizrat Dr. Sigmund Berolzheimer.[16] New owners of other works included Theodor and Meta Harburger, who lived in Munich until 1933, and with whom Berolzheimer was well acquainted. The Harburgers were also collectors of Feuerbach's works.[17]

In addition, Berolzheimer collected sculptures and antiques. He owned several small Roman sculptures as well as colored bas-reliefs in the manner of Andrea della Robbia and Desiderio da Settignano. His acquisition of the more than six-foot tall, bronze statue *St. John the Baptist* by Auguste Rodin, dated 1880 (*fig. 5*), is an unusual exception. Berolzheimer placed it in the garden of his country house in Untergrainau, where its nudity and larger-than-life dimensions must have caused quite a stir. The sculpture was one of the artworks he managed to take with him when he emigrated, and to this day has been one of the main treasures in the sculpture collection at Saint Louis Art Museum since 1946.[18] Berolzheimer bought the work for 6500 francs on the recommendation of

Georg Treu, director of the Sculpture Collection in Dresden. According to Rodin's assistant, Jean Limet, it was one of the finest versions of the bronze sculpture.[19]

Berolzheimer was involved in a number of social activities, and was board member of the Kunstwissenschaftliche Gesellschaft (Fine Arts' Society). He also sat on committees at the Alte Pinakothek art museum and the Staatliche Graphische Sammlung (State Prints Collection), and was one of the assessors at the Bayerischer Verein der Kunstfreunde/Museumsverein (Bavarian Association of Art Lovers/Museums' Association) in Munich, founded in 1905. One of this association's aims was to purchase works of art which public collections could not afford.[20] Head of the Museumsverein was Theodor Freiherr von Cramer-Klett and his deputy was Alfred Pringsheim, Thomas Mann's father-in-law. In 1933, the association was dissolved because of its predominantly Jewish chairmen, and the loans made by the association to museums in Munich were declared to be gifts.[21]

The composition of Michael Berolzheimer's art collection was quite conservative and typical of its time in Munich. It boasted quality works by Munich and other German painters of the nineteenth century and early twentieth centuries. Although there were no masterpieces of museum quality, it did include medium format works by well-known artists of decorative, popular subjects. The collection of works by Feuerbach was certainly influenced by Berolzheimer's acquaintance with collectors such as Harburger and Levi. The collection was built up during the time Hugo von Tschudi, Heinz Braune, and Friedrich Dornhöffer were directors of the Bayerische Staatsgemäldesammlungen in 1909–12, 1912–14, and 1914–33 respectively. Hugo von Tschudi, during whose tenure Berolzheimer gifted works to the Pinakothek museums and the Museum Society, assisted important, private Munich collectors such as Carl and Thea Sternheim, Alfred

fig. 7   Bonaventura Genelli, *Palamedes and Thersites Playing Dice in the Trojan Camp*, c. 1839, graphite, restituted by the Albertina, Vienna

Walther Heymel, and Alfred and Hanna Wolff, whose collections however were more avant-guarde than Berolzheimer's. Buying the large Rodin sculpture would certainly only have been possible through the influential connection of museum directors such as von Tschudi and Treu, both connoisseurs and patrons of Rodin, and their contacts.

Berolzheimer's acquisition of drawings and prints in particular can be considered exceptional. While the Königliche Graphische Sammlung (Royal Prints Collection) in Munich, as it was called after 1905, was much admired by artists and art historians, a collection such as Berolzheimer's would have been reserved for just a small circle of friends, family, and like-minded connoisseurs. His collection included Italian, German, and Dutch drawings of the sixteenth and seventeenth centuries, French and German drawings of the eighteenth century, as well as German drawings of the first half of the nineteenth and early twentieth centuries. These drawings are documented in Alfred Weinmüller's auction catalogue of March 1939. From a total of 1015 items listed in the catalogue, some 800 came from Berolzheimer's collection.[22] The introduction by the authors Franz Kieslinger und Benno Grimmschitz makes no mention of their southern German provenance. Instead, it refers to a collection of Old Master drawings assembled in Vienna around 1870. This inferred the Jolles Collection sold by Boguslav Jolles (Dresden/Vienna, c. 1845–1912), which was auctioned in 1895 by Helbing in Munich and is likely to have been bought largely by Berolzheimer. Other known previous owners of some sheets include Carl Gottlieb Peschel of Dresden (1798–1879) and E. von Oppelzer of Innsbruck.

An early drawing mistakenly attributed to Albrecht Dürer of the Holy Roman Emperor Charles the Bald from the Codex Aureus of St. Emmeram was reproduced in color on the title page of the Weinmüller catalogue. Many of the sheets are illustrated in the plate section, some with accompanying attributions. In his foreword, Grimmschitz especially emphasized the quality of drawings by German and Austrian artists such as Moritz von Schwind (*fig. 6*) and Bonaventura Genelli (*fig. 7*), Julius Schnorr von Carolsfeld and Eduard von Steinle (*fig. 8*), whose works were particularly admired by the National Socialists. The drawings are mostly sketches of scenes from operas or illustrations for poems. Impressive sketches for large church frescoes, the ones for Steingaden in Upper Bavaria by Johann Georg Bergmüller (*fig. 8*) being especially noteworthy, are well represented. Sensitive landscape studies by the Nazarenes complete the collection's exquisite profile (*fig. 9*).

Collectors of drawings and prints comparable to Berolzheimer were the Munich industrialist and banker Hugo von Maffei (1836–1921), the court counselor Sigmund Röhrer (1861–1929)[23] from Unterschondorf on Ammersee, and the Augsburg art historian and collector Albert Hämmerle (1899–1976), who donated works to the Staatliche Graphische Sammlung in Munich and the City of Augsburg. Berolzheimer's collection should be seen in this context to be able to evaluate it appropriately. When a large number of works from the collection were auctioned off in 1939, representatives of the most important museums and dealers of works on paper from Germany and Austria were present and acquired works for their own collections (*see also p. 165 f.*). For a short moment, one section of this intimate, private collection was visible in all its opulence. Then the doors closed again. The high quality of the sheets became apparent again in 2011, more than seventy years after the unlawful dissolution of the collection, as a result of restitution efforts and the associated publication of two catalogues by the Galerie Arnoldi-Livie, detailing the works in the Albertina in Vienna and the Kupferstichkabinett in Berlin returned to the heirs.

fig. 9 Philipp Veit, *The Flight into Egypt*, 1836, graphite, restituted by the Albertina, Vienna

28150.

1 Emily D. Bilsky, *"Only Culture"—The Pringsheims*, Jewish Museum Munich, 2007; Emily D. Bilsky, *The Bernheimer Art and Antiques House*, Jewish Museum Munich, 2007; Monika Ständecke, *Dirndls, Trunks, and Edelweiss. The Folk Art of the Wallach Brothers*, Jewish Museum Munich, 2007; Emily D. Bilsky, *Heinrich Thannhauser's "Moderne Galerie,"* Jewish Museum Munich, 2008.

2 The exact extent of the collection is not known. While mention is made of more than 800 drawings sold through Weinmüller, the collection may well have included several thousand prints and drawings. An indeterminate number of works on paper, which included the Old Master prints and works from the 15th–18th centuries, were taken to America. All or most of the 19th and early 20th-century works on paper were most probably left in Germany. Researched by Horst Kessler for the Jewish Museum Munich.

3 Researched by Horst Keßler for the Jewish Museum Munich.

4 Vanessa Voigt and Horst Keßler, "Die Beschlagnahmung jüdischer Kunstsammlungen 1938/39 in München" (The Confiscation of Jewish Art Collections in 1938/39 in Munich); a research project of the State and Municipal Museums in Munich on the fate of Jewish collectors and art dealers; "Ein Forschungsprojekt der Staatlichen und Städtischen Museen in München zum Schicksal jüdischer Kunstsammler und Kunsthändler" in *Kunst sammeln, Kunst handeln*, Vienna 2012, pp. 37–49.

5 *29 Drawings from the Michael Berolzheimer Collection Restituted by the Albertina*, Arnoldi-Livie cat. no. 27, 2011; *Michael Berolzheimer Collection II. 24 Drawings restituted by the Kupferstichkabinett Berlin*, Arnoldi-Livie cat. no. 28.

6 Inv. nos 1073/ and 8696.

7 Munich no. 41649, restituted on 09/13/1950 to Waldemar Schweisheimer as executor of Dr. Berolzheimer's will, Bundesarchiv 323/686.

8 "Antiques, furniture, sculptures, paintings from the 15th through 20th centuries, east Asian art from a family from Augsburg, as well as items in princely ownership and others from southern Germany," auction 11/30 and 12/01+02/1938; Münchner Kunstversteigerungshaus Adolf Weinmüller. The Berolzheimer lots are marked "Be. i. M.". See also Meike Hopp, *Kunsthandel im Nationalsozialismus: Adolf Weinmüller in München und Wien*, Vienna, Cologne, Weimar 2012, p. 164ff.

9 Munich no. 9038, Linz no. 0830, Ecker cat. raisonné no. 160.

10 Auctioned at Sotheby's on 01/26/2012 for 450,000 US dollars. The work was submitted by Waldemar Schweisheimer's heirs.

11 This may possibly be the picture in question: addendum by Diem to cat. raisonné, no. 104.

12 http://heinemann.gnm.de, as of 09/01/2012.

13 Jürgen Ecker, *Anselm Feuerbach. Kritischer Katalog der Gemälde, Ölskizzen und Ölstudien*, Munich 1991, pp. 356–57, cat. raisonné no. 509.

14 See Alois Schwarzmüller, "Hermann Levi – Hofkapellmeister in München und Ehrenbürger des Marktes Partenkirchen," 2009, under http://members.gaponline.de/alois.schwarzmueller/biografisches/levi_hermann.htm, as of 09/17/2012; Renata Stih and Frieder Schnock, *Zeige Deine Sammlung – Jüdische Spuren in Münchner Museen*, Nuremberg 2008, pp. 47–56.

15 Heinrich Voss, *Franz von Stuck. Werkkatalog der Gemälde*, Munich 1973, no. 309/450.

16 To provide some idea of the value in real terms of the amounts given here and elsewhere in this volume in Reichsmarks, Marks, and francs, together with an approximate equivalent of these sums in US dollars today, please see Appendix.

17 Barbara Staudinger (ed.), *From Bavaria to Eretz Israel. Tracing Jewish Folk Art*, exh. cat., Jewish Museum Munich, Munich 2007. Like Berolzheimer, Harburger was also a member of the Verein für Jüdisch Museen in Bayern e.V., see also the contribution by Bernhard Purin in this volume (pp. 123–29).

18 Saint Louis Art Museum, inv. no. 2:1946.

19 Antoinette Le Normand-Romain, *The Bronzes of Rodin, Catalogue of works in the Musée Rodin*, vol. 2, Paris 2007, pp. 639–40.

20 See foreword by Bruce Livie in *29 Drawings from the Michael Berolzheimer Collection Restituted by the Albertina*, Arnoldi-Livie cat. no. 27, 2011.

21 Bayerische Staatsgemäldesammlungen, archive no. 9/6a, no. 224, Bayerischer Verein der Kunstfreunde (Museums-Verein), e.V. in München

22 "Historical and modern miniatures and original artists' drawings" auctioned by the Kunstversteigerungshaus Adolf Weinmüller, Munich, on 03/09+10/1939. Items owned by Berolzheimer are marked with an * and A.

22 Adolf Feulner, *Die Sammlung Hofrat Sigmund Röhrer im Besitze der Stadt Augsburg*, Augsburg 1926.

ACQUISITION, THEFT, AND RESTITUTION: THE BEROLZHEIMER LEGACY IN RETROSPECT

"Only promise me that they shall have a handsome catalogue.
That will be my monument. I do not want any better."
Stefan Zweig, *The Invisible Collection*

In Stefan Zweig's well-known and touching fictional account of an unsung, elderly, German collector of splendid Old Master prints, the frail, blind gentleman tells the dealer/narrator that a catalogue of his collection, a printed testament to his gathering of masterworks, would be a sufficient memorial. It is not certain that Dr. Michael Berolzheimer (*fig. 1*) would have expected even that. However, when Zweig's old collector states with finality that: "I do not want any better," he expresses a modesty that would have found favor with Berolzheimer. A man who has left but a minimal written record of his thoughts regarding art, Berolzheimer's inclinations seem to manifest strongly in the works of art themselves, their nature and number. Not a classical catalogue of an art collection, this book and its essays endeavor instead to celebrate the life and achievement of Michael Berolzheimer, a remarkable and humble collector who has been all but forgotten because of the life-altering circumstances he experienced in Germany during the formative years of the Nazi terror. To do justice to his efforts as a collector and potential benefactor, but also to memorialize his stature as a respected and contributing member of pre-war German society, has required the labor of many individuals, who have meticulously investigated the whereabouts of his many possessions and pursued their restitution.

THE COLLECTOR IN CONTEXT

In many respects, Michael Berolzheimer's story is but another deeply disturbing tale of the Holocaust. Yet it is one now documented and enriched by recent research of a particularly thorough nature. As the number of Holocaust survivors precipitously diminishes, history is left to piece together what it can of the lives and possessions lost to the catastrophe.[1] In terms of "treasure," both lost and found, public interest is always piqued by an emphasis on those works by major

fig. 1 Michael Berolzheimer, c. 1939,
Little St. Simons Island, Georgia

Old Masters or even by artists who have come to international prominence since World War II—such as Gustav Klimt and Egon Schiele. The scholarly lives and humanistic inclinations of collectors, who devoted their time and knowledge to gathering and preserving highly significant objects of less than the highest monetary value, have often been sidelined in storytelling literature which is frequently more attracted to possessions than persons. Nonetheless, for subsequent generations, this literature has both brought the period to life, and for the sake of impact, neglected less iconic or fashionable (though no less fascinating or aesthetically significant) works of art. Such works were often the goal of knowledgeable and passionate collectors—amateur scholars of means—who were absolutely devoted to their pursuit.

Michael Berolzheimer, an attorney and serious avocational genealogist, was such a collector. Not one addicted to gathering trophies or the resident of palatial quarters intended to display large-scale paintings and sculpture, Berolzheimer was instead in pursuit of works of art that contributed to the understanding of a greater whole—of a culture, a period or a movement. The uniqueness or iconic status of a work did not seem to lure him, or so his collection suggests. In the course of his life, he assembled a notable group of prints and drawings, as well as works in other media. Among his prints were acknowledged masterpieces of graphic art. Of the collector's paintings, one of the most widely known is the oil study for the celebrated work *Der Arme Poet* (The Poor Poet; *fig.* 2), by the German Romantic painter Carl Spitzweg (1808–85). This small and charming painting sold at auction in 2012, fetching $542,500 for the benefit of family members.[2] Of course, there is much about Berolzheimer's possessions that we do not know, and yet much has been discovered through the persistent efforts of a group of researchers led by his dedicated great-nephew and namesake, Michael G. Berolzheimer.

It is clear from what has already been gleaned of Berolzheimer's works on paper that he was not a connoisseur in the Berensonian sense.[3] As an example, the hundreds of prints from his holdings that have been brought to light do not evidence the commitment to quality of impression which is so near and dear to

fig. 2   Carl Spitzweg, *The Poor Poet*, c. 1839, oil on paper on cardboard, sold at Sotheby's, New York, on January 26, 2012

the "art for art's sake" devotee. The unarguable attraction of engravings, etchings or woodcuts preserving the rich contrasts characteristic of early impressions, the seductive impact of burr and texture seen in the best drypoint examples, and those prints classically sought for their rarity and historical caché were really never Berolzheimer's focus. Yet, such stellar examples did exist among his holdings of graphic art. One may point to his selection of prints by Albrecht Dürer as an example. Some of these were evidently both known and noteworthy, as attested to by a piece of correspondence discovered by Gary Zimmerman of the Fiske Genealogical Library, Seattle. It is from the well-known dealer, Dr. von Faber du Faur of the famous Munich firm of antiquarian print and booksellers, Faber & Faber. In a letter of February 18, 1931, von Faber du Faur writes to Berolzheimer at his home in Untergrainau stating that he would be very pleased if he might be allowed to see Berolzheimer's "lovely collection of Dürers."[4] Yet, the evidence of the Berolzheimer collection of prints and drawings, as it has been pieced together, supports the notion that it was directed toward a gathering of prints from the whole range of European graphic art, as opposed to the selection of singular, splendid impressions. His was not the specialist's pursuit of a focused trove of material, but rather an alertness to random opportunities for acquisition. However, by no means should his broad interest in art be misinterpreted as having expressed itself in a capricious or haphazard approach to collecting. As a genealogist devoted to the study of his family and its heritage, Berolzheimer was of course concerned with groups and subgroups, with interrelationships and implications, and with keeping a written record of his pursuits and discoveries. As a trained attorney with a methodical orientation, it is also most likely that he made precise notes relating to his art acquisitions, possibly with comments on how they would serve to enrich the meaning of his growing collection. Typically, such notes would have included dates and costs of purchases.

Though quite unfortunate for our full understanding, the almost complete absence of the collector's written documentation may be the result of what was surely Berolzheimer's most legitimate fear of carrying any sort of documentation which the Nazis might have regarded as evidence of sequestered art assets. Such a discovery could have not only put an instant halt to the Berolzheimers' hurried emigration from Germany; it could have led to a concentration camp and worse. Nevertheless, the suspicion that such documentation may have existed is strengthened by the presence of Berolzheimer's notations on some of his genealogical papers, recording the scholarly catalogue numbers of certain works in his print collection.[5] However, even without a specific, annotated record of his collecting activities or a personal testament to his thoughts or desires, one may still find substantial clues to some presiding motivation in the nature of the collection itself.[6] It seems to have been the display of relationship between styles, movements, and themes in the work of both major and minor artists.

Collections of every period, despite their unique qualities, seem to fall into certain categories, largely determined by sociopolitical and economic conditions. As an example, between 1900 and 1930 a serious collection of drawings might commonly hold several thousand works. By the year 2000, it was more typical to find that good collections had been reduced to several hundred drawings. Artists with international reputations which have grown over the centuries and whose works always add luster to a collection, have most noticeably disappeared from regular availability. Also, scholarly opinions regarding the accuracy of attributions continue to change, with research and fashion making examples of authentic "master" works even harder to find and more costly to acquire.

In the field of print collecting, as differentiated from the pursuit of drawings, examples by the great masters of the medium, such as Dürer and Rembrandt, remained available throughout the twentieth century. However, particularly fine impressions, those revealing the characteristics of early printing, became ever more costly and, with certain intermittent exceptions, more rare to the market. Pursuing the acquisition of many examples that were representative, but not supreme as regards their relative aesthetic stature, was the path followed by Berolzheimer. His collection, as it has been reconstructed, testifies as well to his avoidance of what can be considered a "stamp-collecting orientation." Such collectors are disposed to focus almost maniacally on the integrity of the sheet (tears on the edges or, worse, those extending into the actual image, paper fills, etc.) as well as on the size of margins around the image (the larger, the better).

A collection's character and quality are often related to opportunities, and if stylistic and thematic relationships were the motivations, the actual opportunities may have been, in part, presented by familial as well as random associations. It is possible, for example, that Berolzheimer's wife, Melitta, had an influence on her husband's later collecting, for both her first husband, Eugen Schweisheimer, and her son (Michael's stepson), Robert, had works of art in their homes. Also, it is of some interest that Melitta's brother-in-law was the respected Munich art dealer Julius Drey, whose family had been in the art trade since the 1830s and whose relative, Paul, had owned a gallery in New York since 1920.[7] It seems unlikely that Berolzheimer and his brother-in-law, Julius, would not have discussed works of art on occasion. We do know that in 1906 Berolzheimer exchanged letters with his brother, Emil, regarding art. He wrote informing him of the opportunity to purchase works of art then for sale in Germany.[8] Aside from that letter, however, there is no reliably citable documentation of familial interchange regarding the collecting of works of art. Of course, that is not unexpected, as serious collecting is very commonly a private passion and the acquisition of works of art is often not discussed, especially among family members.

If frank discussion of the pragmatics of acquisition, logistics, and payment was restricted by discretion and/or the preservation of competitive advantage, there were nevertheless rich opportunities in Munich and its environs for sharing ideas and pleasure generated by works of art. Berolzheimer certainly took advantage of these opportunities and many visitors to the Berolzheimer homes in Munich and Untergrainau, documented in the guestbook (1904–13), must have enjoyed both his company and knowledge.[9] Signatures in the book testify as well to the visits of scholars and artists. They include the names of Josef Meder (1857–1934), the great Dürer expert whose well-respected book on drawings, *Die Handzeichnung*, first published in 1919, was to become a classic, as well as that of Max Lehrs (1855–1938), a famous print scholar whose writings were extremely influential in the study of the history of graphic art. Contemporary artists, though not the avant-garde, were also among the Berolzheimers' visitors (*see also pp. 88–93*).

Regarding the print collection as a whole, one might interpret Michael Berolzheimer's response to art as demonstrating an ethnographer's, as opposed to an art curator's, prejudice. That is, he seems to have been motivated to create a collection that would allow studying types and themes as opposed to focusing on

Das Berolzheimerianum 1906

fig. 3   The "Berolzheimerianum" in Fürth, 1906

fig. 4   The auditorium in the Berolzheimerianum, 1906

Ansicht des Vortragsaals im I. Stock gegen das Orchesterpodium.

aesthetic stature and/or rarity. The Berolzheimer print collection simply stresses the primacy of form and content that is the image itself rather than the media-mediated characteristics of its presentation or the state of its preservation.

As collectors go, evidence certainly suggests that Berolzheimer was of the more selfless variety. His inclinations were to share his passion and even works of art themselves with his family. When he and Melitta sent her son, Waldemar Schweisheimer (1889–1986), to the United States to re-establish himself as a physician, Berolzheimer offered a number of his better paintings as collateral in exchange for a four-year stipend from his brother's sons to insure that Schweisheimer and his family could sustain themselves. Also, in 1933, Berolzheimer gave two paintings to his brother Philip, one by Bramantino and the other attributed to Tintoretto.[10] He had owned the Bramantino since 1902.

It may well have been a family trait that personality was subsumed to celebrating or supporting the achievements of others, both living and dead. Berolzheimer's father, Heinrich, an honored native of Fürth in southern Germany, devoted much of his time to civic and charitable duties. Toward the end of his life, he established a kind of grand community center there, the "Berolzheimerianum" (fig. 3) and a similar institution, the "Luitpoldhaus" in Nuremberg.[11] Opening in 1906, the magnificent Berolzheimerianum was founded under an enlightened charter that decreed that it "serve the whole population of Fürth, regardless of social class, religion or political opinions, for the good of the people, the health of the people, the formation of the character, and the political education of the people." The Berolzheimerianum featured a reading room, a free public library (now with over 20,000 volumes) and an 800-seat auditorium (fig. 4). Heinrich also contributed financially to the founding of a Nuremberg art gallery, the "Künstlerhaus," which opened after his death in 1910.

Heinrich's children were similarly motivated toward the benefit of others. Philip Berolzheimer (1867–1942), Michael's younger brother and a New Yorker since his early youth, was described by *Time* magazine (May 28, 1923) as "having a deep, inarticulate devotion to culture that is characteristically Germanic. He tells you, simply and seriously that he has devoted himself to the advancement of music, but he cannot sing, play or compose, and must find his service in the organization of musical affairs; moreover, his philosophy is that musicians are as important people as politicians, big business men, generals or admirals."

Due to the vicissitudes of war, Berolzheimer was not able to fulfill himself philanthropically during his lifetime, as had his father and brother, but the record of his collection affirms that he was most probably on his way to doing so. The graphic arts seemed to have claimed his private devotion, but more publically he had served for a time as a member of the acquisitions committees of the Alte Pinakothek (*fig. 5*), the Munich Graphische Sammlung, and the Deutsche Orientalgesellschaft.

For Berolzheimer, works of art were to be studied as a reflection of a time, a place, and a culture; their provenance was of considerably less interest. There is much to admire in such an orientation, and today's historians are, more than ever, desirous of studying patterns of collecting among the cultural hunters and gatherers of society, for they see these individuals both as the exemplars of the taste and cultural values of their period and occasionally as the very force propelling changes of taste.

ESCAPE AND SACRIFICE

Michael Berolzheimer's drawings, comprising a smaller group of works within his collection than his prints, included both Old Master sheets as well as significant nineteenth-century studies attributed to both major and minor German artists. As a direct result of penalizing financial laws enacted to legalize the ethnic prejudices inflamed by the Nazis, the Berolzheimers, as Jews, were forced to take steps to dispose of the drawings just days before their emigration from Germany.[12] An auction sale was deemed necessary to generate funds to pay the various Nazi taxes imposed on them (*see p. 77*). The only collectors who benefited in prewar Germany were those who were prepared to take material advantage of such forced sales. Unfortunately, national collections were among the knowing exploiters of these ruinous, racist circumstances.

Berolzheimer was not a last-minute escapee. He and his wife departed Germany for Switzerland on July 25, 1938, prior to continuing to the United States in September that same year. This was late to be sure, but for a man of some influence, wealth, and connections, clearly not too late. However, the typically shocking price of departure was the extensive loss of properties and bank holdings to the Reich. Of course there was no choice. As hindsight made abundantly clear, it was literally a matter of losing one's country and worldly goods or almost certainly losing one's life. Essentially, individuals with means bought their way out, usually with little or nothing left to help begin life in the countries to which they fled. Fortunately, the Berolzheimer family's American business, the Eagle Pencil Company (later called the Berol Corporation in the late 1960s), and

fig. 5   The Alte Pinakothek art museum
in Munich, c. 1890

Michael's brother Philip's prominence in the New York business and political communities, provided him the contacts, if not the means, to begin life anew.

The Berolzheimer family had been in the pencil business in one form or another since the 1830s, and Michael's father, Heinrich Berolzheimer, from the age of twenty-three, had very successfully run the family firm of Berolzheimer and Illfelder in Fürth, before leaving Germany to set up the Eagle Pencil Company in 1869 in New York City. Having an American enterprise enabled the Berolzheimers to serve the growing market for pencils in the United States and to avoid the taxation applied to foreign imports that made German pencils too costly to compete. Eagle became a large company and America's leading pencil maker. In essence, Michael Berolzheimer, like his brothers Philip and Emil, represented the third generation of a manufacturing family that had put down multi-generational roots in both Germany and the United States. Of course, this history was in and of itself absolutely no guarantee of safety under the pathological Nazi laws. Many once-affluent Jews, Berolzheimer relatives and close friends among them, failed to respond decisively to the cascade of increasingly bleak events. Those who did not manage to emigrate went to their deaths not fully comprehending the degree of abject national dissolution and the growing danger they faced.

The sequence of events in the dispersal of the Berolzheimer drawings began on July 23, 1938, just two days prior to Michael's and Melitta's emigration, when Berolzheimer delegated power of attorney for his drawings and other possessions to his stepson, Robert Schweisheimer (later Sheridan). Berolzheimer's drawings, protected and studied by their owner for over forty years were, within a few months thereafter, handed over for sale by Robert to help generate 80,000 Reichsmarks (the amount that Berolzheimer was assessed to pay as his share of the Jewish registered assets taxes).[13]

Robert Schweisheimer had Dr. Ernst Wengenmayr, who worked with the Weinmüller auction firm in Munich, appraise Berolzheimer's collection of drawings as well as the prints left in the family home in Untergrainau. On October 10, 1938, George Keller of the Munich tax office became the Nazi regime's administrator for the confiscated Berolzheimer possessions. It is probable that, by early November 1938, Schweisheimer had received a contract from the Weinmüller auction gallery to include works from both the Berolzheimer and Schweisheimer collections in upcoming sales.[14] On November 30 and December 1, 1938, just months after the Berolzheimers had arrived in New York, and again from March 8 to 10, 1939, the Weinmüller firm in Munich conducted auctions that included most of Berolzheimer's known drawings.[15]

Curators of major German and Austrian museums flocked to the Weinmüller sale, and purchases were made by the National Gallery, Berlin (30 drawings); the Kunsthalle, Bremen (12 drawings); the Städel, Frankfurt (1 drawing); the Kurpfälzisches Museum, Heidelberg (9 drawings); the Kurfürstliches Museum, Mannheim (4 drawings); the Jagdmuseum, Munich (2 drawings); the Germanisches Nationalmuseum, Nuremberg (3 drawings); the Städtische Galerie im Lenbachhaus, Munich (12 drawings); the Albertina, Vienna (29 drawings); the Theatermuseum, Vienna (1 drawing); and the Landesmuseum, Weimar (4 drawings). There was very good reason for the curators attending the sale to have had misgivings about their purchases, for although the name Berolzheimer did not appear in the printed catalogue, a telling little asterisk was placed before all works that had come from Jewish collections.[16] Thus, the curators certainly understood what was going on, though they may not have known of the specific Berolzheimer provenance. Technically, of course, they were free to buy whatever they bid on successfully, as the sale was being conducted under the Nazi law of the land.

The deterioration of conditions in the final few months of 1938 marked a watershed moment in the degradations heaped upon German Jews and the history of German aggression. Hitler and his forces annexed Austria that year, and attacks on Jews markedly increased during the spring and summer of '38, capped by the "Reichskristallnacht" on November 9/10. This infamous "Night of Broken Glass," so called because attacks throughout Germany and Austria left streets of buildings with smashed windows, was in fact a nationwide pogrom against Jews and their property, covertly overseen by the authorities to make it appear as the eruption of pent-up, popular sentiment.[17]

The police simply looked on as Jewish homes, businesses, community centers, hospitals, and 267 synagogues were ransacked and burned by SA troops and an excited mob. In addition, approximately 100 Jews were killed and some 30,000 Jewish men arrested. Most of them were transferred to Buchenwald, Dachau, and other concentration camps. This national crime was portentous of the unthinkable evil to come as it marked the first time that the Nazis imprisoned

Jews for their ethnicity alone. Though some of those arrested on "Reichskristall-nacht" died from their brutal treatment in the camps, most were released under the condition that they prepare immediately for emigration. Hermann Göring's remark of November 12, 1938: "I would not like to be a Jew in Germany," had begun to morph from threat into action.[18] It is no wonder, then, that approximately 36,000 Jews fled Germany and Austria in 1938.

Of course, Michael and Melitta Berolzheimer were fortunate that they were able to emigrate to a nation of religious freedom and ethnic diversity, despite the shameful attitudes and practices retained in certain regions of the United States at the time of their arrival. Yet when one considers that Berolzheimer only lived for another four years after arriving in the United States, it gives pause for further appreciation of the consequences that such a wrenching dislocation as emigration, so late in life, can involve. For anyone with a realist's view, uprooting in life's later years has to signal the cessation of many hopes and dreams and requires a

fig. 6 Auguste Rodin, *St. John the Baptist*, 1878, bronze, height 6 ft. 7¼ in., now in the Saint Louis Art Museum

fortitude that the elderly can find hard to muster. This, in fact, was the case with many immigrants who arrived too old, tired, and beaten down to revive whatever strengths had helped them to fashion their younger years. Berolzheimer, at the age of seventy-two, had to have been discouraged and even shocked by the drastic diminishment of his life and influence, his loss of country, home, and possessions. Yet his early experience in the United States and the safe harbor provided by the American nation and his American family members must have provided his generous and pragmatic mind with a resigned comfort, which he well appreciated too few had been able to achieve.

Given the circumstances of his departure, it is extremely fortunate that Berolzheimer was able to get some 600 prints by Old Masters and later artists to the United States. Small works on paper were relatively easy to transport, although it is not known whether Berolzheimer and his wife, Melitta, carried them on their voyage or managed to have others transport them.

Amazingly, the couple's one major sculpture accompanied the Berolzheimers to their new country, exported as a mere garden statue. It was Rodin's *Saint Jean-Baptiste* (*fig. 6*), purchased directly from the artist himself, according to the family, and now in the collection of the Saint Louis Art Museum (*see also p. 54*).[19]

Recently, Berolzheimer's great-nephew and namesake, Michael G. Berolzheimer, presented a gift of 112 works to the Fine Arts Museums of San Francisco and seventy-two works to the Hawai'i Preparatory Academy in Kamuela on the island of Hawai'i in honor of his great-uncle. These significant selections of classical Western European graphic art from the Berolzheimer Collection were among those works taken by Michael and Melitta to the United States in 1938, and had been passed down through the family. The donation brings some closure to what we have good reason to assume would have been the lifetime direction of their collector.

The gift to the Fine Arts Museums of San Francisco provides a sense of the range in the Berolzheimer holdings. It includes a handsome sampling of early German prints, including four woodcuts by Hans Baldung Grien (1484–1545) and six engravings as well as six woodcuts by Albrecht Dürer (1471–1528). Italian works includes two prints by Andrea Mantegna (c. 1431–1506) and three by his school, thirty-three engravings by the Master of the Die (active in the sixteenth century), two engravings by Marcantonio Raimondi (1480–1534), and two etchings by Guido Reni (1575–1642). Among Dutch prints in the Berolzheimer gift are four engravings by Hendrik Goudt (1583–1648) after Adam Elsheimer and three engravings by Lucas van Leyden (1494–1533). Sixteen etchings by Rembrandt (1606–69) top off the Dutch contribution.

RESTITUTION STRUGGLES AND SUCCESSES

Beginning just after the war, survivors of the Holocaust commenced their efforts to claim their property from both individuals and German institutions. Retrieving the Berolzheimer drawings became the ongoing focus of the tedious and almost unavoidably frustrating restitution efforts that have occupied so many collectors and/or their heirs for more than half a century. Fundamentally these are struggles between the descendants of victims and representatives of the postwar "reset" governments and institutions of the perpetrators. Certain institutions adopted enlightened policies regarding restitution and should be so credited; others have been inclined to dig in their heels. It is well to remember that even with negotiations that have resulted in the return of stolen possessions, many collectors, Berolzheimer among them, never lived to be reunited with their possessions. In some cases, Berolzheimer's included, it has required more than one generation of family tenacity to dislodge works from what German and international law have, by now, judged their illegal owners. Some chapters in this publication deal with the gathering of evidence for the restitution of master drawings from the Berolzheimer Collection, and also document the often-contorted trails that such investigation reveals.

Critical to proving Berolzheimer's ownership of the drawings that the Nazis had forced him to sell was the presence of a little inked imprint, called a collector's stamp, on many of his sheets. Most major collectors of the past four centuries marked their works on paper with such unique stamps, usually printed on the back (verso) of prints or drawings. These were intended as perpetual evidence of the linkage of a particular work with a particular collector at a particular time. Collector's stamps are one way of tracing the often fascinating path a print or drawing has traveled through time to its present whereabouts. As one might expect, there are reference volumes dedicated to listing and discussing these marks and the holdings of the collections they represented. Though Berolzheimer's drawings could not be identified by any stamp of his own, it happened that he purchased a large number of works from one collection, which had been dispersed at auction in 1895 by the Hugo Helbing firm in Munich.[20] The auction included drawings assembled over a twenty-five year period by a nineteenth-century collector in Dresden, Boguslav Jolles. The Jolles Collection was rich in drawings by artists of the Dresden School, and—most significantly for identifying sheets purchased by Berolzheimer—Jolles stamped the back of his drawings. The stamp is recorded in the principal tome identifying collector's stamps, Fritz Lugt's magnum opus, *Les marques de collections de dessins & d'estampes,* as nos. 381–82.

Attempts to prepare for the restitution of Berolzheimer's drawings and other sections of his collection began in 1947 and 1948. Robert Held was the American attorney for Dr. Waldemar Schweisheimer, Berolzheimer's stepson, now deceased, and executor of Melitta's and Michael's estates. Held was assisted in Germany by attorney Alfred Holl of Munich.

Held corresponded with representatives of the military government for Germany, first requesting in April 1947, on behalf of Schweisheimer, that the Berolzheimer works be traced and that, in particular, a canvas by the important German painter Anselm Feuerbach (1829–80) be located.[21] Held refers to the 1939 Weinmüller auction and suggests that a copy of the sale's catalogue, which included many of Berolzheimer's works, could certainly be found.[22]

In the aftermath of the war, there were the usual denials of culpability, with both innocent and guilty parties telling similar stories. Often the evidence was provided by recovering a written record, but not always. Testimony from participating parties was sought. As the responsibility for the acceptance of and cataloguing of the Berolzheimer drawings in 1938 had been that of Ernst Wengenmayr, his written testimony was officially requested. Wengenmayr had been in charge of artistic research at the Weinmüller auction house and, in that capacity, had presided over the evaluation of the Berolzheimer collection.

fig. 8   Bernardino Lanino, *The Church Fathers Ambrose and Gregory*, 1560–64; study for a fresco in San Magno in Legnano, near Milan; brush in brown and light gray with brown wash, heightened with white on blue paper, restituted by the Albertina, Vienna

In a statement to the Landesamt fur Vermogensverwaltung (March 5, 1947) investigating the circumstances of the Berolzheimer sale, he wrote that it was Professor Dr. Heinrich Leporini who catalogued the Berolzheimer collection for the Weinmüller sale. Given Leporini's scholarly reputation and curatorial position at the Albertina in Vienna, this statement seems suspect, as do many other statements in Wengenmayr's testimony. Leporini was a known Nazi sympathizer, and his was one of the Art Looting Intelligence Unit's "red flag names," for he is reported to have removed anti-Nazi staff members and modern works of art from the Albertina.[23] No matter whether or not Leporini was complicit in helping Wengenmayr or the Weinmüller firm dispose of Berolzheimer drawings, it is not surprising that Wengenmayr was trying to place himself safely above blame for the forced sale of Jewish Art. When Weinmüller himself was interviewed a few days later, he made several statements conflicting with Wengenmayr's testimony.

In the recovery process of the immediate postwar period, seven portfolios containing eighty-six works were turned over by Wengenmayr to the authorities pursuing Waldemar Schweisheimer's claims. Most of these were twentieth-century prints, many by Jewish artists who had interested Berolzheimer, such as Emil Orlik and Eric Wolfsfeld. In addition, twenty-seven empty portfolios were also returned. It has not been ascertained what these portfolios contained. Most probably, it was material that was included in the 1939 auction. However, there is the possibility that the portfolios contained unsold works that were retained after the auction and have not been located. What is certain is that not all of Berolzheimer's works included in the 1939 sale have as yet been located, and may well never be.

Crucially, and in a matter-of-fact manner that belies the obvious satisfaction in his discovery, Held notes in a letter of June 28, 1948, that he had located Berolzheimer works from the Weinmüller sale in the collection of the Albertina, and he cites their numbers in the Weinmüller catalogue as well as their Albertina inventory numbers.[24] Evidence enough. So, the obvious question that arises is why did more than sixty years elapse between the time of Robert Held's discovery and the conclusion of this matter, with the return of the drawings to the family of their rightful owner?

In a move that appears unexpected and difficult to understand today, research has revealed that in 1951, Waldemar Schweisheimer declared his restitution claims to be *erledigt* (settled). This is surprising considering that his attorney, Held, had filed and begun to pursue claims against a number of museums for the return of the Berolzheimer drawings. In discussing this potentially disappointing discovery, there are two possible explanations for Schweisheimer's declaration at the time.[25] One is that some of the Berolzheimer drawings had been removed to the Soviet Union as war booty, as had many thousands of works of art belonging to museums and private collectors. Given the onset of the Cold War, this would have, of course, presented an impossible stalemate in terms of restitution. The other is that some of the Berlin drawings were in East Germany at the time (the early 1950s), an equally uncompromising site in terms of likely restitution. These suggestions from today's cooperative German authorities, though not definitive, help to provide insight into the complexities of immediate postwar negotiations between individual claimants and states under physical and cultural repair and political reorganization.

Despite the 1950s impasse resulting from the *erledigt* declaration, which effectively halted efforts to return works from the Albertina in Vienna and the National Gallery in Berlin to the Berolzheimer family, Schweisheimer did have success in effecting restitution (either by return of the drawings or compensation payments) to the family by three other institutions.

In June 1950, three years after Held initially contacted the Städtische Galerie im Lenbachhaus in Munich, the museum became one of the first public institutions to agree to restitution, returning the twelve drawings that it had purchased from the Weinmüller auction in 1939. Works from this group included two drawings by Gustav Canton (1813–85); two by Bonaventura Genelli (1798–1868); two by Peter von Hess (1792–1871); one by Christoph Maurer (1558–1614); and two by Eugen Neureuther (1806–82)—all German artists—and three drawings by the

Austrian Moritz von Schwind (1804–71).[26] In addition to the Lenbachhaus, the Kurpfälzisches Museum in Heidelberg, and the Germanisches Nationalmuseum in Nuremberg also cooperated in successful negotiations.[27]

Waldemar Schweisheimer's cases against private individuals who had acquired Berolzheimer drawings at Weinmüller were not as successful. He filed claims against Dr. Albert Hügelin of Ebershausen, as well as against a Dr. Graff, who had both bought drawings at the sale. On June 8, 1953, the decision of the German Court assigned to such cases (the Wiedergutmachungskammer) was that Schweisheimer's claims against both these individuals were "baseless."[28] It is interesting to reconsider these two judgments in the light of the works listed in the dispute. Hügelin's group of nine works included sheets assigned to artists such as Claes Berchem, Gaetano Gandolfi, Johann Rottenhammer, and Alexandrine Calame. Graff's group included works supposedly by Albert Cuyp, Allart van Everdingen, Jan van Goyen, Claude Lorrain, and Rembrandt.[29]

Considering the names of the artists and their considerable fame, it seems rather shocking that the claims were rejected as "baseless" because of low value.[30] It was a judgment that suggested the effort was not worthy of the court's, the

claimant's or the defendants' time. Setting aside for the moment the question of whether or not the attributions of the drawings would be judged as correct by today's academic standards, it is true that, at the time of the case, drawings in general were remarkably inexpensive. However, sheets by the greatest names had value that was certainly not negligible. Thus, in good conscience, drawings believed to be by Claude Lorrain, Rembrandt, and Albert Cuyp, as examples, really could not be dismissed responsibly as of minimal value. The court, in effect, was saying that these drawings, that admittedly belonged to "your stepfather" and that were purchased from a forced sale, do not have sufficient value to be worth the effort of being returned to the family. However, in reading the documents and considering their judgments, there is a sense of annoyance on the part of the court which seems reflective of the mindset of some sectors of postwar German governance. At least in retrospect, the unseemly implication, however subtle, that the pursuit of Jewish possessions was an imposition that was resented and would not be encouraged, seems manifest. To be sure, anti-Semitism of the almost unprecedented virulence which had been inculcated for over a decade was not to be eradicated merely by an Allied military victory.

fig. 10 Carl Spitzweg (1808–85), *A Compendium of Humorous Figures, some Relating to the Artist's Paintings,* n.d., graphite, restituted by the Kupferstichkabinett Berlin

NOT FORGOTTEN: RESTITUTION EFFORTS
IN THE TWENTY-FIRST CENTURY

A half-century had passed since Waldemar Schweisheimer's unsuccessful attempt to restitute his stepfather's drawings from two of Europe's most important cultural institutions, Vienna's Albertina and Berlin's National Gallery, when in February 2000, Maren Gröning of the Albertina requested information from the Holocaust Victim's Information and Support Center of the Jewish Community of Vienna (HVISC) regarding Berolzheimer, Waldemar Schweisheimer, and their heirs.[31] In March of 2000, Gröning was informed by HVISC that they had located the family of Schweisheimer and, in May of that year, Gröning completed her listing of the Berolzheimer drawings held by the Albertina. In June 2001, the Austrian Federal Ministry for Education, Arts, and Culture (AFMEAC) requested any information that HVISC could provide regarding the heirs of Dr. Michael Berolzheimer.

Four years later, in 2005, the HVISC inquired whether the Albertina was still pursuing the quest for Berolzheimer heirs. The answer was yes, and the HVISC continued its search. In May 2007, the HVISC was able to provide the AFMEAC with the death certificates of Waldemar Schweisheimer and his wife, Irmgard, along with Waldemar's probate file, and the names of his two heirs— his grandchildren, Michael Thrope and Douglas Sherwood. Other heirs were identified during 2009, and their names and status forwarded by the Department of Restitution Affairs of the Jewish Community of Vienna to the AFMEAC, including the probate files of Berolzheimer's other stepchildren and heirs, Nelly Friedberg and Robert Sheridan, as well as the death certificate of Anna J. Sheridan, (Robert's widow).

Finally, in August 2009, an expert opinion could be rendered detailing the legal succession of Dr. Michael Berolzheimer. The opinion enumerated the seven rightful heirs as Michael Thrope, Douglas P. Sherwood, Erica Ruth Friedberg, Ernest Michael Friedberg, Suzanne Schiessel, Max Eugene Friedberg and the Anna J. Sheridan 1999 Revocable Trust.[32] To effect a transfer of drawings formerly purchased by the Albertina to these heirs, signed powers of attorney and statements of liabilities had to be submitted to the AFMEAC. This was completed in May 2010, and the Federal Ministry was then able to permit the Albertina to release the drawings at issue to Michael Friedberg, the representative of the rightful heirs of Dr. Michael Berolzheimer.

In 2010, Vienna's Albertina Museum (one of the world's greatest public collections of Old Master drawings), restituted twenty-nine drawings to the Berolzheimer family—some seventy years after the initial attempts to retrieve the works. The transfer of these drawings to the Berolzheimer descendants concluded a decade-long process of extensive research and documentation by the HVISC, conducted from February 2000 to February 2009, and from 2009 by the Department for Restitution Affairs of the Jewish Community of Vienna. To mark the occasion and memorialize the collector, in 2011, the Arnoldi-Livie Gallery, a fine art dealer in Munich, prepared a catalogue of the drawings. The gallery sold the works on behalf of the family, allowing the rightful heirs of Berolzheimer to finally dispose of their patrimony as they themselves chose (*figs 7, 8*).

The history of the Berolzheimer drawings purchased by the National Gallery in Berlin provides a more poignant look at the tangled path of the restitution process and the diligence required by multiple generations of the family seeking justice. The National Gallery purchased thirty-two works at the Weinmüller sale, thirty of them from the Berolzheimer consignment, and the director who attended the sale was obviously pleased with his acquisitions, reporting back to his museum that: "…I think I have bought quite well overall."[33] Apparently, two of the works purchased (Weinmüller catalogue no. 670 by Friedrich Kaiser and no. 810 by Friedrich Daniel Reichel) were lost during the war, either destroyed or perhaps removed to the Soviet Union as were most, if not all, the Berolzheimer Berlin drawings. However, claims specialist Rebecca Friedman of New York State's Holocaust Claims Processing Office cautions: "Experience has taught us to regard postwar allegations by art dealers (particularly those, like Weinmüller, who were intimately tied to the Nazi machinery and notorious for selling Jewish art), that works of art were destroyed either during or in the aftermath of World War II, with skepticism."

Robert Held's correspondence from the late 1940s on behalf of Waldemar Schweisheimer eventually led to a case being brought against the National Gallery in 1949 for the return of Berolzheimer property. However, as discussed previously, the matter was declared "settled" in 1951. Recent research, documented in a letter from Carola Thielecke of the National Gallery's Prussian Cultural Heritage Foundation (Stiftung Preussischer Kulturbesitz), and summarized in the following discussion, provides the history.[34]

Thielecke writes: "The only reason we know that the works from the Berolzheimer collection were among those that went to Russia is that they have Russian numbering on the back. We don't have a concise list telling us what exactly the Russian army removed. Also, we don't know exactly what is still in Russia."[35] Of the remaining twenty-eight Berolzheimer works identified in the collection of the National Gallery in Berlin, nineteen were originally from the Jolles Collection and bore the distinctive collector's mark. Thielecke reports that the National Gallery recently investigated the "settled" declaration of 1951, in order to determine whether the institution may have paid damages at the time—the point being not to compensate the heirs twice (by returning the drawings and paying money). Once the museum confirmed that the Berolzheimer claim had certainly *not* been settled in 1951, the museum expressed its willingness to find a fair and just solution to the situation. In 2012, the Arnoldi-Livie Gallery prepared another testamentary catalogue.[36] It featured twenty-eight drawings restituted by the Berlin Museum of Prints and Drawings (Kupferstichkabinett), part of the National Gallery and the largest collection of graphic art in Germany (*figs 9, 10, 11, 12*).[37]

In negotiating the possibility of restitution, the National Gallery was initially concerned that it would not be able to differentiate Berolzheimer from Schweisheimer property so as to effect proper restitution, but Thielecke notes that they appreciated that the heirs might be identical. As it turned out, all of the restituted drawings were from the Berolzheimer collection.

In addition to the Albertina, Vienna and the National Gallery, Berlin, a few other institutions have been forthcoming in their desire to restitute Berolzheimer drawings. The Landesmuseum in Weimar purchased four sheets at the Weinmüller auction. They were an ink drawing by Friedrich Preller of Tivoli (lot 805), a drawing by Moritz von Schwind, *Design for the Fairytale of the Seven Ravens* (lot 880), and two ink drawings by Karl Sprosse, *Interior of the Castle Chapel of*

fig. 11 Gustav Adolf Friedrich (1824–89),
A Farmer Plowing, watercolor, restituted by the
Kupferstichkabinett Berlin

Altenbur, and *Cathedral of Speyer* (lot 905). In the latter half of 2011, the Landesmuseum requested help finding the Berolzheimer heirs. This, of course, signaled
their willingness to consider restitution. At the time of writing (spring 2014), the
restitution process has been successfully completed.

Without the Jolles collector's stamp and without, in its stead, the existence of
photographic documentation of individual drawings or prints, paperwork or
snapshots of rooms that included an image of a disputed work of art, substanti-
ating the claim of the Berolzheimer family would have been far more difficult
and, in some cases, perhaps impossible. Nevertheless, despite the invaluable
evidence established by the presence of a collector's stamp and the undisputed
aid that it provided the investigators who sought to establish the Berolzheimer
ownership of drawings, the fact that Berolzheimer did not design or employ a
collector's stamp of his own is, in and of itself, the most persuasive evidence of
his orientation as a collector. It reinforces the contention that his prints and
drawings were collected to constitute an informative gathering of cultural relics

rather than to stand as a testament to some then-current fashion of refined taste or as a way of perpetuating a self-imagined link to artistic genius.

As the elderly collector in Stefan Zweig's tale had lost his eyesight and, unbeknown to him, his beloved collection as well, Berolzheimer lost his native country together with a substantial portion of his collection. These were profound losses, to be sure, representing many years of knowledgeable effort, financial commitment and undoubtedly dreams of donation. Yet, circumstances and the moral compass of a dedicated descendant have moved assiduously to identify and recover as many of Berolzheimer's scattered possessions as possible. This chapter provides only an overview of the work of discovery and restitution and the revelations that have resulted. One of the remarkable organizations engaged in these efforts is discussed by Rebecca Friedman of the New York Holocaust Claims Processing Office in her essay in this publication (*see pp. 207–13*).

Her work and essay as well as this chapter are, of course in a larger sense, a reminder and indictment of the political crimes against millions of innocents directed by an abominably evil and historically disgraced regime. However, these pages are also a celebration of the largely successful efforts on behalf of and in the memory of one man, Michael Berolzheimer, to right a terrible wrong.

fig. 12 Ferdinand Anton Krüger, *St. Maurus*, 1827, graphite; restituted from the Kupferstichkabinett Berlin

1 As this essay is being written, the death at 108 of the world's oldest Auschwitz survivor, a non-Jewish Polish citizen, Antoni Dobrowolski, has been reported by the Associated Press. See: http://www.dailynews.com/news/ci_21828097/worlds-oldest-survivor-auschwitz-concentration-camp-dies-at

2 See Sotheby's catalogue, *Important Old Master Paintings and Sculpture*, 01/26/2012, lot 84, listed only as "property from a Private Collection," but with a provenance that cites Dr. Michael Berolzheimer. This painting was apparently sold to a Professor Meissner in the November 30–December 2 Weinmüller sale, cat. 18, no. 158. This work was restituted to Dr. Berolzheimer's executor, stepson Waldemar Schweisheimer through his representative, Dr. Alfred Holl, in 1948. See Holl's letter of 09/16/1948, in Records concerning the Central Collecting Points ("Ardelia Hall Collection"), Munich Central Collecting Point, 1945–51, Restitutions Claim Records, Jewish Claims, numbered 0043–0044, p. 174: http://www.fold3.com/document/270071609/

3 Bernard Berenson (1865–1969) was a Lithuanian-born, American art connoisseur of legendary distinction who–though a graduate of Harvard–was self-educated in the history of art. More a diagnostician than a historian, he became a prolific writer of scholarly tomes, and through his association with the immensely talented, though famously self-aggrandizing dealer, Joseph Duveen, became very wealthy. Berenson's opinion on the attribution of early Italian through Renaissance paintings was sought internationally, and a high percentage of his attributions have stood the test of time. His reputation stands tarnished in the opinions of those who view the fact that he was beholden to Duveen for his livelihood as being in conflict with the impeccable impartiality that should govern acts of attribution. Others find his achievement remarkable and do not begrudge him his affiliation with a merchant and its implications for scholarly compromise.

4 The Berolzheimer Collection, Fiske Genealogical Library Archives, 1325–1942.

5 Such an example was recently called to our attention, also by Gary Zimmerman of the Fiske Library, who noted a listing in Berolzheimer's hand of prints by Agostino di Musi after Raphael on the verso of one of the collector's genealogical drafts. This listing includes the Barstch (catalogue raisonné) numbers of the listed prints.

6 The Berolzheimer Collection, as it is now understood, has been reconstructed from the prints that either accompanied him to the United States when he immigrated in 1939 (and there is the possibility that some were sent to the States at an earlier time or accompanied Berolzheimer on an earlier trip, such as that of 1937), from those drawings illegally acquired by German and Austrian institutions and returned to the Berolzheimer heirs through restitution, and from family sales at public auction.

7 The heirs of a number of prominent German Jewish art dealers of the prewar period have been in the news in the last decade with regard to their own efforts to have works returned that were forced from their families. See: Melissa Müller and Monika Tatzkow, *Lost Lives, Lost Art/Jewish Collectors, Nazi Art Theft and the Quest for Justice*, New York 2010. To appreciate the decades-long pursuit that can transpire, the text (pp. 10–27) presents a discussion of the restitution challenges faced by Lily Cassirer in an ongoing fight to retrieve one of the Cassirer paintings, Camille Pissarro's *Rue de Saint Honoré*. Legal proceedings were initiated by Lily after the war, and the German government conceded her ownership in 1958. At the time, the painting was still missing, and so she was paid 120,000 Marks in compensation for suffering and provided papers acknowledging that she retained full rights to the work. By the time of her death in 1962, the Pissarro painting had still not been found. It was only at the very beginning of this century that *Rue de Saint Honoré* turned up and was noticed in a book on Pissarro by a friend of Cassirer's heir. Listed as belonging to the Thyssen Collection, itself now part of the Spanish National Collections, it has been the focus of the Cassirer ownership debate for the last twelve years.

8 Letter from Dr. Michael Berolzheimer from Munich, dated 11/03/1906, with a personal typographic letterhead and with the address Franz-Joseph-Strasse 21/III.

9 Berolzheimer Untergrainau guestbook, property of Anita Sheridan, Fairfield, California.

10 See letter of 05/29/1933, from Berolzheimer to Philip Berolzheimer with provenance and other information relating to the two paintings. Other art objects collected by Philip can be found in Philip Berolzheimer's art inventory books located in the Berolzheimer Family Archives (California Cedar Products Company Archives) in Stockton, California. Upon Charles' death, the family sold the two paintings at auction.

11 For an introductory discussion of the Berolzheimerianum, see R. Bruce Livie, "Forward" in: *29 Drawings from the Michael Berolzheimer Collection Restituted by the Albertina*, Gallerie Arnoldi-Livie, Munich, and *Berolzheimerianum: "100 Year Anniversary Celebration"* on: Pencil Community website: http://community.pencils.com/content/berolzheimerianum-100-year-anniversary-celebration

12 The confiscatory taxes imposed by the Reich in 1938 were intended to eliminate gradually all Jewish participation in German financial life of any kind. The impact was not only to stifle Jewish business but also to make responsibilities associated with the personal lives of Jews and their families painfully hard, if not impossible, to fulfill. Part of the greater program of Aryanization, these taxes followed five years of pressure to liquidate Jewish businesses, and by the end of spring 1938, in fact, 60–70% of all German Jewish businesses had been liquidated. This incredible situation followed the *Decree on the Registration of the Property of Jews* of 04/26/1938. Only seven months later, on November 12, the compulsory stage of Aryanization began with the imposition of the racially accusatory *Suhneleistung* (Atonement Tax). It was 20%, (later raised to 25%) on registered assets of Jews. Another tax of 25% on registered assets, the *Reichsfluchtsteuer* (Escape Tax or Reich Flight Tax), was imposed on Jews sufficiently panicked and/or prescient to leave Germany, but also (most cruelly) on those who were deported to concentration camps outside Germany. The final nails in the coffin of Jewish economic survival were the regulations following these taxes that prohibited all Jewish economic activity except for services applicable soley to Jews. Also, all Jewish businesses were placed under government control so that their sale to Germans was the only way of realizing a pittance in remuneration, as a large portion of the sales price was to be taken by the government. These taxes are clearly discussed and summarized in "Expropriation (Aryanization) of Jewish Property" under: http://www.edwardvictor.com/Holocaust/Expropriation.htm

13 To provide some idea of the value in real terms of the amounts given here and elsewhere in this volume in Reichsmarks, and some approximate equivalent of these sums in US dollars today, please see Appendix.

14 See: Staatarchiv Munich WB1a4347; see also Meike Hopp, *Kunsthandel Im Nationalsozialismus/Adolf Weinmüller in München und Wein*, Cologne 2012.

15 It is worthy of note that there seemed to be no further acquisitions of drawings by the collector on the scale of the 1895 purchase of Jolles' works at Helbing. This fact almost certainly indicates that Berolzheimer had taken a conscious decision to limit his graphic art collection to prints.

16 Petra Winter (see also note 33) has researched the asterisk in the Weinmüller catalogue and states: "It was required since April 1938 by the National Socialists to distinguish works consigned by Jews." It was "meant to prevent efforts to hide before the State any liquidation of Jewish wealth through dissolution of households and the sale of valuables like art objects."

17 Regarding the Reichskristalnacht see: http://www.ushmm.org/wlc/en/article.php?ModuleId=10005201 and for a summary of events in 1938, see United States Holocaust Museum website: http://www.ushmm.org/wlc/en/article.php?ModuleId=10005468

18 The transcription for this remark appears in the Stenographische Niederschrift (Teilübertragung) der interministeriellen Konferenz im Reichsluftfahrtministerium (11/12/1938); see: http://germanhistorydocs.ghidc.org/docpage.cfm?docpage_id=2409&language=german

19 The Saint Louis Art Museum's cast (accession no. 2.1946) was purchased through Kurt Valentin, an eminent New York private dealer representing the Berolzheimer family. It was on extended loan to and exhibited in the sculpture garden of the Museum of Modern Art in New York from 1941 to 1945 and again in 1953 in an exhibition "Sculpture of the Twentieth Century." http://www.moma.org/docs/press_archives/1888/releases/MOMA_1955_0003_1a.pdf?2010

20 It may be that Berolzheimer's purchase of drawings at the 1895 Helbing sale comprised most of the studies that he came to own, for it seems that subsequent purchases of drawings, if any, did not add greatly to the numbers substantiated by the Jolles and Helbing provenance. His interest after the Jolles sale seemed to be focused on prints.

21 Letter of 04/25/1947, from Robert O. Held to the Office of Military Government for Germany (U.S.). See Holocaust Collection, Ardelia Hall Collection: Wiesbaden Administrative Records; Restitution Claim records, Claim [United States]-Internal Restiitution (cases 51–128) case 71, Held to MFAA. (Note: The Wiesbaden Central Collecting Point was the site for deposit of mostly German-owned works of art subject to restitution). It is interesting to note that from the time of its delivery to the official U.S. Collecting point in Wiesbaden to its restitution to Dr. Waldemar Schweisheimer in the United States, just over five years elapsed (10/13/1945–11/13/1950). Research in response to Held's request discovered that the painting by Feurbach remained unsold at the Weinmüller auction, but was subsequently purchased by the Reichskanzlei for 6,500 Reichsmarks for eventual inclusion in Hitler's museum, planned for Linz, Austria. In June 1949, the painting was restituted to Waldemar Schweisheimer, acting as executor of the Berolzheimer estate. See Bundesarchiv, Koblenz B 323/663; inventory card 9038.

22 Ibid.: Held.

23 See records of the American Commission for the Protection and Salvage of Artistic and Historical Monuments in War Areas (The Roberts Commission), 1943–1946 "Subject File" Art Looting Investigation Unit: Final Report, p. 58. Also: http://www.lootedart.com/MVI3RM469661

24 Op. cit. (note 21): Holocaust Collection.

25 See letter from Carola Thielecke (in-house lawyer to Michael G. Berolzheimer, 22/12/2010, p. 2).

26 Irene Netta, Collections Archives, Städtische Galerie im Lenbachhaus, Munich.

27 A letter from Holl of 10/10/1950, mentions the three works restituted by the Germanisches Nationalmuseum, Nuremberg, though a final settlement did not occur until October 19.

28 Op. cit. (note 21): Bundesarchiv, Koblenz, pp. 1–9. Court decision made by the Wiedergutmachungskammer.

29 Budesarchiv, Koblenz, Bestand B 323/360.

30 Op. cit. (note 16).

31 The Albertina, Vienna, had been cooperative with restitution efforts even before the much publicized Washington Agreement of 2001 that concluded the Claims Conference. The agreement compelled Austria to face the wartime persecution of its Jewish Community.

32 The chronology and names included in the process of restitution summarized in this text are entirely based on a letter from Eva Holpfer, Abteilung für Restitutionsangelegenheiten (Department for Restitution Affairs) Jewish Community, Vienna, Austria, to Michael G. Berolzheimer, 08/10/2010.

33 See: Rave's correspondence with Perlwitz, Nationalgalerie, 03/10/1939, SMB-ZA, I/NG 874, sheet 85 (see also pp. 197–204).

34 Carola Thielecke, letter to Michael G. Berolzheimer, 12/12/2010.

35 Ibid. Thielecke quotes a report from Max Heiss, a Nazi bureaucrat employed by the Landeskulturverwalter, which states: "Weinmüller was commissioned by the fiduciary for the Jews, Berolzheimer and Schweisheimer installed by the Devisenstelle (foreign currency bureau), Herr Keller, to auction the cultural property of these two Jews. In the case of Berolzheimer, this concerned an important collection of graphic art, in the case of Schweisheimer several good paintings, including a preliminary oil sketch for Spitzweg's picture 'The Poor Poet.'' Heiss was incorrect in that it was Berolzheimer, not Schweisheimer, who owned *The Poor Poet*.

36 Of the twenty-eight drawings, twenty-four works were offered for sale. The remaining four were retained by the family.

37 Staatliche Museen zu Berlin, Collections/Institutes. http://www.smb.museum/smb/sammlungen/details.php?lang=en&objID=8&n=1&r=7http://www.smb.museum/smb/sammlungen/details.php?lang=en&objID=8&n=1&r=7

THE FATE OF THE
BEROLZHEIMER COLLECTION

fig. 1   Joseph Anton Koch (1769–1839), *Study of an Ash Tree*, n.d., graphite, black and brown chalk, restituted by the Albertina, Vienna

Between 1895 and 1938, Michael Berolzheimer assembled a diverse art collection consisting of more than 800 Old Master and 19th-century European drawings and watercolors. Added to this was a group of over 1,000 Old Master and modern prints by German and other European artists of the 15th to early 20th centuries, along with a small group of paintings and a few 19th-century sculptures, including Auguste Rodin's *St. John the Baptist*, now in the Saint Louis Museum of Art, Missouri, USA. However, just as Berolzheimer's commitment to the arts and culture has since faded into oblivion, so has the knowledge of his extensive collection.

In June 1938, in the face of the ever increasing persecution of Jews by the Nazi regime, the Berolzheimers applied for permission to emigrate to the United States. Not only did Berolzheimer have to pay a substantial government levy before being granted an exit visa, his art collection also had to be valued. A representative of the "Reichskulturkammer" (Reich Chamber of Culture), Dr. Ernst Wengenmayr, went to Untergrainau to determine which artworks of "German cultural value" were to stay in the country. As mentioned in other essays in this volume, it was these works which were sold at the two auctions in 1938 and 1939.

Back in October 1895, a collection of artworks owned by Boguslav Jolles of Dresden was auctioned by the art gallery and auction house Hugo Helbing in Munich (*fig. 2*). This sale provided Berolzheimer with the initial impetus to build up a collection of prints and drawings.[1] With the purchase of almost 600 sheets on that occasion, Berolzheimer established the basis of his own collection. Through this sale, Helbing—who was reputed to be a very suave, knowledgable, influential, and tenacious salesman—created a long-standing, loyal customer in Berolzheimer.

The purchase of the Jolles drawings collection provided Michael Berolzheimer with an important group of works, to which he added many others. His collection of graphic art and works on paper ultimately formed what may be considered one of the major, private collections of its type in southern Germany in the first half of the twentieth century. With the acquisition of such a large number of prints and drawings, Berolzheimer also gained the respect of his peers as a collector, likely contributing to his appointment as honorary member of the

The Jolles Collection

Who was Boguslav Jolles and why was his collection of prints and drawings auctioned in 1895? There is very little information about Jolles himself. The only official document known is his death certificate, mentioned in a Swiss court order concerning a claim entered by his grandson, Hans Eppenberger, showing that Jolles died on July 17, 1912, in Dresden.² The Jolles family lived in Berlin between 1855 and 1864, where Boguslav's father, Ber, is listed in the municipal address book as a banker and the proprietor of a transport company.³ Operating later under the name "Jolles & Co.," he built up a plant for artificially manufacturing carbonated water, and also traded in champagne and fruit juice.

At the end of the 1860s, Ber Jolles and his family moved to Dresden where he is mentioned in the city's address books in 1869 and 1870 as a "Privatier (Particulier)"—"a gentleman of independent means." From 1869–72, Boguslav lived with his parents at An der Elbe 20, to the south of the river, in a park fronting the water. From 1871 through 1874, Boguslav is listed as a factory director, which would suggest that he was probably born around 1845, and between 1875 and 1893, worked as a building contractor in Dresden.⁴

Although no evidence exists to date, Boguslav's father may well have started collecting prints and drawings while living in Berlin, which at that time enjoyed a reputation as a center of the arts. Ber died in 1874 and was buried in the New Jewish Cemetery in Dresden.⁵ Twenty years later, Boguslav was registered at Rabenerstrasse 5, and recorded as being a banker in 1894–96 and an engineer from 1897 onward. If is fair to assume that he sold his parents's house and disposed of its contents some time before 1895—the year the collection was sold through Helbing.

Acquisitions Committee at the Alte Pinakothek and the Prints Collection in Munich. Judging from the enthusiastic entries in Berolzheimer's guestbook, he loved to show his collection to his often knowledgable guests in Munich and later in Untergrainau, where Rodin's bronze statue could be admired in the garden (*see p. 54*).

When the decree was issued in April 1938 by the Nazis ordering all Jewish property to be registered, the Berolzheimers made final preparations for their emigration. They left Untergrainau on July 25, 1938, as recorded in a note from the District Authority in Garmisch to the Gestapo (the Secret State Police) in Munich.⁶ On July 26, they picked up their American immigration visas in Stuttgart and traveled that same day to Zurich, Switzerland. Six weeks later, on September 8, they sailed for the United States from Le Havre, France (*see also p. 99 f.*).⁷ On July 23, two days before leaving Untergrainau, Berolzheimer signed over his property, giving full power of attorney to his stepson, Robert Schweisheimer.⁸ This included the house and land in Untergrainau, as well as a significant part of the art collection, deemed too important by the authorities to leave the country.⁹ A photo of Berolzheimer in his study shows his holdings of old and valuable books. He was forced to leave many behind, but as he never saw a need for *ex libris* plates (*fig. 3*), the whereabouts of these volumes can no longer be traced.

In May and June, 1938, the representative of the Reich Chamber of Culture, the art historian Wengenmayr, who also worked for the Munich art auction house

Adolf Weinmüller, had valued the Berolzheimer art collection for the purposes of the asset declaration. Since Berolzheimer's emigration application was already being processed at that time, Wengenmayr also had to determine what works "of German cultural value" were to be left in Germany. His assessment was most likely based using a list Berolzheimer had drawn up. This list was taken by Berolzheimer to America and is mentioned in correspondence by his executor, but has subsequently been lost or destroyed. No records exist of Berolzheimer's German asset declaration, which was either lost during the war or perhaps never actually filed.[10] Robert Schweisheimer was required to submit a similar declaration of his own assets. He had plans to emigrate to England and therefore had to abide by the same government procedures concerning asset declaration and art valuation. Schweisheimer's assets included the large house he had had built at Am Priel 25 in Munich, his share in the private bank "E. & J. Schweisheimer Bankgeschäft," which he owned jointly with his father, as well as other investment shares and luxury items.[11] Wengenmayr was also instructed by Schweisheimer to value the works of art in his own house in Munich in June 1938. The asset declaration list Wengenmayr compiled as a result, included paintings by Paul Bril, Heinrich von Zügel, Hans von Marées, Carl Spitzweg, Joseph Wenglein, and Toni Stadler, as well as works by Italian painters, faience, and carpets.[12] There will have been a lot of conflicting interests among those parties involved in such valuations.

Shortly after the Berolzheimers had left the country, the district court in Garmisch-Partenkirchen appointed an "absentee guardian"—Georg Keller—to supervise Berolzheimer's real estate in Untergrainau. Those works in Berolzheimer's art collection not allowed to leave the country were taken to Munich for auction.[13] On November 2, 1938—one week before the "Night of Broken Glass" (Kristallnacht)—and under pressure from the trustee, Schweisheimer signed an agreement with the Weinmüller auction house for the sale of those artworks Berolzheimer had had to leave behind.[14] Seven paintings, including works by Anselm Feuerbach, Carl Spitzweg, Max Liebermann, and Franz Simm, as well as five sculptures from Berolzheimer's collection, marked in the catalog with the abbreviation "Be. i. M." (Berolzheimer in Munich) came up for auction on November 30, 1938.[15]

Catalog number 98 was the painting *Portrait of a Parisian Lady with a Small Dog* by Anselm Feuerbach (*fig. 4*). It was not until after the war that the whereabouts of this painting was clarified in the course of restitution efforts initiated by Michael Berolzheimer's heirs.[16] In January 1947, attorneys representing the family asked the American research official in Germany at the "Monuments, Fine Arts and Archives Section" (MFA&A) to help trace this painting. In March that year, Weinmüller was questioned about its whereabouts. He declared that the picture had not sold at auction on two occasions and had finally been acquired for 6,500 Reichsmarks by the "Sonderauftrag Linz" (Special Commission Linz),[17] which at that time was in the process of amassing an art collection for the "Führermuseum," planned by Adolf Hitler for Linz in Upper Austria. One year later, the MFA&A in Bavaria discovered that the former "Reichsleiter," Martin Bormann, had acquired the portrait from Weinmüller directly and had sent it to the Reichskanzlei in Berlin, or to Hitler himself, for the museum.[18] The painting was restituted to Berolzheimer's executor, Waldemar Schweisheimer, in June 1949.

With the largest part of Berolzheimer's remaining art collection still waiting to be sold through Weinmüller, works of art were also passed to the Munich art dealer Hellmut Lüdke "for further sale." On March 9 and 10, 1939, the rest of Berolzheimer's collection of drawings, also valued by Wengenmayr in early summer 1938, was sold in 803 lots—for a total of 33,686 Reichsmarks[19] by the same auctioneers.[20] Many of the works on paper originally formed part of the Jolles Collection (*see box*) as shown by the collector's stamp. The same auction also included 159 works of art confiscated from the Jewish art and antiques dealer, Siegfried Lämmle, of Munich. After deducting the commission payable to Weinmüller and the cost of printing the elaborately produced auction catalog, the trustee—Keller—reported sales totaling 17,925 Reichsmarks after the auction.[21] Proceeds from all these sales were paid into an account at the Dresdner Bank.[22] By July 1941, however, all Berolzheimer's property and bank deposits had been seized by the state. The proceeds from the auctions never reached Berolzheimer.

Through these sales, an important collection of drawings was broken up and the cultural commitment of the collector Michael Berolzheimer has since been forgotten. Only with the help of the respective Weinmüller auction catalogs has it been possible to define the former scope of this collection more precisely. Restitution claims for works in the collection, launched after the war by Berolzheimer's executor and stepson, Waldemar Schweisheimer, testify to a complex and arduous process, rendered all the more difficult by false statements con-

fig. 4 Anselm Feuerbach, *Portrait of a Parisian Lady with a Small Dog*

28134

sciously made by art dealers and resolutions passed at various levels by different authorities.[23]

Initially, only the restitution of a total of twelve works took a positive course in 1948. These had been acquired by Konrad Schießl, director of the Historisches Museum in Munich (known as the Münchner Stadtmuseum from 1955 onward), at the Weinmüller auction in March 1939 for the Städtische Galerie im Lenbachhaus, Munich.[24] The 800 or so other artworks auctioned by Weinmüller in March 1939 could not be located at first, as Weinmüller stubbornly maintained that he no longer had any documentation on the sales.[25] It was only in the course of restitution proceedings that an auction catalog with entries written in his associate Wengenmayr's hand came to light, indicating who had purchased each work. This annotated copy was loaned to Waldemar Schweisheimer's attorneys, Alfred Holl and Fritz Hamann, by the Central Collecting Point in Munich in 1948.[26]

After examining the catalog, Weinmüller came increasingly under pressure. It emerged that he had not auctioned all the works of art submitted for sale from Berolzheimer's collection in March 1939, consciously withholding 239 items. It should be mentioned that there was also a group of late 19th and early 20th-century prints by German artists which were sent to Weinmüller along with the drawings. These were never auctioned by Weinmüller and their respective

post-war locations are only partially known. The art dealer stated to the authorities that he had sold part of this batch privately and that a large number of works had been destroyed in air raids.[27] This claim was only partially true as, shortly afterward, American investigators discovered a part of Berolzheimer's art collection not submitted for auction in one of Weinmüller's depots.[28]

Holl and Hamann managed to identify several buyers who had attended the Weinmüller auctions thanks to the notes written in the margin of the catalog. As a result, a total of 36 restitution claims were opened before April 1950.[29]

fig. 6 Carl Gottlieb Peschel, *Design for an Altar in Staucha near Oschatz (Saxony)*, 1851; depicting the Crucifixion (middle panel), the Birth of Christ (left wing), the Angels at the Tomb (right wing), and the Last Supper (predella); graphite, partially washed, restituted by the Kupferstichkabinett Berlin

The attorneys subsequently returned the catalog to the respective authorities.[30] Another annotated copy of the catalog, together with other sale catalogs, was discovered in spring 2013 in the cellar of his post-war successor, the Munich art auction house Neumeister. These catalogs are now being digitized.

The catalog notes confirm that works from Berolzheimer's art collection were largely acquired by museums and other public institutions in March 1939, although there are also a number of art dealers and private individuals listed.[31] The following museums were among the successful bidders; the number of works acquired is given in parentheses: Nationalgalerie, Berlin (29; *fig. 6*); Albertina, Vienna (28; *figs 1, 5, 7*); Kunsthalle Bremen (12); Städtische Galerie, Munich (12); Kurpfälzisches Museum, Heidelberg (10); Kulturamt, Heidelberg (5); Germanisches Nationalmuseum, Nuremberg (3); Kurpfälzisches Museum, Mannheim (3); Landesmuseum, Weimar (3); Staatliche Graphische Sammlung, Munich ("several works," according to reports in various newspapers); Jagdmuseum, Munich (2); Städelsches Kunstinstitut, Frankfurt am Main (1); Theatermuseum, Vienna (1).[32]

However, the notes did not make it possible for Schweisheimer's attorneys to identify accurately the individual art dealers and private individuals. First names and addresses were either not mentioned, only given as initials or noted in abbreviated form. What could be proven, however, was that Wengenmayr—not forgetting that he worked for Weinmüller and had valued Berolzheimer's art collection in mid 1938 as an art expert—was among those who benefitted from the auction. Five portfolios, comprising 86 works of graphic art and drawings were found in Wengenmayr's possession[33] and were confiscated by officers working for the Central Collecting Point in Munich, as was the portait of a "nobleman" by the Cranach School. When questioned by the authorities, Wengenmayr maintained that the latter had been a gift to him from Robert Schweisheimer, in lieu of payment for valuing the art collection.[34] Although plausible given the circumstances at the time, this has never been proven either way.

Several drawings by Carl Spitzweg were acquired on behalf of the Bornheim Kupferstichkabinett in Gräfelfing, near Munich, in March 1939, through Weinmüller. During restitution proceedings launched after the war, the successor to the Bornheim Kupferstichkabinett claimed that all drawings and prints had been destroyed. As it was not possible to confirm or refute this statement, the claim was ultimately dropped. Nevertheless, restitution efforts by Berolzheimer's heirs are still ongoing, based on the names of successful bidders at the auction.

Private individuals who acquired works of art, and against whom restitution proceedings were opened after 1945, included Dr. Alfred Hüglin from Ebenhausen to the south of Munich, a certain Dr. Graff from Herford in Westphalia, and Richard Holtkott from Cologne.[35] Hüglin acquired nine drawings from Berolzheimer's art collection in March 1939. These were *Study with Three Women* by Nicolaes Pieterszoon (Claes Pietersz.) Berchem; a work by Cornelius Bois, *Fisherman on the Water*; a 17th-century Flemish drawing, *Portrait of a Man in a Hat*; a sheet by Gaetano Gandolfi, *The Holy Family*; *Two Farmers on a Hill* by Pieter de Molyn; a drawing by Parrogel Charles *Head of a Rider*; a sheet by Johann Rottenhammer, *Venus und Amor*; one by Georg Philipp Rugendas, *Cohort of Riders*; and a drawing by Alexandre Calame, *Rocky Mountains*.[36]

Similarly Dr. Graff acquired several important works including Albert Cuyp's *Dutch River Landscape*; one sheet by Allart von Everdingen, *Fishing Harbour with Old Tower*; a drawing by Jan van Goyen, *Plain Landscape with Trees*; a work by Claude Lorrain, *Italian Seaport*; Jacopo Palma il Giovane's *The Entomb-ment*; as well as two works attributed to Rembrandt in the auction catalog, *The Nativity* and *Farewell*; a *Study of a Seated Man* by David Teniers the Younger; and the *Sketch for "Hermannsdenkmal" near Kassel* by Ernst von Bandel.[37] Hüglin and Graff paid between 5 and 180 Reichsmarks per sheet at this auction.[38]

Although it was proven that all the drawings mentioned were still in the possession of the said buyers even after 1945, the "Wiedergutmachungskammer" (Claims Committee) at the District Court in Munich dismissed these restitution claims submitted by Schweisheimer's attorneys in June 1953, insisting that "the Generalbevollmächtigter" (authorized representative) of Berolzheimer's assets—which included his art collection—had offered the collection for sale through the Weinmüller auction house after the owner had emigrated.

The Claims Committee also based its decision on the understanding that the collection had been submitted for auction at Weinmüller's in March 1939 at the request of a private individual.[39] The committee may have quoted this date incorrectly or else it had been wrongly informed, Robert Schweisheimer having fled Germany after the "Night of Broken Glass" on November 9/10, 1938. The actual commission to sell the artworks at auction was most likely made by Wengenmayr himself at a much earlier date, following his initial valuation of Berolzheimer's collection. The committee's decision was based in particular on statements made by Weinmüller and Wengenmayr, who attested that the agree-ment to auction Berolzheimer's art collection had been signed by Robert Schweisheimer on November 2, 1938.[40] It disregarded the fact that the artworks had been auctioned because the owner had not been allowed to take them out of the country, and that the proceeds from the sale had been confiscated in 1941 by the government, when the "law for the Aryanization of all Jewish property" came into effect.

The dispersal of this collection is just one example of the fate of numerous Jewish collections in territories under National Socialist rule between 1933 and 1945. During this period, the Nazi regime confiscated, sold or destroyed innu-merable artworks and cultural objects, resulting in a significant loss to Europe's cultural history.

fig. 7 Wilhelm von Kügelgen, *Illustration for the Poem "Täubchen" by Adolf Krummacher*, 1827, graphite, restituted by the Albertina, Vienna

1 Catalog published by the Kunstauktionshaus Hugo Helbing, Munich, for the auction held on October 28–31, 1895, of the collection of original drawings and watercolors, works by Old Masters and more modern artists from a variety of different schools owned by Boguslav Jolles of Dresden/Vienna.

2 http://www.crt-ii.org/_awards/_apdfs/Jolles_Heinz_and_Gertrud_trans.pdf (07/31/2013).

3 See Berlin books of addresses, 1850–74, http://adressbuch.zlb.de/searchResultAdressbuch.php?&CatalogName=adre2007&CatalogCategory=adress&CatalogLayer=2&ImgId=37661 (07/31/2013).

4 All information on the Jolles family in Dresden has been taken from the city's books of addresses. See: http://adress-buecher.sachsendigital.de/startseite (08/12/2013).

5 http://www.juden-in-mittelsachsen.de/verzeichnis/index.html.

6 Staatsarchiv München, LRA GAP 63049, Garmisch District Authority to the Secret Police in Munich, dated August 5, 1938.

7 Before being given permission to leave the country, the Berolzheimers had to pay a "Judenvermögensabgabe" (Jewish Asset Fee) and "Reichsfluchtsteuer" (Reich flight tax), like all Jews who had submitted applications to emigrate, calculated according to the owner's assets. As can be seen in a note from the tax authorities in Garmisch to the tax office in Moabit-West in Berlin, dated July 1, 1939, the Bayerische Hypothek und Wechselbank Garmisch transferred the payment of 10,000 Reichsmarks, representing the "Judenvermögensabgabe" for Michael Berolzheimer, to the tax office, shortly before the Berolzheimers left Germany. See: Staatsarchiv München, FinA 16853, Berolzheimer, Michael.

8 Staatsarchiv München, WB Ia 4347, document signed by the notary's office, Munich XIII, dated July 23, 1938.

9 The Berolzheimers did succeed in taking several items from their art collection to America. These included a print cabinet, an armoire, and miscellaneous furniture, along with the Rodin sculpture—which was identified for export as a "garden sculpture"—thereby allowing it to leave Germany. The most important part of the exported material was the large collection of Old Master prints that formed the best part of the Berolzheimer art collection. We are not certain as to how and when these prints were sent to America, but it is assumed that they accompanied Berolzheimer when he emigrated to America or that he had sent them previously through associates or friends.

10 Staatsarchiv München, WB Ia 4347, Schweisheimer, Robert, as well as Meike Hopp, Kunsthandel im Nationalsozialismus: Adolf Weinmüller in München und Wien, Cologne/Weimar/Vienna 2012, p. 166.

11 Staatsarchiv München, Fin A 19327, Declaration of Assets of Robert Schweisheimer 08/15/1938.

12 Ibid.

13 Staatsarchiv München, WB Ia 2996, Berolzheimer./. Weinmüller; letter from Max Heiß to the Ministry of the Interior of June 26, 1940.

14 Staatsarchiv München, WB Ia 4347, WB 2996, copies of the auction instruction dated November 2, 1938. See also Hopp, op. cit. (note 11), p. 166f.

15 Auction catalog, Antiquitäten, Möbel, Plastik, Gemälde des 15.–20. Jahrh., Ostasiatica einer Augsburger Bürgerfamilie sowie aus fürstlichem und anderem süddeutschen Besitz, Kunstversteigerungshaus Adolf Weinmüller, Munich November 30–December 2, 1938. See also Hopp, op. cit. (note 11), pp. 166ff., 318. It may well be that the paintings listed as having been submitted by "Be. i. M." were works in Schweisheimer's possession or grouped together with those from Berolzheimer's art collection, after Keller had been appointed trustee for Schweisheimer's assets as well. A study for The Poor Poet by Carl Spitzweg was auctioned by Waldemar Schweisheimer's heirs at Sotheby's in New York on January 26, 2012.

16 Online research at the National Archives Washington D.C. (NARA), Records Concerning the Collecting Points (Ardelia Hall Collection): Wiesbaden Administrative Records, Restitution Claim Records, Claim (Germany), Berolzheimer, Michael, digitalized excerpt from letters from Robert O. Held to OMGUS of January 21, 1947. The painting by Anselm Feuerbach was given the number 9038 at the Munich Collecting Point; a painting attributed to the Cranach School depicting a "nobleman" from the Berolzheimer/Schweisheimer collections was given the number 41649.

17 Staatsarchiv München, VK Garmisch, K4, Menacher, statement made by Adolf Weinmüller on March 3, 1947. The painting was given the so-called Linz No. 830.

18 Die Reichskanzlei (Reichs Chancellery) was the name of the office of the Chancellor of Germany (Reichskanzler) in the period of the German Reich (Deutsches Reich) from 1871 to 1945. Since 1933 the Reichskanzlei was the "bureau" of the Hitler Cabinet. The chief of the Reichskanzlei was Martin Bormann. Most of the acquisitions for the planned "Führermuseum" in Linz were carried out by the Reichskanzlei.

19 To provide some idea of the value in real terms of the amounts given here and elsewhere in this volume in Reichsmarks, Marks, etc., and some approximate equivalent of these sums in US dollars today, please see Appendix.

20 Auction catalog, Buchminiaturen und Handzeichnungen aus älterer und neuerer Zeit. Zwei Münchner Sammlungen und andere Beiträge (Old and Modern Miniatures and Original Drawings. Two Munich Collections and other Entries), Kunstversteigerungshaus Adolf Weinmüller, Munich March 9–10, 1939. Submitted by A: Dr. Michael Berolzheimer; B: Dr. Siegfried Lämmle, Munich. See also Hopp, op. cit. (note 11), p. 319.

21 Bundesarchiv Koblenz, B 323/360, Berolzheimer restitution proceedings. See also Hopp, op. cit. (note 11), p. 166f.

22 Bundesarchiv Koblenz, B 323/360, Berolzheimer restitution proceedings, unpaginated, minutes taken at a public meeting of the Claims Committee at the District Court in Munich on 10/19/1950: Dr. Walter Schweisheimer as trustee of Dr. Berolzheimer's estate vs. Adolf Weinmüller.

23 On December 8, 1948, Waldemar Schweisheimer filed a restitution claim at the "Zentralanmeldeamt" in Bad Nauheim, north of Frankfurt-am-Main, "against persons unknown," with regard to the graphic works and drawings in Berolzheimer's ownership auctioned in March 1939 at Weinmüller's. See: Staatsarchiv München, WB Ia 2992.

24 Städtische Galerie im Lenbachhaus, acquisitions archive files (up until 10/31/1949), restitution correspondence re. Dr. Michael Berolzheimer (December 1947–June 1948), former inv. no. G5035-G5046. See also Hopp, op. cit. (note 11), p. 167.

25 Staatsarchiv München, WB Ia 2996, Berolzheimer./. Weinmüller.

26 Ibid., see also: Bundesarchiv Koblenz, B323/360, fol. 9, 12–13, fol. 14, 37.

27 Staatsarchiv München, VK Garmisch, K4, Menacher 19. Statement by Adolf Weinmüller of March 3, 1947. See also: Hopp, op. cit. (note 11), p. 167f. Adolf Weinmüller reported a pen-and-ink drawing of Charles the Bald, attributed to Albrecht Dürer in the auction catalog, which was not sold in March 1939, to the authorities months after the opening of restitution proceedings. See also the auction catalog, Buchminiaturen und Handzeichnungen aus älterer und neuerer Zeit. Zwei Münchner Sammlungen und andere Beiträge, Kunstversteigerungshaus Adolf Weinmüller, Munich March 9–10, 1939, cat. no. 198, and Hopp op. cit. (note 11), p. 167f., note. 610.

28 These artworks were sent to the Wiesbaden Collecting Point and restituted to Berolzheimer's heirs. See also: Bundesarchiv Koblenz, B 323/360, Berolzheimer restitution proceedings.

29 Bundesarchiv Koblenz, B 323/360, Berolzheimer restitution proceedings, letter from the attorney Alfred Holl to the Wiesbaden Collecting Point, of April 18, 1950. See also: Staatsarchiv München WB Ia 2992, 2995–3003, 4324–4330, 4342–4353, 4415, 5328, 5509.

30 This immensely important annotated document, needed for tracing the whereabouts of works from Berolzheimer's art collection, was considered lost until recently.

31 In documentation concerning compensation proceedings (1948–53), now in the Federal Archive in Koblenz, the names of a number of buyers who acquired works of art at the Weinmüller auction in March 1939 are listed, Wengenmayr having noted the names of purchasers in a copy of the auction catalog. The first section lists public institutions which bid successfully, followed by art dealers and private individuals. See: Bundesarchiv Koblenz, B 323/360, Berolzheimer restitution proceedings.

32 Works on paper acquired by the Albertina, Vienna, and the Nationalgalerie in Berlin at the Weinmüller auction in March 1939 have since been returned to the heirs. The 29 drawings restituted by the Albertina in 2010 were sold in 2011 through the Galerie Arnoldi-Livie in Munich. See 29 Drawings from the Michael Berolzheimer Collection restituted by the Albertina, Vienna 2010, Galerie Arnoldi-Livie, Munich, catalog no. 27, Munich 2011.

33 Staatsarchiv München, WB Ia 5328, Berolzheimer./. Wengenmayr. Also: The National Archives Washington D.C. (NARA), Records Concerning the Collecting Points (Ardelia Hall Collection): Wiesbaden Central Collecting Point, 1945–1952, M 1947, Record Group 260, Cultural Object Movement and Control Records I, Out-Shipment 237 through Out-Shipment 243 (11/10/1950–12/15/1950), Out-Shipment 238, 11/13/1950, Berolzheimer, pp. 10–24, here p. 12 (copy of "Wiedergutmachungsbehörde I Oberbayern, München", agreement made between the heirs of Michael Berolzheimer and Ernst Wengenmayr, Munich, 11/03/1949).

34 Ibid., see also: Hopp, op. cit. (note 11), p. 169.

35 The names of other art dealers and private individuals on the list (many incomplete) are: Richard Friedrichsen & Co, Buch- und Kunstantiquariat, Hamburg; Walz, Antiquariat, Munich; Reinhard Puppel, Antiquariat, Berlin; Köberlin, Antiquariat, Munich; Wilhelm Heinrich, Frankfurt am Main; Gustav Hobrack, Neuwied am Rhein; Heinrich Dörfler, Niedertraubling; Kunsthandlung Eymer, Kohlmarkt, Vienna; Heinrich Wendel, Kunsthändler, Munich; Hans Beyerlein, Kunsthändler, Munich; Maria Almas-Dietrich, Munich; Ilserer; Sauerwein, Munich; Reindl, Freising; Freytag; Funk, Berlin; Hauser; Gstättner; Siedhoff, Feldafing, near Munich; Ruff; Maden [?]; Eberl, Schloss Grünwald; Kroner [?]; von Ritter; Dr. Michailow; Scheidwimmer, Munich; Kirstell [?]; Prof. Schneider; Hoehn [?]; Dr. Lu(t)z, Berlin; Brüschwiler, Chiemsee; A. Vetter, Munich; A. Schwarzwalder; Gerstenberger, Chemnitz [?]; L. Rech, Maisach, near Munich; Spangenberg [?]; Meisner, Munich; Dr. Kisslinger, Vienna. [?] denotes those not definitively identified.

36 Bundesarchiv Koblenz, B 323/360, Berolzheimer restitution proceedings.

37 Ibid.

38 Bundesarchiv Koblenz, B 323/360, Berolzheimer restitution proceedings, also The National Archives Washington D.C. (NARA), Records Concerning the Collecting Points (Ardelia Hall Collection): Munich Central Collecting Point, 1945-1951, M1946, Record Group 260, Restitution Claim Records, Jewish Claims, No. 0043-0044 (Michael Berolzheimer).

39 Ibid.

40 Ibid.

THIRTY DRAWINGS FROM
THE BEROLZHEIMER COLLECTION IN
THE NATIONALGALERIE, BERLIN

ACQUISITION IN 1939 FOR THE DRAWINGS COLLECTION AT THE NATIONALGALERIE

The auction of book miniatures and original drawings held on March 9 and 10, 1939, at the art dealer Adolf Weinmüller in Munich, caught the interest of private collectors and museums alike. A comprehensive catalogue had been sent out beforehand to potential buyers—art dealers, prints collections, and private individuals. One copy also arrived at the Nationalgalerie in Berlin, which the acting head, Paul Ortwin Rave, scrutinized extensively and became especially interested in the upcoming auction. On March 4, he wrote to the auction house: "Please confirm whether the more recent drawings in your catalogue no. 19, listed as nos. 490 onward, are to be auctioned on March 10 or not. If this is the case, I would like to ask you to reserve a seat for me, if at all possible in one of the front rows, as it will not be possible for me to arrive in Munich before the morning of March 10."[1] The answer arrived a few days later. An employee at the auctioneers wrote "that the original drawings will be auctioned strictly according to the numbering in the catalogue. On the first day, March 9, numbers 1 to 550 will be auctioned."[2] Rave consequently traveled to Munich already on the first day of the auction, as proven by the artworks that he bought for the Nationalgalerie (*fig. 2*).

The Nationalgalerie's exclusive interest in "more recent drawings" was due to the fact that the museum already owned a collection of original nineteenth-century drawings and was always looking to expand it. The policy of the Nationalgalerie was to collect German art in three genres—painting, sculpture, and graphic works. The so-called "Drawings Collection" was established in 1878 and also included sketches and preliminary drafts of sculptures and paintings. A decree by the Prussian Minister of Culture in December 1877 ordered the transfer of original drawings by nineteenth-century German artists from the Kupferstichkabinett (Prints' Collection) to the Nationalgalerie, thereby establishing the basis for a new department at the gallery. From 1879 onward, the collection was exhibited in several rooms on the upper floor of the Nationalgalerie. Several hundred drawings were permanently displayed, hung very closely together over the whole wall space.

fig. 1   Gottlob Friedrich Thormeyer,
The Royal Palace in Dessau, c. 1799, watercolor over graphite, restituted in 2011

fig. 2   Nationalgalerie stamp

In the first few years of its existence, its expansion was impressive. In 1878, fifty-eight drawings by Julius Schnorr von Carolsfeld were acquired; in 1880 and 1881 a total of twenty-four drawings by Max Klinger; in the same year 170 studies by Adolph Menzel for the coronation painting were added, and finally, two years later, a comprehensive collection of works by Carl Blechen (849 sheets). Lionel von Donop, the curator responsible, drew up the first inventory in 1902, which listed an impressive 8,552 sheets, even though "artistically insignificant sheets" were not included. Another hugely important and voluminous addition was the purchase of drawings from Adolph Menzel's estate in 1906, comprising some 4,400 works.

In 1919, the Drawings Collection was moved to the former Kronprinzen-palais (Crown Prince's Palace), which had been taken over by the Nationalgalerie and located in the boulevard Unter den Linden, where it was given a study room in addition. Ludwig Justi, director of the Nationalgalerie from 1909 onward, divided the collection into two—one section to be exhibited and the other stored for study purposes. In the 1920s, important acquisitions of drawings from nineteenth-century and German Modernist artists were added. The latter suffered greatly during the "Degenerate Art" campaign in 1937. 369 sheets from the prints' collection in the Nationalgalerie alone were confiscated, as well as more than 400 Modernist paintings and sculptures.[3] Due to the National Socialists' art policies, which denounced Expressionist and avant-garde artists, the National-galerie focussed its attention after 1933 once again on nineteenth-century art. This way, an attempt was gradually made to fill the gap in the collection, made through the confiscation of extensive holdings in 1937, with works ranging from Classicism and Romanticism to Impressionism.

The drawings, largely by nineteenth-century German artists, purchased at the auction in March 1939, are to be seen in this context. Right after the auction, Rave reported back to his office in the Nationalgalerie from Munich: "... I am sending you herewith the confirmation slips from the auction, at which I think I have bought quite well over all."[4] The confirmation slips that Rave mentioned, pasted on several pages in the respective files at the Nationalgalerie, have survived and are now in the archives of the Staatliche Museen zu Berlin. They confirm the purchase of thirty-two lots for the Drawings Collection and state the price of each individual work.[5]

Thirty of the thirty-two drawings acquired were marked with an asterisk in the auction catalogue—a distinguishing mark ordered by the National Socialists to be added to works submitted by Jews from April 1938 onward. This compul-sory form of identification was intended to prevent Jewish assets or the sale of household effects and other valuables, such as works of art, from being concealed from the state and, therefore, not being taken into consideration when calculating the amount of tax due ("Reichsfluchtsteuer"—Reich flight tax, and the so-called "Judenvermögensabgabe"—tax on Jewish assets). It can certainly be assumed that museum staff familiar with the fine art trade would have understood the real meaning of works marked with an * in an auction catalogue. Whether, in this case, the exact provenance of the drawings was generally known is, however, questionable and has to remain speculation. Without doubt, Michael Berolz-heimer's collection of graphic works would have had a certain reputation, at least in southern Germany, not simply because Berolzheimer was the son of a very well known and respected entrepreneur and patron of the arts in the

fig. 3   Carl Christian Vogel von Vogelstein
(1788–1868), *Portrait of the Author Freiherr Alexander
von Ungern-Sternberg*, n.d., pastel chalks on brown
paper, restituted in 2011

Nuremberg/Fürth region, but also as a result of his own honorary work for the arts as a member of the acquisitions committee at the Alte Pinakothek and the Graphische Sammlung München.

It is very likely that the collection of Boguslav Jolles from Dresden was also known to potential buyers at the auction. After 1870, Jolles started to assemble a collection of mostly nineteenth-century German drawings, with an emphasis on artists from Dresden or those who had worked in Dresden, in keeping with his own roots. The collection was auctioned in 1895 at Hugo Helbing in Munich; a great number of sheets from the former Jolles Collection found their way into Berolzheimer's collection, which was created much later. The Weinmüller auction catalogue listed the provenance of these sheets from the Jolles Collection. These

were easily identifiable through the collector's stamp which was registered at Frits Lugt (Lugt 381, 381a) and to be found on the back of the sheets (*see also p. 187 f.*).

As Paul Ortwin Rave did not return to Berlin after leaving Munich, he sent the confirmation slips to the Berlin office so that the purchase with the auction house could be completed. He himself went abroad, presumably to Switzerland: "Greetings to everyone. Tomorrow I'll be crossing the border!"[6] At the National-galerie in Berlin, the acquisition was processed as usual. First, Weinmüller sent the invoice for the lots purchased from catalogue no. 19. A few days later, the respective drawings arrived at the museum, were added to the collection's inventory (inv. nos. F III 2744–F III 2773) by the custodian responsible for the drawing collection, Anni Paul-Pescatore, and kept with the collection in the Kronzprinzenpalais. The two sheets by Schinkel were assigned to the Schinkel Museum, which was also part of the Nationalgalerie, where they were added to the inventory, and stored in the "Bauakademie."[7] Finally, at the end of March, payment amounting to a total of 1656.50 Reichsmarks[8] was made to the Weinmüller auctioneers by the accounts department at the Staatliche Museen zu Berlin.

fig. 4 Carl Gottlieb Peschel (1798–1879), *The Flight of Lot*, n.d., graphite and black chalk on gray-green paper, restituted in 2011

THE WAR AND POSTWAR YEARS

Just a few months after the auction, World War II broke out. The museums in Berlin were closed to the public on September 1, 1939. As in all other museums, the artworks in the Nationalgalerie were, at first, put in the basement of the respective buildings to protect them from damage. For the Drawings Collection, this meant being stored in the cellar at the Kronprinzenpalais which dates back to around 1730, to the first building on the site.

Just over a year after the outbreak of war, in December 1940, the roof of the rear wing of the Palais, where the library of the Nationalgalerie was located, was set on fire by incendiary bombs. The books were transferred to the Bauakademie building in which the painting collection and the works in the Schinkel Museum were already being stored in the cellars. A collection of photographic plates as well as the remaining holdings of original drawings that were of less value, were also being stored there. In the course of heavy fighting during the Battle of Berlin in 1945, the Kronprinzenpalais was extensively damaged. Fire broke out in the cellars as well, causing the loss of the photographic plate collection, museum catalogues, and a small number of drawings of minor importance. It is indeed possible that the two sheets from the Berolzheimer Collection still

fig. 5   Moritz von Schwind, *Allegory of the Neckar and Main Rivers*, 1846–47, pen in brown ink, restituted in 2011

missing (Friedrich Kaiser's *Die Düppler Schanzen nach dem Sturm* and Friedrich Daniel Reichel's *Kiefernwald mit gestürztem Baum*) may have been among these works.

The increasing number of bombing raids on Germany and Berlin by the Allies led to a search for other places to safeguard the museums' artworks.[9] The newly constructed Deutsche Reichsbank building (now the Foreign Office building on Werderscher Markt) was suitable for the collections on the "Museumsinsel." In January 1941, the paintings, sculptures, and drawings were moved into two underground bunkers in the Reichsbank. The collection of drawings permanently on display was also moved there, along with drawings from the estate of Adolph Menzel. Although by the end of the war this building had been totally burned out above ground level too, the underground bunkers remained untouched except for some water damage in summer 1944. This in turn effected the Schinkel Museum folders, among others. In late summer 1944, these were moved to the Flak tower "Am Zoo" (an anti-aircraft gun blockhouse tower). This is how the two Schinkel sheets from the Berolzheimer Collection most probably came to be in the Flak tower and shared the same fate as the other drawings.

fig. 6   Johann Hermann Kretzschmer, *A Caravan in a Sandstorm*, 1842; preparatory drawing for the painting of 1844 in Leipzig Museum; graphite with light brown wash, restituted in 2011

In 1940 and 1941, several anti-aircraft towers were built in Berlin which also
contained a system of above-ground shelters, intended from the outset for the
storage of artworks from museums. Preliminary inspections had shown that these
Flak towers were in fact one of the safest storage places in Berlin. The choice of
works to be taken there was based on several years of planning by museum
employees. Finally, in summer 1941, the Nationalgalerie moved a number of
paintings, as well as sculptures and original drawings, into three rooms in the
Flak tower near Berlin Zoo. Every batch of works and every crate was documented. Some lists include the entry "Vorrat" (Reserve), however, which would
suggest that the drawings stored here were of secondary importance and formed
part of the study collection. Bearing in mind the substantial holdings of works
by well-known artists such as Menzel, Schinkel, Blechen, and others, mentioned
above, the newly acquired drawings from Berolzheimer's collection probably
belonged to the study collection stored in the Flak tower at the zoo. One list
documents a batch of drawings taken there in October 1943. It is entitled:
"Additional delivery to the Flak tower of new acquisitions and recently made
artists' drawings."[10] This list, noting only the names of the artists but not the title

or the dimensions of the sheets, contains—among others—works by Adolf Friedrich (3 works), Eduard von Steinle (84 works), Gottlieb Friedrich Thormeyer (3 works), Carl Christian Vogel von Vogelstein (4 works). These are the names of the artists of several sheets which had been bought in March 19 from Berolzheimer's collection (*figs 1, 3*).

The story of what happened later to the artworks stored in the Flak tower is as follows. In March 1945, on orders from the "Führer" and at considerable risk, the most valuable works of art—provided that they could be transported easily—were moved to disused mine shafts in central Germany to ensure that they did not fall into the hands of the Red Army, should Berlin be captured. The large-format paintings from the Gemäldegalerie, for example, were left behind. The collection of original drawings was not part of the holdings moved at the last minute and remained in Berlin. The so-called "Reserve" drawings in the Flak tower were in fact later confiscated by the Soviet occupying forces in summer 1945 and taken to the Soviet Union. For years, the fate of holdings in German museums remained unknown. These included such world famous treasures as the friezes of the Pergamon Altar and the *Sistine Madonna* from the Gemäldegalerie, Dresden. In the German Democratic Republic (East Germany), searching for artworks relocated during the war was taboo. It was not until the mid 1950s that a certain politically-driven, mutual dynamism generated the return of museum holdings between the two halves of Berlin. The West German states of Hesse and Lower Saxony, which had looked after artworks confiscated by the Western Allies in central Germany in 1948/49, transferred these items to the newly established state museums in Berlin-Dahlem in West Berlin. The Soviet Union returned the paintings from the Gemäldegalerie in Dresden in 1955, followed by the vast holdings in the state museums to East Berlin and other museums in East Germany.

The following journey can be reconstructed for the thirty drawings from the Berolzheimer Collection which had found their way into the Nationalgalerie in 1939. At least twenty-four sheets were in the Soviet Union between 1945 and 1958. In all likelihood, they were in the Hermitage in Leningrad (now St. Petersburg) during that time, as copious lists accompanying the return of the artworks in 1958 would suggest. They were subsequently integrated into the holdings of the Drawings Collection at the Nationalgalerie in East Berlin. Four drawings remained in Berlin after the war (three sheets by Carl Gottlieb Peschel and one by Moritz von Schwind) and were kept in the Nationalgalerie (*figs 4, 5*). The whereabouts of two drawings (one by Friedrich Kaiser, the other by Friedrich Daniel Reichel) is unknown. They either remained in the Soviet Union and are possibly still there, or—if they were still in the Kronprinzenpalais at the end of the war—must be considered as having been destroyed.

Following the amalgamation of the museums in West and East Berlin after the reunification of Germany, the Drawings Colltection in the Nationalgalerie in East Berlin was dissolved in 1993 and its holdings reassigned to the Kupferstichkabinett as part of the Staatliche Museen zu Berlin, where the twenty-eight drawings from the Berolzheimer Collection were kept until their restitution to the family in 2011 (*figs 6, 7, 8*).

fig. 8   Carl Hummel (1821–1907), *The Kochel Waterfall in the Riesengebirge*, n.d., brush in brown wash, restituted in 2011

1   Rave to Weinmüller, 03/03/1939, in Staatliche Museen zu Berlin – Zentralarchiv (SMB-ZA), I/NG 874, sheet 83.

2   Weinmüller to the Nationalgalerie, 03/04/1939, SMB-ZA, I/NG 874, sheet 84.

3   On the Drawings Collection, see Elke Blauert, "Sammlung der Zeichnungen" in: Peter-Klaus Schuster (ed.), *Die National-galerie*, Berlin 2001, p. 378f.

4   Rave to Perlwitz, Büro der Nationalgalerie, 03/10/1939, SMB-ZA, I/NG 874, sheet 85.

5   Compare with SMB-ZA, I/NG 874 sheets 94 and 95.

6   Rave to Perlwitz, Büro der Nationalgalerie, 03/10/1939, SMB-ZA, I/NG 874, sheet 86.

7   Ibid., sheets 87–95.

8   To provide some idea of the value in real terms of the amounts given here and elsewhere in this volume in Reichsmarks, Marks, etc. and some approximate equivalent of these sums in US dollars today, see Appendix.

9   For a more detailed account of the rescue and transport of artworks from the Nationalgalerie to a new place of safekeeping during the war, see: Paul Ortwin Rave, "Bergungsmaßnahmen der Nationalgalerie" in: *Dokumen-tation der Verluste*, vol. II: Nationalgalerie, Berlin 2001, pp. 12–14.

10 SMB-ZA, V/documentation of items from the collections at the Staatliche Museen zu Berlin moved to safe storage, missing or returned, file "Sammlung der Zeichnungen" (Drawings Collection).

CURRENT BEROLZHEIMER COLLECTION RESTITUTION EFFORTS

The New York State Department of Financial Services' Holocaust Claims Processing Office (HCPO) was created in June 1997 in recognition of the need for an agency to assist individuals attempting to navigate the emotionally charged maze of Holocaust-era asset restitution. Though initially intended to help individuals hoping to recover assets deposited in Swiss financial institutions, the HCPO expanded its mission by the end of 1998 to assist in the recovery of assets held in non-Swiss banks, proceeds from Holocaust-era insurance policies, and works of art that were lost, looted or sold under duress between 1933 and 1945.

The HCPO is currently the only government agency in the world that assists individuals, regardless of their background and current residence, with a variety of restitution processes worldwide. Claimants pay no fee for its services, nor does the HCPO take a percentage of the value of the assets recovered. As such, the Office is able to pursue a claim regardless of the value of the object, and successful resolution is not dependent on the item's recovery. The goal of the HCPO is to advocate for claimants by helping to alleviate any cost and bureaucratic hardships they might encounter in trying to pursue claims on their own.

The office has successfully helped original owners and current possessors of looted art reach mutually agreeable solutions by engaging in candid discussions about the ownership histories of lost objects. The HCPO relies on moral persuasion as articulated in the applicable international principles on Nazi-confiscated art. To date, the office has 134 open art claims from claimants in nineteen states and thirty four countries and has recovered sixty artworks.

The Office became involved in the Berolzheimer claim when Michael G. Berolzheimer approached the HCPO in April 2011 to request assistance in locating and recovering the artworks from the March 9/10, 1939 Weinmüller auction that had not yet been restituted. After reviewing the comprehensive documentation the Berolzheimer Research Team (BRT) amassed concerning the Berolzheimer collection and the diligent postwar compensation efforts of Michael Berolzheimer's stepson, Waldemar Schweisheimer, the Office opened an art claim and immediately began research.

While the sheer number of works in the claim was daunting, the archival documentation and information compiled by the BRT particularly with regard

fig. 1 Christian Ferdinand Hartmann, *The Wager of Tarquinius with Collatinus*, c. 1835, black chalk, heightened with white on light-brown paper; restituted by the Kupferstichkabinett Berlin

207

to the private parties and institutions that purchased works from the 1939 sale[1] provided a strong foundation from which to begin the search for the missing works. Initially the Office focused on the institutional purchasers, but we first had to ascertain whether the works were still in these respective collections. After all, fitty-two years had passed since their acquisition, and it was certainly possible that some pieces might have have been de-accessioned and subsequently re-entered the art market in the intervening years.[2]

Claims were submitted for the works that today remain in these institutions, primarily in Germany. While the majority of these claims are still pending, they have generally been well received. The Landesmuseum in Weimar, which purchased four drawings[3] from the 1939 sale and in the aftermath of the Albertina restitution contacted the Israelitische Kultusgemeinde Wien (IKG Vienna) in an attempt to locate the Berolzheimer heirs, was fully cognizant of the provenance of the drawings and anxious to restitute them (*figs 2, 3, 4*). Some of the other institutions were completely unaware of the circumstances under which the Berolzheimer works were acquired but equally as responsive to claims. For example, the Deutsches Theatermuseum München, which purchased Louis Letronne's charcoal drawing *Portrait of the Singer Ranuzio Pesadori* at the Weinmüller auction[4] immediately replied and set the wheels in motion for restitution.

The Office next concentrated on those works which were purchased either by private or unidentified individuals or that allegedly remained unsold at the 1939 auction. Thorough research into the identities and collections of the private buyers was conducted. The archival documents, while instrumental, provided varying amounts of information regarding these parties ranging from full names with complete address to only last names, sometimes with alternate spellings. Some of the art collectors and dealers such as Bernhard Funk, Richard Holtkott,[5] the Antiquariat Ackermann und Sauerwein, Munich, and Hollstein & Puppel, Berlin were widely known and thus easily identifiable. In some cases, works from the 1939 sale reappeared years later in sales by the very same dealers; a handful of drawings even resurfaced at subsequent sales at Weinmüller itself. However, the names of other purchasers, who were most likely smaller collectors and antique shops, were entirely unrecognizable.

Simultaneously, we researched each of the individual missing works in the 1939 auction. Given that Dr. Berolzheimer seemed to have acquired the bulk of the drawings in his extensive collection from the October 31, 1895, sale of works in Dresden known as the Boguslav Jolles Collection, the first port of call was to obtain a copy of the 1895 sales catalogue. The catalogue has proved to be an invaluable resource as it not only contains provenance information and images that were omitted from the 1939 Weinmülller catalogue, but in many cases provides detailed descriptions of artworks that were largely un-illustrated in either catalogue. Moreover, works from the Jolles Collection, that re-emerged on the art market after the war, frequently cite Jolles in their provenance, which has been helpful in locating and identifying them. The pre-1895 provenance of the artworks has also been a useful tool since many of the previous owners, particularly those like Count Sternberg-Manderscheid[6] and Baron Carl Rolas du Rosey,[7] who were renowned and significant collectors, consistently reappear in the ownership histories of works. Additionally, catalogues raisonnés, monographs, exhibition, auction and dealer catalogues, art historical publications (the mainstays of provenance research), and other resources were examined.

28136.

1821

fig. 2 Ferdinand Anton Krüger, *Garden in Florence with Fiesole in the Background,* 1821, graphite; restituted by the Albertina, Vienna

In the course of research, we noticed an interesting and useful trend in the postwar auctions in which Berolzheimer works appeared. Curiously, the drawings did not tend to travel alone. Rather, where one Berolzheimer drawing materialized, the same sale commonly included one additional Berolzheimer drawing or more, suggesting that these works were purchased together by the same parties. For example, eight Berolzheimer works appeared in the sale of Ingeborg Tremmel's Munich collection on May 5–6, 2003, at the Ketterer art auctioneers, and two drawings appeared at the sale on February 27–28, 1941, of Heinrich Beckmann's collection at Reinhold Puppel, Berlin. By far the largest assemblage (eighteen drawings) appeared in the sale of works from the collection of the Bedberg industrialist, Richard Holtkott, on December 6, 1997, at Kunsthaus Lempertz. Holtkott was an avid purchaser of works at the 1939 sale, at which he acquired approximately ninety-seven drawings.

28/29.

A number of challenges in locating the missing works have arisen during research, many of which are endemic to provenance research. Probably the biggest obstacle has been identifying the specific works. While the 1895 and 1939 auction catalogues do contain descriptions and images of some artworks, they do not do so for all of them. Drawings with vague, generalized titles, especially those depicting subjects typical of a prolific artist's oeuvre, have been the hardest to identify.

The issue of reattribution has further complicated the process of identification. While the Berolzheimer collection contained a myriad of high-quality works on paper, numerous works were misattributed and subsequently reattributed in the years after the war. Some of the misattributions are more glaring than others, such as the attribution of the pen and watercolor drawing *Charles the Bald* to Albrecht Dürer. Other misattributions are much less conspicuous and were deemed by later art historians based on stylistic grounds or scholarly research to have been executed by the "school of," "circle of" or "after" a known artist or by an altogether different one.[8]

The Office was also faced with the problem of determining whether specific works had been destroyed since their appearance in the 1939 auction, and thus should be eliminated from our search. In postwar correspondence, Ernst

fig. 3 Heinrich Franz Dreber, *View across a Mountain Valley*, 1840/41, pen in gray and brown ink over graphite; restituted by the Albertina, Vienna

fig. 4 August Leopold Vogel, *Illustration for the Fairy Tale "The Magic Forest,"* c. 1870, watercolor, brown ink, black chalk, and graphite; restituted by the Albertina, Vienna

Wengenmayr, art historian and managing director of Weinmüller between 1936 and 1939, stated that the unsold works from the 1939 auction were stored in Weinmüller's warehouses, where they were destroyed during internecine bombing.[9] Experience has taught us to regard postwar allegations by art dealers (particularly those, like Weinmüller, who were intimately tied to the Nazi machinery and notorious for selling Jewish art), that works of art were destroyed either during or in the aftermath of World War II, with skepticism. We per-severed in our search for the ostensibly decimated works, and lo and behold, a number of them have resurfaced.

Once the Office was able to identify some of the artworks and discern details of their post-1939 provenance, we were confronted with the problem of ascertaining the identities of their past and current owners. While information about institutional owners is commonly available and usually appears in publications, the identity of private owners is much more difficult to discover. Private owners typically prefer to remain anonymous for obvious reasons, and it is virtually impossible to uncover their identities when a piece appears on the art market. Due to privacy concerns, auction houses have strict confidentiality policies that guarantee the anonymity of both consignors and purchasers, and art dealers are

similarly tightlipped about the identities of their clients. Furthermore, neither is under any obligation to disclose such information.

The challenges so far have been not limited to the research of the artworks and their owners but have also permeated the restitution component of the claim. The research aspect is only half the battle, as once an object has been identified and located, a claim must then be submitted to the current owner requesting that the object be restituted to our claimant. One of the primary impediments to resolving restitution claims is the lack of enforceable laws governing restitution. As mentioned above, the HCPO relies solely on moral persuasion and applicable international principles such as the eleven principles (the "Washington Principles") resulting from the 1998 Washington Conference on Holocaust-era assets and the 2009 Terezin Declaration, which were developed to guide the resolution of issues related to stolen art. Some countries have also implemented their own policies in demonstration of their commitment to the Washington Principles.[10] However, these principles, though endorsed by the forty-four governments participating at the conference, as well as many of the decrees enacted by several European countries, are not legally binding, and enforceable laws governing restitution have long since expired in the majority of them. Additionally, many interpret the principles as only applicable to public institutions such as state-funded museums. This means that current possessors of artworks, particularly private owners, sometimes choose to flout these principles. Although the HCPO's reliance on moral persuasion may not always yield the desired results, it is a preferable, often more effective alternative to litigation, which can be costly, time consuming, and antagonistic.

A second complication is that of the so-called "good faith" purchaser. More often than not, an owner (either public or private) purchased a work of art with no knowledge of its tainted provenance. The provenance of many Berolzheimer works is far from complete, and the name Berolzheimer is often omitted,

fig. 5 Christian Leberecht Vogel, *Joseph Reveals his Identity to his Brothers,* 1782, gray brush over graphite, gray and brown wash; restituted by the Kupferstichkabinett Berlin

whether deliberately or inadvertently, often due to lack of documentation. When presented with a restitution claim, the good faith purchaser is usually placed in the unenviable position of wanting to do the right thing by restituting the artwork and wanting to either recoup the price paid for it or keep the work, which may have sentimental value or be integral to a collection as a whole. This must be taken into consideration when crafting a fair and just solution that benefits both the current owner and the party making the restitution claim.

Despite these difficulties, the Office has had several notable successes over the past year and a half. Since the Berolzheimer claim was opened in April 2011, the HCPO's research has yielded a great deal of valuable information and resulted in six successful restitutions to the Berolzheimer heirs. In December 2011, a settlement was reached with the owner of Ludwig Elsholtz's watercolor *Sunday Afternoon in the Hare's Moor* with the assistance of the Ketterer auction house in Munich, to whom it had been consigned and who, upon discovery, immediately pulled it from the October 27 sale in 2011. Hendrick Potuyl's red chalk drawing *Two Farmers at an Inn* was found in the possession of a private art dealer in New York and recovered in May 2012 with the help of US Immigration & Customs Enforcement (ICE) and the office of the US Attorney. More recently, a settlement was reached with the École national supérieure des beaux-arts, Paris, for the restitution of Nicolas Bertin's red chalk drawing *Apollo and the Cumean Sybille*. Three additional drawings were restituted in 2013.

While the majority of Berolzheimer drawings that have reappeared in recent years were in Germany, a number of them continue to turn up in the United States and other European countries as well—a true testament to the fluidity of the art market. Further restitution claims have been made to nine institutions in Germany, the United States, and France for a total of seventeen Berolzheimer works. Claims for six drawings have been resolved in principle, although no money has changed hands yet, nor have settlement agreements been countersigned. Other claims are currently under review.

1   Dr. Alfred Holl's letter of September 24, 1948, to Dr. Breitenbach at the Munich Central Collecting Point.

2   In the case of the Kunsthalle Bremen, at least six of the twelve drawings the museum purchased at the 1939 sale are no longer in its possession.

3   Friedrich Preller's *View of Tivoli*, Moritz von Schwind's *Design for the Fairytale of the Seven Ravens*, and Karl Sprosse's *Interior of the Castle Chapel of Altenburg* and *Cathedral of Speyer*

4   Archival documents erroneously list the drawing as having been acquired by the Österreichisches Theatermuseum, the curator of which was invaluable in verifying the correct purchaser and passing on our inquiry to the museum in Munich.

5   Richard Holtkott (1866–1950) was a Nazi party member and businessman who owned a once-prosperous linoleum-manufacturing company with approx. 1,000 employees, which he took over from its Jewish owners at the time of Austrian Aryanization in 1938. He was exposed recently as a treacherous individual by his nephew, who—during the Nazi era—had paid his uncle in exchange for his promise to save his Jewish in-laws. They were however killed in the camp to which they were sent. See: Stewart Ain, "German Scam to Save Jews Revealed: World Jewish Congress' Bronfman makes Disclosure at House Banking Probe of Swiss Nazi Complicity" in: *The Jewish Week*, 12/13/1996.

6   Count Sternberg-Manderscheid's collection was sold at J.G.A. Frenzel, Dresden, on November 10, 1845, and contained at least thirteen drawings later acquired by Berolzheimer.

7   The first of several sales of the extensive collection of the Prussian general, Baron Rolas du Rosey (L. 2237), was in Dresden on April 8, 1863, and approx. five drawings later acquired by Berolzheimer were formerly in the collection.

8   Carlo Cignani's *Portrait of Two Ladies in Oval Medallions*, pen and bister, was reattributed to the Circle of Jacopo Amigoni at the sale at Christie's London on April 16, 1991 (lot 169). Ambrosius Francken the Elder's *Lamentation of Christ*, pen and bister on yellowish paper, was reattributed to Frans Francken the Elder at the sale at Sotheby's London, on October 28, 1969 (lot 125). Rembrandt's pen drawing *Adoration of the Child* was attributed to Nicholas Maes in the Hauswedell & Nolte sale on July 11/12, 1941 (lot 31), and subsequently to Samuel Hoogstraaten by Joseph Fach, while David Teniers the Younger's *Study of a Seated Man*, red chalk, was reattributed to the Dutch School at the April 13, 1992 (lot 292) sale at Sotheby's, London.

9   Dr. Wengenmayr's letter of March 5, 1947, to the Landes-amt für Vermögensverwaltung und Wiedergutmachung in Garmisch-Partenkirchen.

10 In Austria, there are three "laws": The Federal State Act on the Return of Cultural Objects from Austrian Federal Museums and Collections (December 4, 1998); the Styrian Provincial Law of March 14, 2000, on the Return or Taking into Account of Works of Art or Cultural Assets confiscated from their owners during the Nazi Regime; and the Resolution of the Vienna City Council of 29 April, 1999, on the Return of Artistic and Cultural property from the Museums, Libraries, Archives, Collections, and other Holdings of the City of Vienna. In the Czech Republic, there is Law No. 212/2000 of June 23, 2000, and in the United Kingdom the Holocaust (Return of Cultural Objects) Act of 2009. The Statement by the Federal Government, the Länder (federal states) and the national associations of local authorities on the tracing and return of Nazi-confiscated art, especially from Jewish property, was issued on December 14, 1999, and pursuant to a decision dated November 16, 2001, by the Secretary of State for the Dutch Ministry of Education, Culture, and Science (OCW), The Netherlands established the Advisory Committee on the Assessment of Restitution Applications for Items of Cultural Value and World War II. Additionally, there is the Vilnius Form Declaration of October 5, 2000, Resolution 1205 of the Council of Europe of November 1999, and the 1999 ICOM Recommendations Concerning the Return of Works of Art Belonging to Jewish Owners.

APPENDICES

THE NAME "MICHAEL"

At least eight people in the extended family have been named "Michael" after Michael Berolzheimer. Charles, who since his youth had been very fond of his uncle, named his second son, the Publisher and Editor of this book, after him (*see also p. 108*). On hearing this news, "Dr. Michael" wrote a long letter in English outlining the history and provenance of the name, which has been transcribed by Dietlind Bratengeyer and is reproduced below. Berolzheimer had intended to carry out further research for his great-nephew's third birthday, but was unable to complete the task.

Dr. Michael Berolzheimer

Untergrainau
(Oberbayern)

Now: Mount Vernon, N.Y. December 2nd, 1939
300 Heywood Ave. – Fleetwood

Dear Lois and Charles,

For your official announcing of the arrival of your child and for your letter, dear Charles, and not the less for your renewing for me subscription of the most interesting "Economist" for the coming year, we thank you most heartily. And moreover I thank you for the great honour you rendered me and for the joy you gave me to get a new and distinct prove of the fact perceived at any time, that both of you are attached to me as much as I am to you.

As you perhaps know I got my first name because of my grandfather Michael Schnebel, born in Redwitz on the little Rodach River, not far away from Lichtenfels, the place where your mother's family came from.

My grandfather again got his name because of his grandfather, who came from Bohemia to Redwitz. The family name Schnebel is to be found in some Bohemian registers of the 18th century.

Their, my, and your little boy's name, Michael, is of very old provenience, going back even until the ancient Babylonians and expressing human ideas of cultures also of Jews, ancient and modern Christians, Greeks, Romans, middle ages peoples and even the most modern science, and so pointing at the future, since we don't know yet the meaning of the character neither of the old theological "angel" nor of the modern scientific comprehension "energy".

For if you say "energy", you dont know at all, where the energy comes from, and if you say "angel", you dont know, where an angel comes from. The only difference is that you can make yourself a picture out of an angel—though in different comprehensions, yet a picture: an angel speaks, makes music, can fly, in short is a human-like young apparition, but the essence of his character is, that he is a messenger from God, id est, from the "quite other" we dont know anything about.

On the other hand the "energy" is a power we dont know where it comes from. The angel so is the same being in concrete way than the energy in abstract way; the former is poetical, condensed, the latter is thought, but both: human invention because of human smallness.

As I said before the angels were well known with the Babylonians. The Jews already in the epoche before the Babylonian captivity knew angels, only they had no name for them. Only during the captivity they learned names of Babylonian angels, who symbolized also planetary. (The Hebrew word "malek" = messenger is the same as the Greek word "angelos" = messenger [seili est: from God] = angel).

On the head of the army of angels were the archangels, and one of these archangels was "Michael", who was the greatest success of all his colleagues, because already the Jews acknowledged him as their special guardian angel and because he himself had a most powerful patron, the emperor Constantine "the Great".

The name "Michael" is Hebrew: "who is like God?"; it means the fight of the good principle against the bad one and the victory of the good ones. It is in the book "Daniel" and in the Apocalypsis of Johannes, where the fight of Michael with his sword against the stoped down dragon (a Satan) is described, and also in the "letter of Juda", where Michael fights and wins over Satan the body of Moses. The later story Goethe used in his "Faust", second part; for the performance of the fight of the angels against Mephistopheles for the body of Faust. The former story was used by many painters and sculptors.

The *fighting* archangel Michael took charge of the fighting functions of Greek hero Herakles and the *messenger* – flying Michael of the messenger from Olympus, the God Hermes, and from the same Hermes came a third function of archangel Michael, as judge of dead men. This later function is reproduced by two works of art, the function of Hermes as judge over the deads by a marble-relief, one of the most beautiful Greek sculptures, now in the Museum of Boston, Mass., belonging to the relief in the museum of therms, Rome, Italy, the latter reproducing "the birth", the former: "the death", Hermes with the weighing-machine and the weights in form of human dead souls. The other work of art, a fresco painting of the beginning 13th century A.D., in the porch of the church San Lorenzo fuorile mure in Rome: the archangel Michael holds in his hand the balance in favour of the pious emperor Henry II.

The legend relates that the emperor Constantine I. erected in Byzantium (Constantinopolis) three crosses of bronze, and every year three times archangel Michael came down from heaven, made a procession around these crosses singing a hymn.

This emperor built, to honour this angel, outside the walls of the city of Byzantium a church, the so-called "Michaelium" and also four other churches he is said to have built for Michael.

The emperors of the East Roman Empire continued this way, the emperor Justiniane alone is said to have built six churches in honour of Michael, whom the Greek, as before the Jews, venerated as their patron-saint. Therefor you can find out so often the Christian name Michael in families of Byzantine emperors and other families as well as in families of Russian Czars.

Since the Greek settled in Lower Italy, they brought along with their cultures their gods, their holies, first of all Maria (also a Hebrew name, translated Greek) and Michael. This latter took his fight over the sea and came down to the Cape Garganus in Apulia (the "spur" on the "boot" of Italy) in the year 493 A.D., where already in ancient times, according to the statement of Strato, two sanctuaries existed, an oracle-place of Podalyrios, son of Aestulaps, connected with a curing-spring, and another temple, of the seer Kalchae, mentioned by Homer (and Jacques Offenbach). Little by little the Christianity became more powerful and exerted herself to expand from the East-Roman empire also to the West-Roman empire, beginning with the country already in Byzantine hands, where, on the Mount Garganus, the heathen tempel had to be supplied by a christian church.

In the city of Sipontum, situated below the promontory lived a rich man call Garganus. One day a pretty bull belonging to him disappeared. After looking for him a long time in the mountains at last they found him on the entrance to a grotte. Garganus, growing angry about the long times they had been looked around in vain, tried to shoot the bull, but the arrow turned back against the shot and wounded him. This story was related to Laurentius, bishop of Sipontum, who ordered three days fastening. On the third day, the eight day of May of the year 493 appeared to him the archangel Michael, announcing that the grotte is sanctified by himself and should be a place of worship in his and the other angel's honour in future. The faithfull, entering into the grotte, found it enlightened by a celestial light, transformed into a chapel by hands of angels, and at the rock an altar erected, covered with purple. Laurentius built a church before the entrance to the grotte and consecrated the sanctuary to the archangel Michael, September 29th, 493, after getting concession from pope Gelasius.

The Catholic Church celebrates on the 8th day of May the apparition of the archangel to the Mount Garganus and on the 29th day of September the apparition of Michael generally. The "Kerwa" = "Kirchweih" church festival & Kermess in Fürth is celebrated, because of the consecration of the Fuerth-church to St. Michael still now (the church is since Luther protestant), with beer drinking and carp eating, and when I was still a boy, the term for rent-paying and –ending was not the 1st of October but "Michaeli" = 29th of September.

In the 6th century, around the church upon Mount Garganus arised a fortified place, called to-day Sant'Angelo. For possession of this fortress different peoples fighted: Lombards of the duchy of Benventum, Greek emperors since Constats II., the Saracines in the ninth century (still now a part of the Cap is called Monte Saracino). After the defeat of emperor Otto II. near Shlo in Calabria (982) the Greek emperors again conquered the whole country, and at that time the emperor Otto III., son of Otto II. and the Greek princess Theophano, came as a pilgrim to this place, bare-footed from Rome via Beneventum and Sipontum, up to the Cap, in 998. Henry II., successor of Otto II., came to Apulia in 1022 and snatched this country away from the Greeks. He also came as a pilgrim to the Mount Garganus, which became Norman in the 11th century. Then the Hohenstaufen emperor Henry VI. got the whole country inclusive Sicily, where he now lays in the cathedral of Palermo in a marvellous porphyry-sarcophagos. After the Hohenstaufen, the Anjou-Kings conquered the country; Charles I. builded a new chapel up on the Mount Garganus for Michael, existing, not much changed, yet now.

This church on the "monte Sant Angelo" was the mother-church of all churches, consecrated to Saint Michael, in the whole western world, so in England, France, Italy, Spain, Germany, upon mountains, in caves, at sea-coasts – instead of the sanctuaries of the ancient gods of the various countries.

In Rome, the oldest church of St. Michael was in the via Salara, but the most celebrated apparition of Saint Michael and his most celebrated chapel was upon the Tomb of the emperor Hadriane. In 590 the plague ruled. The great pope Gregorius guided a procession to the church of St. Peter. Suddenly St. Michael appeared hovering above the tomb of Hadriane, putting his blazing sword in the sheath, whereupon the plague died away. On the top of the tomb a chapel in honour of St. Michael was built, who still now is puting there his sword into the sheath. Since then the tomb of the emperor Hadriane is called "Castel Sant Angelo" (angel – is Michael).

In the eight century S. Angelo in Rocaria was built into the fragments of the "Ponticus Octaviae", giving the name to a quarter of the city of Rome.

In the ninth century San Michele in Sassia was built in the "Borge" of the Vaticane. "Sassia" = Anglo-Saxon. So you may learn, that already in these early times the English people venerated St. Michael.

At the council of Mayence in 813 St. Michaels-day, September 29th, got acknowledged as an ecclesiastical holiday.

In the 16th century the greatest Michael, the architect, sculptor and painter Michelangelo Buonarotti built the glorious Santa Maria degli Angeli into the Therms of the emperor Diocletiane.

Not only in Rome of course but in many other cities of Italy churches, consecrated to St. Michael, became erected, for instance San Michele in Affrisco in the city of Ravenna (6th century, then Greek). San Michele in the city of Pavia: In this church the kings Beringold and Adalbert and Frederic I. of Hohenstaufen became crowned with the iron Lombardian crown, which is now still preserved in Monza, where the Kings of Italy use to be crowned with.

In similar manner as the church upon Mount Garganus also the French St Michael's church originated. The archangel made his apparition to the bishop Aubert of Arranchu, Normandy, and ordered him to build a church in his honour upon a rock on the shore of ocean, where the old sanctuary of Gaul Druids, called Tumba, has been. After an other apparition the bishop became obedient, built and consecrated a chapel in 710 and them Benedictines. Such was the beginning of the sanctuary "Mont Saint-Michel", Normandy, celebrated in the whole world. The Normans after conquering this country made out of this church a great place for pilgrims, the people of France and of England made pilgrimages thither, and this church became immense rich. From this sanctuary the highest order of France established by king Louis XI originated. (Also the Bavarian kings established an order of St. Michael, and your grandfather Henry was Knight of this order).

In Germany the emperor Henry II. in 1009 founded a church in honour of St. Michael and also an abbey of Benedictines upon the so-called "Michaelsberg" – Mount Michael in the city of Bamberg, founded by himself as a strategic place for Germanication of the Slaves.

Your little boy, dear Lois, got also an other first name, George, because of your late father, I think. And in my opinion that choice is a good one, as well, because he was your good father, whose name now continues with his grandson, as also because the two names, Michael and George, are well matched. For also Saint George was, although not even an angel so a holy man and a dragon-killer too, and he also came from Asia, and he also was a protector, not even of a whole people but of innocent women, and he also was successor to an ancient hero, not Hermes and not Herakles, but Theseus.

"George" is a Greek name and means "farmer". The St. George came from Kappadokia in Asia Minor, where early Christians lived in rock-caverns (confer the latest edition of the National Geographic Magazine, pag 763). He was an officer and became executed because of his confession to be christened. He killed with his lance a dragon, being about to devour a virgin, liking Theseus of Athens, saving a princess by killing a dragon.

Crusaders perhaps brought the veneration of St. George to the occident. The Norman kings made him patron-saint of England.

So we hope your boy will become – in peace – a fighter for good and right and true, in harmony with his elder brother, like this older generation of friendly and affectionate brothers, your father and myself, as you, dear Charles wrote so very truly.

With renewed thanks and warm wishes for both of you and both of your children Aunt Melitta's and my best love!

Yours affectionately

Uncle Michael

HONORING THE MEMORY
OF FAMILY AND FRIENDS

This list, researched and compiled by Dietlind Bratengeyer, includes some of the known victims of the Holocaust, who are connected in some way to the Berolzheimer family. Many are mentioned elsewhere in this publication.

Names shown **IN BOLD** are known blood relatives of Michael Berolzheimer

BAUER, GISELA (Bertha Berolzheimer and Heinrich Bauer's daughter)
Born: December 25, 1872, in Augsburg, Bavaria
Place of residence: Munich
Committed suicide: September 23, 1941, in Munich

BEROLZHEIMER, HANS DAVID MARTIN (Sigmund and Clara Berolzheimer's son)
Born: August 1, 1882, in Nuremburg
Place of residence: Munich
Interned in November 1938, in Dachau concentration camp, later released
Deported from Munich April 3/4, 1942, to Piaski ghetto (Poland)
Died: Piaski
Death officially confirmed

BEROLZHEIMER, FRANZ SALOMON (Julius Berolzheimer and Lina Bloch's son)
Born: October16, 1882, in Munich
Place of residence: Munich
Interned November 10, 1938–December 19, 1938, in Dachau concentration camp
Deported from Munich November 20, 1941, to Kaunas (Lithuania)
Died: November 25, 1941, in Kaunas

BEROLZHEIMER, RICHARD THEODOR (Julius Berolzheimer and Lina Bloch's son)
Born: December 26, 1883, in Munich
Place of residence: Munich
Interned November 10, 1938–December 19, 1938, in Dachau concentration camp, later released
Deported from Munich November 20 1941 to Kaunus (Lithuania)
Died: November 25, 1941, in Kaunas

DISPECKER, SIGMUND (Melitta's uncle)
Born: November 7, 1875, in Fürth
Place of residence: Munich
Imprisoned November 10, 1938, in Dachau concentration camp,
released November 21, 1938
Died: 9 hours later at home on November 21, 1938

DRIESEN, FRIEDA (née Friedberg; Nelly Friedberg's sister-in-law)
Born: September 23, 1883, in Karlsruhe
Emigrated to Belgium, later to Paris
Deported from Marseille June 23, 1943 to Drancy internment camp (Paris);
later with Convoy No. 55 to Auschwitz death camp

DRIESEN, OTTO (husband of Nelly Friedberg's sister-in-law)
Born: 1875 in Segnitz (Bavaria)
Wartime spent in France
Deported March 25, 1943, with Convoy No. 53 from Drancy internment
camp (Paris) to Sobibór extermination camp (Poland)

EINSTEIN, HINA HINDEL IRINA (née Schweisheimer; Eugen's sister)
Born: November 16, 1859, in Ederheim (Bavaria)
Place of residence: Munich
Deported from Munich June 23, 1942, to Theresienstadt ghetto
Died: October 1, 1942, in Theresienstadt

ENOCH, IDA EVA (née Wolf, daughter of Moritz (Moses) Wolf,
granddaughter of Wolf and Jette Wolf, granddaughter of Voegele Berolzheimer
and David Hirsch Wolf)
Born: October 15, 1875 in Neumarkt in der Oberpfalz (Upper Palatinate)
Place of residence: Munich
Arrested March 13, 1942, Munich, detained in camp at Knorrstrasse 148,
Munich
Deported from Munich on June 23, 1942, to Theresienstadt ghetto
Died: September 25, 1942, in Theresienstadt

FELS, PAULA (née Stettauer, Johanna Wertheimer's daughter, David Moses
Wertheimer's granddaughter)
Born: September 12, 1866 in Fürth
Emigrated to Italy
Deported from Italy to Auschwitz death camp
Died: December 14, 1944, in Ravensbrück concentration camp

FRIEDBERG, ELISABETH (LISEL) (Nelly Friedberg's sister-in-law)
Born: July 28, 1888, in Karlsruhe
Place of residence: Karlsruhe
Deported from Baden October 22, 1940, to Gurs internment camp (southwest
France); 1942 to Drancy internment camp (Paris); September 16, 1942,
to Auschwitz death camp

FRIEDBERG, HANS (Nelly Friedberg's brother-in-law)
Born: March 23, 1898, in Karlsruhe
Place of residence: Karlsruhe
Emigrated 1936 to France
Deported from Drancy internment camp (Paris) March 25, 1943,
to Sobibór extermination camp (Poland)

FRIEDBERG, JULIUS (cousin of Nelly Friedberg's husband Leopold)
Born: April 23, 1875, in Bruchsal (Baden)
Place of residence: Freiburg i. Brsg.
Deported November 11, 1938 to Dachau concentration camp
Died: December 25, 1938, in Dachau

HAAS, WILLIE (Emilie Berolzheimer and Samuel Bloch's grandson)
Born: June 17, 1893 or 1896 in Nuremburg
Place of residence: Nuremburg
Emigrated to France
Deported from Drancy internment camp (Paris) September 2, 1942,
to Auschwitz death camp
Death officially confirmed

HARBURGER, BETTY (née Berolzheimer; Sigmund and
Clara Berolzheimer's daughter)
Born: November 11, 1869, in Nuremburg
Place of residence: Munich
Deported from Munich November 20, 1941, to Kaunus (Lithuania)
Died: November 25, 1941, in Kaunus

HARBURGER, CHARLOTTE (LOTTE) (Betty's daughter;
Sigmund and Clara Berolzheimer's granddaughter)
Born: October 9, 1893, in Munich
Place of residence: Munich
Deported from Munich November 20, 1941, to Kaunus (Lithuania)
Died: November 25 1941, in Kaunus

HEINEMANN, LEONORE (Bertha Berolzheimer and
Heinrich Bauer's granddaughter)
Born: May 1, 1892, in Mannheim (Baden-Württemberg)
Place of residence: Heidelberg
Deported from Berlin January 19, 1942, to Riga ghetto (Latvia)

ISRAELSOHN, ERNA (née Müller; Ricke Berolzheimer and
Samuel Rosenthal's granddaughter)
Born: March 5, 1899, in Minden (Westphalia)
Places of residence: Erfurt, Minden
Deported from Münster via Osnabrück and Bielefeld December 13, 1941,
to Riga ghetto; later to Stutthof concentration camp on August 9, 1944
Died: February 1945, in Stutthof

ISRAELSOHN, GERDA (Ricke Berolzheimer and Samuel Rosenthal's granddaughter)
Born: August 23, 1925 in Minden (Westphalia)
Places of residence: Ahlem, Minden
Deported from Münster via Osnabrück and Bielefeld December 13, 1941, to Riga ghetto; later to Stutthof concentration camp on August 9, 1944

ISRAELSOHN, GÜNTER (Ricke Berolzheimer and Samuel Rosenthal's grandson)
Born: December 22, 1928 in Minden (Westphalia)
Place of residence: Minden
Deported from Münster via Osnabrück and Bielefeld December 13, 1941, to Riga ghetto; later to Kaunus ghetto; to Stutthof concentration camp on August 9, 1944; and to Auschwitz death camp on September 10, 1944

ISRAELSOHN, JULIUS (Erna's husband)
Born: October 29, 1898 in Vörden (Westphalia)
Place of residence: Minden
Interned November 12, 1938–December 12, 1938, in Buchenwald concentration camp
Deported from Münster via Osnabrück and Bielefeld December 13, 1941, to Riga ghetto
Died: September 26, 1944, in Riga

MERZBACHER, ERNST (Helene Berlin's son, Zerline Berolzheimer and Samuel Berlin's grandson)
Born: February 11, 1871, in Nuremburg
Place of residence: Munich
Interned November 10, 1938–December 1, 1938, in Dachau concentration camp, later released
Deported from Munich July 2, 1942, to Theresienstadt ghetto
Died: May 27, 1943, in Theresienstadt

MEYER, FANNY (née Bauer; Bertha Berolzheimer and Heinrich Bauer's daughter)
Born: May 8, 1869, in Augsburg (Bavaria)
Place of residence: Munich
Committed suicide: September 25, 1941, in Munich

NEUBURGER, HEDWIG (HEDI) (née Berlin; daughter of Ernst Berlin, granddaughter of Zerline Berolzheimer and Samuel Berlin)
Born: May 17, 1892 in Nuremburg
Place of residence: Nuremburg
Deported from Nuremburg on November 29, 1941, to Jungfernhof concentration camp (Riga, Latvia)

LÖB, FRIDA (née Berolzheimer; Michael Berolzheimer's sister)
Born: July 30, 1870 in Fürth
Places of residence: Munich, later Bendorf-Sayn (Rhineland-Palatinate)
Deported from Koblenz via Cologne and Düsseldorf to Sobibór
extermination camp (Poland) on June 15, 1942
Died: June 30, 1942
Death officially confirmed

PRAGER, MICHAEL SIGMUND (family friend of the Berolzheimers)
Born: December 28, 1866, in Fürth
Place of residence: Fürth
Emigrated to The Netherlands
Deported from Westerbork March 30, 1943, to Sobibór
extermination camp (Poland)
Died: April 2, 1943, in Sobibór
Death officially confirmed

PRAGER, PAULINE (family friend of the Berolzheimers)
née Sahlmann
Born: July 9, 1869, in Fürth
Place of residence: Fürth
Emigrated to The Netherlands
Deported from Westerbork, March 30, 1943, to Sobibór
extermination camp (Poland)
Died: April 2, 1943, Sobibór
Death officially confirmed

PRESSBURGER, ALBERT (Waldemar Schweisheimer's father-in-law)
Born: April 9, 1866, in Rexingen/Horb (Baden-Württemberg)
Places of residence: Horb, Stuttgart, Eschenau
Deported from Stuttgart August 22, 1942, to Theresienstadt ghetto
Died: October 2, 1942, in Theresienstadt

REIF, BERTHA (née Neuhäuser; Bertha B. Berolzheimer and
Michael Rothschild's granddaughter)
Born: February 6, 1866, in Idar-Oberstein (Rhineland-Palatinate)
Places of residence: Stuttgart, Eschenau
Deported from Stuttgart August 22, 1942, to Theresienstadt ghetto;
later to Treblinka death camp on September 26, 1942
Death officially confirmed

SCHWEISHEIMER, BENNO (son of Gabriel Schweisheimer,
Melitta's brother-in-law)
Born: July 28, 1898 in Nördlingen (Bavaria)
Place of residence: Nördlingen
Deported from Munich April 3/4,1942, to Piaski ghetto (Poland)

SCHWEISHEIMER, EUGEN (Melitta's first husband)
Born: February 18, 1858, in Ederheim (Bavaria)
Place of residence: Munich
Deported from Munich June 24, 1942 to Theresienstadt ghetto
Died: July 26, 1942, in Theresienstadt

SCHWEISHEIMER, JULIUS ISAAK (Melitta's brother-in-law)
Born: December 16, 1863, in Ederheim (Bavaria)
Place of residence: Munich
Deported from Munich June 23, 1942, to Theresienstadt ghetto
Died: November 23, 1942, in Theresienstadt

SCHWEISHEIMER, MATHILDE (née Mendle; Moritz's wife
and Melitta's sister-in-law)
Born: September 5, 1873, in Fischach (Bavaria)
Place of residence: Nördlingen
Deported from Munich August 7, 1942, to Theresienstadt ghetto
Died: December 19, 1942, in Theresienstadt

SCHWEISHEIMER, MORITZ MODEL (Melitta's brother-in-law)
Born: October 4, 1862, in Ederheim (Bavaria)
Place of residence: Nördlingen (Bavaria)
Deported from Munich August 7, 1942, to Theresienstadt ghetto
Died: November 14, 1942, in Theresienstadt

SCHWINK, ELISABETH (née Löb, widowed Meussdoerfer;
Frida Löb's daughter)
Shot by SS soldiers on May 3, 1945, near Jachenau, Upper Bavaria

SCHWINK, RUTH (Frida Löb's granddaughter)
Shot by SS soldiers on May 3, 1945, near Jachenau, Upper Bavaria

SELZ, LAURA (née Wassermann; Marie Dispeker's mother-in-law)
Born: October 15, 1857 in Munich
Place of residence: Munich
Deported from Berlin August 25, 1942, to Theresienstadt ghetto
Died: September 23, 1942, in Treblinka death camp

SELZ, OTTO (Marie Dispeker's father-in-law)
Born: February 14, 1881, in Munich
Place of residence: Mannheim
Interned November 11, 1938, in Dachau concentration camp
Emigrated to The Netherlands on May 17, 1939
Deported from Westerbork August 24, 1943, to Auschwitz death camp
Died: August 27, 1943, in Auschwitz
Death officially confirmed

REICHSMARKS AND DOLLARS: CONVERSIONS AND COMPARISONS

THE WEIMAR REPUBLIC AND HYPERINFLATION

In the first few years following the end of World War I, inflation grew at an alarming rate. The government reacted by simply printing more banknotes to pay the bills. By 1923, the Republic could no longer afford reparation payments imposed on Germany, as stipulated in the Versailles Treaty. As a result, French and Belgian troops seized control of most mining and manufacturing companies in the Ruhr region in January 1923, Germany's most productive industrial area at the time, leading to strikes which lasted eight months and further damaged the economy and social structure.

During Germany's hyperinflationary period (1922–23), the Reichsmark lost value rapidly against the US dollar. In June, 1922, there were 272 Reichsmark (RM) to 1 US$. This value increased monthly in leaps and bounds. By the end of that same year, it had risen to an incredible 500,000 RM to 1 US$. In February 1923, the Reichsbank attempted to stabilize the currency at 20,000 RM to 1 US$. By May 4, 1923, this had doubled; by August 15, 1923, there were 4,000,000 RM to 1 US$; by September 1, 1923, 10,000,000 RM. Around September 10–September 25, 1923, prices reportedly rose hourly in several German cities:

September 30, 1923: 60,000,000 RM = 1 US$; November 15, 1923: Rentenmark issued; pegged to the Gold Standard; Rentenmark 4.2 = 1 US$. By this time: Old Reichsmark 4,200,000,000 = 1 US$. 1 New Rentenmark = 1 Billion Old Reichsmarks.

1 US$ = 4.2 RM

An interim currency, the Rentenmark, served to stabilize the economy and provide a more gradual transition. The Rentenmark was backed by the *Deutsche Rentenbank*, which had assets from industrial and agricultural real estate. The Reichsmark joined the Gold Standard at the same rate previously given to the Goldmark: 1 US$ = 4.2 RM; 100,000 RM = $23,800 (roughly the equivalent of $340,000 in 2014).

THE GREAT DEPRESSION

The devastating effects of the Wall Street Crash of 1929 led to the Great Depression, during which Germany was effectively forced to take the Reichsmark off the Gold Standard when it imposed exchange controls in July 1931.

After the National Socialists had seized control of Germany, the Reichsmark was used to finance Germany's rearmament. Radical wage cuts and price controls were put into effect, foreign currency exchange rates were manipulated, and interest rates increased in an effort to stem inflation.

REICHSFLUCHTSTEUER

Reich Flight Tax was a capital control law introduced on December 8, 1931. It was levied when a German citizen intended to emigrate, provided that the individual had assets exceeding 200,000 Reichsmarks or had a yearly income over 20,000 RM. The tax rate was set at 25 percent. During the Third Reich, the use of the *Reichsfluchtsteuer* shifted away from dissuading wealthy citizens from moving overseas. Rather, the departure of Jewish citizens was desired and permitted by the Nazi government—even after the Invasion of Poland—until a decree forbade Jewish emigration on October 23, 1941. The *Reichsfluchtsteuer* was used as a "partial expropriation" of the assets of Jewish refugees who were persecuted and driven to flee their homeland.

CONVERTING REICHSMARKS TO DOLLARS IN 1938

In 1938, 2.50 RM were approximately equivalent to US$1. Although it is impossible to provide precise conversion values, comparisons can be made. Taking 6000 RM to be the rough equivalent of $2500, this would approximately be worth the following by today's standards and exchange rates:

$35,500   (according to the Consumer Price Index)
$30,000   (GDP deflator)
$85,000   (consumer bundle)
$76,000   (based on unskilled wages)
$166,500 (based on the nominal GDP per capita)

For the value of a simple commodity (bread, gas, etc.), refer to the CPI
For a salary or annual income, refer to the consumer bundle or GDP per capita
For the cost of a building or public works project, refer to the GDP deflator

These figures are a rough guidance only. Further conversion tables and examples can be found on the Internet.

PUBLISHER AND EDITOR

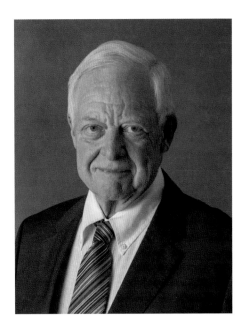

MICHAEL G. BEROLZHEIMER, born in 1939 in Oakland, California, lives in Saitama, Japan. His MBA from Harvard Business School laid the foundation for his long career in the family businesses of wood products. He is a founding partner of Early Stages, a venture-capital firm and co-founder and President of Duraflame, Inc. the leading fireplace firelog company. Michael served on the Board of Directors of several private and public companies as well as the Board of YPO (Young Presidents' Organization).

CONTRIBUTING AUTHORS

ANDREA BAMBI, born in 1964 in Amberg in der Oberpfalz, studied art history, theater studies and modern German literature in Munich and wrote her doctorate on the collector Adolf Friedrich Graf von Schack. Since 2008 has been in charge of the Department of Provenance Research at the Pinakothek Musuems in Munich, having worked there since 1998, is responsible for the export of cultural artifacts in Bavaria, and the coordinator of diverse provenance research projects funded by third parties.

DIETLIND BRATENGEYER, born in 1943 in Poznan, Poland, grew up as a war refugee in southern Germany. She graduated in 1965 from the Hessische Bibliotheksschule in Frankfurt/Main and worked at the Institute for Political Sciences, University of Freiburg im Breisgau before emigrating in 1968 to Canada. She worked for the Simon Fraser University Library in Burnaby, BC, the EXPO 86 in Vancouver, and the human resources consulting firm Wilson Banwall & Associates, among others.

SVEN H. A. BRUNTJEN, first studied fine arts and philosophy, followed by history of art at Stanford University, California, where he gained his doctorate in 1973. He worked at the British Museum, the Royal Academy, and the V & A Museum in London on a Kress Foundation Fellowship, before becoming Assistant Director and Chief Curator at Stanford University Museum of Art. He now works as a private art dealer, consultant, and appraiser.

REBECCA FRIEDMAN, born in 1974 in New York City, studied art history at Columbia University and the Courtauld Institute of Art, London. An art historian and a licensed attorney, she has worked as an art claims specialist at the New York State Department of Finance's Holocaust Claims Processing Office (HCPO) since 2006. Prior to joining the HCPO, she worked at a number of museums, art galleries, and non-profit arts organizations.

JOSEPH GOLDYNE, born in 1942 in Chicago, studied medicine in San Francisco and art history at Harvard. He has worked as an artist for forty years and had exhibitions at many major museums including the Smithsonian Institution, Washington, D.C., and San Francisco Museum of Modern Art. He has written critical appraisals on artists and lectured at the Getty Center for Education in the Arts and at the College Art Association of America on approaches to attribution.

UWE HARTMANN, born in 1959 in Rostock, Germany, studied art history at Humboldt University, Berlin. He worked at the Coordination Office for the Loss of Cultural Objects in Magdeburg and was, from 1989–99, research assistant at the Art History Department at Humboldt University. Since 2008, he has been head of the Department for Provenance Research at the Institute for Museum Research of the Staatlichen Museen zu Berlin—Stiftung Preußischer Kulturbesitz.

ANDREAS HEUSLER, born in 1960 in Calw, has a doctorate in history having studied history and political science in Tübingen and Munich. Since 1994 he been working at the Munich City Archives as head of the department for contemporary and Jewish history. Between 1998 and 2006 he was responsible for the Jewish Museum in Reichenbachstrasse. He is a member of the academic advisory council for the projected Nazi Documentation Center in Munich.

HORST KESSLER, born in 1957 in Augsburg, Germany, is a historian. From 2001–11 he worked in the field of provenance research in art collections and museums in Augsburg, largely responsible for dealing with the estate of the art dealer Karl Haberstock. His work has included research on the confiscation of Jewish art collections in Munich in 1938/39, and coordinated provenance research work between Munich and Berlin.

BERNHARD PURIN, born in 1963 in Bregenz, Austria, is Director of the Jewish Museum in Munich. He studied Cultural Science and Modern History at Tübingen University. From 1995–2002 he was Director of the Jewish Museum of Franconia—Fürth and Schnaittach; and 1993–95 Curator of the Jewish Museum in Vienna. He has served as a board member of the Association of European Jewish Museums (AEJM) and is an advisory board member at several Jewish museums.

PETER J. SCHWARZ, born in 1945 in Garmisch-Partenkirchen, is a retired electrical engineer now living in Grainau. He worked at the Max-Planck-Institut and Technical University in Munich. As a local historian, he was for many years president of the local historical society in Grainau, director of the "Dorfgalerie" in Grainau for ten years, and a voluntary independent contributor to the Werdenfels Museum in Garmisch-Partenkirchen.

VANESSA-MARIA VOIGT, born in 1975 in Bückeburg, studied art history at the University of Münster, writing her doctorate thesis on art dealers and collectors of modern art during the Nazi period, with a special focus on the Sprengel Collection. Since 2009 she has been part of a research team looking into the confiscation of Jewish art collections in Munich in 1938/39, and provenance researcher for the Munich Stadtmuseum since September 2011.

PETRA WINTER, born in 1972 in Berlin, studied history and archival studies at Humboldt University, Berlin, and at the University of Applied Sciences in Potsdam. She wrote her doctorate thesis on the history of the Staatliche Museen zu Berlin—Stiftung Preußischer Kulturbesitz from 1945–58, where she has been working since 2000 in the Central Archive, first as an archivist, and since 2008 as Deputy Director. She is also responsible for provenance research at the Staatliche Museen zu Berlin.

GARY A. ZIMMERMAN, born in 1938 in Seattle, Washington, is a genealogist, educated at the California Institute of Technology and the University of Wisconsin at Madison. He is president of the Fiske Genealogical Foundation and Library. His primary focus is on genealogical records of North American and Western Europe. He is a retired professor of chemistry and university administrator from Seattle University (1964–88) and Antioch University Seattle (1988–98).

ACKNOWLEDGMENTS

Tracing the life and times of my great-uncle and his art collection involved a considerable number of people around the globe—researchers and museum staff, authors and editors, family and friends—over a period of several years. I am indebted to the commitment and enthusiasm shown in this undertaking, and thank everyone for their efforts. While it is not possible to list all names individually, I would like to mention several people who have accompanied this project.

First is Peter Selz, grandson of Melitta's sister, Marie Dispeker Drey. We met in 1998 during a dinner-reception sponsored by my friend Lonna Wais. The event was to honor my gift of some of Dr. Michael's etchings to the Legion of Honor in San Francisco. Peter began his speech by declaring he had visited my great-uncle's home in Untergrainau in 1936, where he had seen Rodin's statue of St. John the Baptist standing in the garden. Peter then pointed to a different cast of the very same statue standing next to my table.

In 2003, my grandson, Pierce, and I tried to find Dr. Michael's home, but failed. My friend Ed Quinnan narrowed the search later that year, and in 2005, Michael Kelbel was able to finally identify the house in Untergrainau and arranged for my first visit in 2009. Inspired by that visit and the encouragement of my late wife, Yoshiko, the quest of discovery began to germinate. Eric Rosenbaum uncovered Internet information about US Army restitutions to Waldemar Schweisheimer, leading to my first meeting with Andrea Bambi of the Bavarian State Picture Collections in Munich in 2010.

Andrea Bambi, Andreas Heusler from the Munich City Archives, and Bernhard Purin from the Jewish Museum Munich provided the initial conceptual framework for this book, namely to have several experts write on subjects related to my great-uncle's life and work, and Tom Zuckerman and Andreas Heusler suggested the preliminary chapter sequence. I am indebted to the authors, all of them authorities in their respective fields, who subsequently analyzed and illuminated different aspects of Dr. Michael's biography: Andrea Bambi, Dietlind Bratengeyer, Sven Bruntjen, Rebecca Friedman, Joseph Goldyne, Uwe Hartmann, Andreas Heusler, Horst Kessler, Bernhard Purin, Peter J. Schwarz, Vanessa Maria Voigt, Petra Winter, and Gary A. Zimmerman. *Michael Berolzheimer, 1866–1942: His Life and Legacy* reflects their knowledge.

The book's rich and detailed content is largely the result of painstaking research in family archives. A special thanks goes to Anita Sheridan Mitchell who provided access to the vast collection of her father Robert's material. Noeline Friedberg's collection of Nelly's letters and memorabilia from other members of the Friedberg family provided information about the family's escape to New Zealand. Michael Thrope, Melitta's great grandson, introduced me to the Schweisheimer family, and both Michael and his mother, Elsieliese, provided interviews and family documents critical to understanding Waldemar's restitution efforts. I am equally grateful to the Meussdörffer and Hopf families (Frida's descendants), for their interest and support. I also gratefully acknowledge the support of my brother, Philip, who made important material in our father's archives accessible by computer with the help of Alex Ortiz.

Dietlind (Dee) Bratengeyer performed every role imaginable during the four-year project. Fluent in both English and German, her insatiable intellectual curiosity uncovered both large and small details related to the historical chains of events in Dr. Michael's life. Her prodigious memory, knowledge, and eye for detail greatly enhanced the work on this publication.

With fourteen contributing authors and writing styles in two languages, the task of translating and editing manuscripts is a daunting one. Thanks to the intelligent, knowledgeable, and patient work of Christopher Wynne, *Michael Berolzheimer, 1866–1942: His Life and Legacy* flows together as a historical document while also capturing the real life events of people who faced difficult circumstances.

I would like to thank museum and gallery staff at a number of institutions, as well as other individuals around the world who have provided invaluable information and material: Rebecca Friedman from the New York State Department of Financial Services' Holocaust Claims Processing Office (HCPO) for her on-going efforts regarding restitution; the Albertina, Vienna, especially Maren Gröning and Katja Fischer, as well as Monika Wulz and Eva Holpfer of the Restitutions Section of the Israelitische Kultusgemeinde, Vienna; the Kupferstichkabinett Berlin, especially Heinrich-Theodor Schulze-Altcappenberg, and the Nationalgalerie Berlin, especially Petra Winter from the Zentralarchiv der Staatlichen Museen zu Berlin; Carola Thielcke of the Stiftung Preussischer Kulturbesitz, Berlin; Michael Friedberg—Melitta's great-grandson—who greatly assisted in recovering the Berlin group of drawings; Eric Rothschild Rosenbaum and Sven Bruntjen for their invaluable help in the restitution process; Peter Selz, mentioned above, also helped me early on with the translation of German documents related to Waldemar's affairs; Erika Kraemer Sanchez (Julius Schweisheimer's granddaughter) showed an active interest in the book from the outset; and Ransom Place provided very insightful information; Rivca and Amotz Amiad, Sally Levine, and Karl Berolzheimer; the Leo Baeck Institute where Dr. Michael's manuscripts are held; Liza Hickey for assisting Sven Bruntjen during the entire project; Wendy Berol Gifford for information about the Torah wimpel; Bruce Livie and Cornelia Muessig of the Arnoldi-Livie gallery in Munich, and Sebastian Winkler of the Verlag und Bildarchiv Sebastian Winkler in Munich, for the provision of exceptional pictorial material and for their spontaneous enthusiasm and support; Maria Schuster and Anton Reindl, both of Unter-grainau, for providing Peter Schwarz with invaluable information while compiling his essay; the Stadtsparkasse München, the proprietors of Hügel am Weg, for their cooperation and hospitality; Regina and Hubert Müller, owners of Hotel Hirth next door, for their repeated hospitality and active interest in their interconnected history with my ancestors; and to the Mayor of Markt Berolzheim who gave me such an interesting tour of the town in 2009.

I am grateful for the creative ideas and dedication of the graphic designers Petra Lüer and Rainer Lienemann, and to the printer and binder, who ensured this publication's high quality.

Finally I would like to thank my family and friends for their encouragement and support over the past four years.

Michael G. Berolzheimer

SELECTED BIBLIOGRAPHY

ANGERMAIR, Elisabeth, "Eine selbstbe-wusste Minderheit (1892–1918)" in: Richard Bauer, Michael Brenner (eds), *Jüdisches München. Vom Mittelalter bis zur Gegenwart,* Munich 2006

BADER, Josef, "Entwicklung eines Berg-bauerndorfes in den Bayerischen Alpen zu einem Fremdenverkehrsdorf, dargestellt am Beispiel von Grainau im Werdenfelser Land," unpublished manuscript, Grainau 1979

BADER, Josef, "Das Haus des Juden Berolzheimer (Grainau 1902–1945)" in: *Groana Heft 19,* December 2006

BAERWALD, Leo and Ludwig Feuchtwanger (eds), *Festgabe. 50 Jahre Hauptsynagoge München, 1887–1937,* Munich 1937

BAUER, Richard, "Stadt und Stadtverfassung im Umbruch" in: Hans-Rüdiger Schwab (ed.), *Geschichte der Stadt München,* Munich 1992

BEROLZHEIMER, Michael, *Geschichte der Familie Berolzheimer* (handwritten manuscript), Berolzheimer Family Archives, Stockton, USA

BILSKY, Emily D., *"Only Culture"—The Pringsheims,* Jewish Museum Munich, 2007

BILSKY, Emily D., *The Bernheimer Art and Antiques House,* Jewish Museum Munich, 2007

BLAUERT, Elke, "Sammlung der Zeich-nungen" in: Peter-Klaus Schuster (ed.), *Die Nationalgalerie,* Berlin 2001

BRAUNSTEIN, Susan L., *Five Centuries of Hanukkah Lamps from the Jewish Museum: A Catalogue Raisonné,* New Haven/London 2005

CENTRAL ARCHIVES for the History of the Jewish People and the Jüdisches Museum Franken—Fürth & Schnaittach (eds), *Theodor Harburger, Die Inventarisation jüdischer Kunst- und Kulturdenkmäler in Bayern,* 3 vols, Fürth 1998

COHEN GROSSMAN, Grace, *Jewish Museums of the World,* Southport 2003

ECKER, Jürgen, *Anselm Feuerbach. Kritischer Katalog der Gemälde, Ölskizzen und Ölstudien,* Munich 1991

GALLERIE HUGO HELBING, "Die Judaica-Sammlung S. Kirschstein Berlin. Kultgeräte für Haus und Synagoge / Manuskripte / Gemälde / Miniaturen / Graphik / Urkunden / Bücher. Versteigerung in der Gallerie Hugo Helbing München," Munich 1932

GALLERY ARNOLDI-LIVIE (ed.), *29 Drawings from the Michael Berolzheimer Collection, Restituted by the Albertina, Vienna 2010,* cat. 27, Munich 2011

GALLERY ARNOLDI-LIVIE (ed.), *Michael Berolzheimer Collection II, 24 Drawings restituted by the Kupferstichkabinett Berlin,* cat. 28, Munich 2012

GROSSMAN, Cissy, *The Jewish Family's Book of Days,* New York 1989

HAMM, Margot et al., *Good Bye Bayern Grüß Gott America. Auswanderung aus Bayern nach Amerika,* Haus der Bayerischen Geschichte (ed.), Augsburg 2004

HOPP, Meike, *Kunsthandel im National-sozialismus: Adolf Weinmüller in München und Wien,* Cologne et al. 2012

KLARSFELD, Beate and Serge, *Le Mémorial de la deportation des juifs de France,* Paris 1978

LE NORMAND-ROMAIN, Antoinette, *The Bronzes of Rodin, Catalogue of works in the Musée Rodin,* vol. 2, Paris 2007

LOEWY, Hanno and Gerhard Milchram, "Alpen 2010: 'Hast du meine Alpen gesehen?' Eine jüdische Beziehungsgeschichte," exh. cat., Hohenems/Vienna 2010

MANN, Vivian B. and Richard I. Cohen, *From Court Jews to the Rothschilds: Art, Patronage, and Power, 1600–1800,* The Jewish Museum New York, Munich/New York 1997

MÜLLER, Melissa and Monika Tatzkow, *Lost Lives, Lost Art/Jewish Collectors, Nazi Art Theft and the Quest for Justice,* New York 2010

OGILVIE, Sarah and Scott Miller, *Refuge Denied: The St. Louis Passengers and the Holocaust,* Madison 2006

PURIN, Bernhard, *City without Jews: The Dark Side of Munich's History,* Munich 2008

RAVE, Paul Ortwin, "Bergungsmaßnahmen der Nationalgalerie" in: *Dokumentation der Verluste,* vol. II: Nationalgalerie, Berlin 2001

RUBENS, Alfred, *A Jewish Iconography,* London 1981

SCHERER, Benedikt Maria, *Der Architekt Carl Sattler. Leben und Werk (1877–1966),* Munich 2007

SCHMOLL gen. Eisenwerth, J.A., *August Rodin and Camille Claudel,* Munich 2000

SCHWAB, Hans-Rüdiger (ed.), *München. Dichter sehen eine Stadt,* Stuttgart 1990

SCHWARZMÜLLLER, Alois, "Melitta und Dr. Michael Berolzheimer" in: http://members.gaponline.de/alois.schwarz-mueller/juden in gap biographien/berolzheimer melitta und dr. michael.htm

SCHWARZMÜLLER, Alois, " 'Juden sind hier nicht erwünscht!' Zur Geschichte der jüdischen Bürger in Garmisch-Partenkirchen von 1933 bis 1945" in: Verein für Geschichte, Kunst und Kulturgeschichte im Landkreis Garmisch-Partenkirchen (ed.), *Mohr-Löwe-Raute. Beiträge zur Geschichte des Landkreises Garmisch-Partenkirchen,* vol. 3, 1995

INDEX OF PROPER NAMES

STADTARCHIV MÜNCHEN. *Biographisches Gedenkbuch der Münchner Juden, 1933–1945*, Munich

STÄNDECKE, Monika, *Dirndls, Trunks, and Edelweiss. The Folk Art of the Wallach Brothers,* Jewish Museum Munich, 2007

STAUDINGER, Barbara (ed.), *From Bavaria to Eretz Israel. Tracing Jewish Folk Art,* exh. cat, Jewish Museum Munich, Munich 2007

STIH, Renata and Frieder Schnock, *Zeige Deine Sammlung— Jüdische Spuren in Münchner Museen,* Nuremberg 2008

VOIGT, Vanessa-Maria and Horst Keßler, "Die Beschlagnahmung jüdischer Kunstsammlungen 1938/39 in München" (The Confiscation of Jewish Art Collections in 1938/39 in Munich): in Kunst sammeln, Kunst handeln, Vienna 2012

VOSS, Heinrich, *Franz von Stuck. Werkkatalog der Gemälde*, Munich 1973

For personal correspondence and information on Michael Berolzheimer:

LEO BAECK-INSTITUT, Center for Jewish History, New York, Michael Berolzheimer Collection 1325–1942

Front cover: Michael Berolzheimer in his study at Hügel am Weg, c. 1935 (*see also p. 136*).

p. 1: The south front of the Berolzheimers' house, Hügel am Weg, in Untergrainau, with Melitta in the garden she created, c. 1920.

pp. 2/3: The east façade of Hügel am Weg and the north entrance gable end, looking south-west toward the village of Untergrainau, showing the raised garden and the drive below (in the foreground). The lower slopes of the Zugspitze can be seen in the top left-hand corner.

pp. 4/5: The view from below Hügel am Weg looking directly south at the Wetterstein mountains, with the Alpspitze on the far left, the Waxenstein group in the middle, and the Zugspitze on the far right. The stream in the foreground is the Krepbach with the "Krepbach Meadows" on either side.

pp. 6/7: Aerial view of Munich city center looking east, c. 1927, with the Frauenkirche (the cathedral church) in the middle. Marienplatz, the central square, is just to the right at the top of the right-hand tower, with St. Peter's church—"Alter Peter"—further to the right. The Opera House is on the far left, with Maximilianstrasse leading eastwards to the top of the picture.

pp. 8/9: Marienplatz, c. 1905

p. 14: Portrait of Dr. Michael Berolzheimer, photograph, c. 1910

pp. 28/29: A view over the rooftops of Munich looking west, c. 1920, with "Alter Peter" on the left, the Frauenkirche center right, and the ornate City Hall on the right.

pp. 118/19: The old synagogue in Munich, c. 1890, to the right, with the towers of the Frauenkirche, the cathedral church, to the left.

pp. 148/49: Johann Georg Dillis (1759–1841), *Weathered Tree Trunk*, c. 1790, graphite and black chalk with brown wash, restituted by the Albertina, Vienna

PUBLISHED BY
Michael G. Berolzheimer
POB 150
Stockton, CA 95201
USA
mgb@berolzheimer.net

Translated from the German (essays by Bambi, Hartmann, Heusler, Purin, Schwarz, Voigt/Kessler, Winter, Zimmerman) by: Dietlind Bratengeyer, Christopher Wynne

Edited by: Michael G. Berolzheimer, Dietlind Bratengeyer, Christopher Wynne

Research and project coordination: Dietlind Bratengeyer

Editorial direction and production management: Christopher Wynne

Design and layout: WIGEL, Munich
Origination: Repro Bayer, Munich
Printing: Weber Offset, Munich
Binding: Conzella, Pfarrkirchen

Printed in Germany on acid-free paper

ISBN 978-3-00-047128-5

PHOTOGRAPHIC CREDITS

Architekturmuseum der TU, Munich: p. 50 bottom; Archiv Peter Adam, Garmisch-Partenkirchen: p. 56; Arnoldi-Livie, Munich, and Michael G. Berolzheimer: pp. 19, 21, 146/47, 150, 153, 154, 159, 160, 161, 163, 174, 177, 179, 180, 183, 184, 186, 191, 192, 194, 196, 199, 200, 201, 202, 203, 205, 206, 209, 210, 211, 212; Bayerisches Hauptstadtarchiv, Munich: p. 50 top; Bayerische Staatsgemäldesammlungen, Munich: p. 155; Thomas Dashuber, Munich: pp. 122, 128, 135; Jewish Museum Munich: p. 126; Jewish Museum New York: p. 127; Monika von Rosen, Berlin: p. 113; Sammlung Peter Schwarz/Photo © Peter Schwarz, Grainau: pp. 4/5, 44, 46, 47, 51 bottom, 52 bottom, 53, 54 top, 57 bottom, 58, 59, 62, 63, 66, 67, 68, 80, and Tables pp. 47, 48, 77; Schuster Family, Grainau: p. 60; Foto Seichter, Grainau: p. 64; Stadtarchiv München, Munich: pp. 33, 34 bottom, 35, 37, 38, 51 top, 73; Verlag und Bildarchiv Sebastian Winkler, Munich: pp. 6/7, 8/9, 28/29, 32, 34 top, 36, 39, 40, 41, 42, 93, 118/19, 123, 171; Wien Museum, Vienna: p. 125

All other illustrations have been taken from the extensive Berolzheimer family archives as well as from other private collections.

Every effort has been taken to identify the copyright owners of the pictorial material. Should however a name have been inadvertently omitted or a picture incorrectly attributed, please contact the Publisher.